Men, Work, and Family

Research on Men and Masculinities Series

Series Editor:
MICHAEL S. KIMMEL, SUNY Stony Brook

Contemporary research on men and masculinity, informed by recent feminist thought and intellectual breakthroughs of women's studies and the women's movement, treats masculinity not as a normative referent but as a problematic gender construct. This series of interdisciplinary, edited volumes attempts to understand men and masculinity through this lens, providing a comprehensive understanding of gender and gender relationships in the contemporary world. Published in cooperation with the Men's Studies Association, a Task Group of the National Organization for Men Against Sexism.

Volumes in this Series

1. Steve Craig (ed.)
   MEN, MASCULINITY, AND THE MEDIA
2. Peter M. Nardi (ed.)
   MEN'S FRIENDSHIPS
3. Christine L. Williams (ed.)
   DOING WOMEN'S WORK: Men in Nontraditional Occupations
4. Jane C. Hood (ed.)
   MEN, WORK, AND FAMILY

Other series volumes in preparation

Men, Work, and Family

Edited by Jane C. Hood

Published in cooperation with the Men's Studies Association, A Task Group of the National Organization for Men Against Sexism

SAGE Publications

International Educational and Professional Publisher

Newbury Park London New Delhi

For information address:

SAGE Publications, Inc.
2455 Teller Road
Newbury Park, California 91320

SAGE Publications Ltd.
6 Bonhill Street
London EC2A 4PU
United Kingdom

SAGE Publications India Pvt. Ltd.
M-32 Market
Greater Kailash I
New Delhi 110 048 India

Printed in the United States of America

Library of Congress Cataloging-in-Publication Data

Men, work, and family / edited by Jane C. Hood.
p. cm.—(Research on men and masculinities series ; 4)
Includes bibliographical references and index.
ISBN 0-8039-3890-X (cloth).—ISBN 0-8039-3891-8 (pbk.)
1. Men—Cross-cultural studies. 2. Work and family—Cross-cultural studies. 3. Fathers—Cross-cultural studies. 4. Family—Cross-cultural studies. 5. Sex roles—Cross-cultural studies.
I. Hood, Jane C. II. Series.
HQ1090.M452 1993
305.31—dc20 93-27756
CIP

93 94 95 96 10 9 8 7 6 5 4 3 2

Sage Production Editor: Judith L. Hunter

Contents

Foreword

This volume is the fourth in the Sage Series on Research on Men and Masculinities. The purpose of the series is to gather together the finest empirical research in the social sciences that focuses on the experiences of men in contemporary society.

Following the pioneering research of feminist scholars over the past two decades, social scientists have come to recognize gender as one of the primary axes around which social life is organized. Gender is now seen as equally central as class and race, both at the macro structural level of the allocation and distribution of rewards in a hierarchical society, and at the micro psychological level of individual identity formation and interpersonal interaction.

Social scientists distinguish gender from sex. Sex refers to biology, the biological dimorphic division of male and female; gender refers to the cultural meanings that are attributed to those biological differences. Although biological sex varies little, the cultural meanings of gender vary enormously. Thus we speak of gender as socially constructed: the definitions of masculinity and femininity are the products of the interplay among a variety of social forces. In particular, we understand gender to vary spatially (from one culture to another); temporally (within any one culture over historical time); and longitudinally (through any individual's life course). Finally, we understand that different groups within any culture may define masculinity and femininity differently, according to subcultural definitions; race, ethnicity, age, class, sexuality, and region of the country all affect our different gender definitions. Thus, it is more accurate to speak of *masculinities* and *femininities* than to posit a monolithic gender construct. It is the goal of this series to explore the varieties of men's experiences, remaining mindful of specific differences among men and also of the mechanisms of power that inform both men's relations with women and men's relations with other men.

One of the central arenas of change in men's lives in the past two decades has been the efforts to renegotiate the relationship between work experiences and family life. Women have increasingly entered the paid labor force, thus raising the painful choices associated with balancing work and family commitments. Historically, working women have also been responsible for what sociologist Arlie Hochschild calls the "second shift," the child care and housework that must be accomplished when the workplace shift is over.

In the 1980s, "having it all" became a new motto for U.S. women. Could U.S. women have it all: a loving, devoted family life and access to rewarding and personally fulfilling careers? Of course, the chief barrier to women having it all was that for centuries it was *men* who had it all—and only because women took primary and exclusive responsibility for the second shift.

Along with signs of backlash and stalled transformation, there are also signs of change. In this volume, Jane Hood has collected some of the most current and innovative social science research on the way men are negotiating this balancing act of work and family commitment. Some chapters provide comparative contexts for analysis, both between U.S. men and men in other countries, and among different groups of U.S. men. Other chapters examine the impact of public policy on men's experience of family and work. Still others address the changing balance between shifting attitudes and behaviors. Using a variety of methodological tools, from in-depth interviews to quantitative analysis of large data sets, this volume will become a standard work in both intellectual and policy discussions of men's family and work experiences.

MICHAEL S. KIMMEL
Series Editor

Acknowledgments

In addition to the authors listed in the table of contents, many others worked behind the scenes to bring this volume to press. Michael Kimmel, Joseph Pleck, and Scott Coltrane scouted for manuscripts. Donna Watkins and Emily Griffiths at the University of New Mexico and Brian Beaman at Indiana University helped with mailings and typing. My research assistant, Cheryl Temple Thompson, checked and copyedited references, and my spouse, John Krogman, entered the changes, checked spelling, and revised idiosyncratic WordPerfect formatting. Stephanie Hoppe, who copyedited the manuscript for Sage, did a particularly careful job.

Mitch Allen and Michael Kimmel variously encouraged, cajoled, and pushed me first to start the volume and then finally to finish it. Through work on this volume, I have profited from the knowledge and friendship of several new colleagues. I thank all of them for their patience, cooperation, and kind words.

My son, Robert Devon Hood Krogman, joined our household shortly after I signed the contract for this volume. I am grateful to him and his dad for giving up several "family" days for my work.

Lastly, the University of New Mexico supported this project though a sabbatical in 1991-1992, and some time released from teaching in 1990-1991.

Introduction

When Rosabeth Moss Kanter wrote *Work and Family in the United States: A Critical Review and Agenda for Research and Policy* in 1977, she was exploring a social science frontier. As she pointed out, because sociologists had bought the myth of separate worlds (Kanter, 1977, p. 8), we rarely studied people's work and family lives together. Since the pioneering research of scholars like the Rapoports (1971, 1978), Pleck (1977), and Bailyn (1970), the sociology of work and family has become a major subfield within the discipline. Among the most common themes in this literature are the incursion of family demands on work and vice versa, and the impact of one set of roles on the other.

A subtext running through much of this work is the image of the balancing act or "juggling" (Crosby, 1991). Juggling, however, is something women are assumed to do far more often than men. As Pleck argued in "The Work-Family Role System" (1977), the boundaries between men's and women's work and family roles are "asymmetrically permeable," so that family is allowed to intrude upon women's work, whereas for men, work intrudes upon family (1977, p. 423). Pleck says, "Husbands are expected to manage their families so that their family responsibilities do not interfere with their work efficiency and so that families will make any adjustments necessary to accommodate the demands of husbands' work roles" (1977, p. 424). Although Pleck's observations about the importance of gender are still true today, the image of the workaholic upper-middle-class husband has splintered into myriad images of husbands and fathers. Now, in addition to Bailyn's early examples of family-oriented middle-class men (Bailyn, 1970), we have research on working-class fathers who put their families first (Hood, 1983; Lein, 1983); and on men who avoid the provider role (Ehrenreich, 1983) as well as those who are trapped by it (Weiss, 1990).

In spite of this diversity, many social scientists still unquestioningly accept the unbroken image of the father-provider. To the extent that social scientists have accepted the social construct of "masculinity" as social reality, we have ignored the lived experiences of most men, particularly minority and working-class men. Although feminist theorists and social scientists have been busy pulling apart cultural definitions of women and attacking essentialist notions about "femininity" (Stacey & Thorne, 1985), only a few have recently turned their attention to masculinity (Carrigan, Connell, & Lee, 1987; Risman, 1987). Thus, we know that it is wrong to think of women as wives and mothers to the exclusion of their work roles, but we have little difficulty thinking of men as workers first and fathers second. Feminist researchers have called for a new look at the intersection of class, race, and gender in women's lives, particularizing women's experience and giving voice to the variety of women's experiences, yet most of us fail to do this for men.

Each contributor to this book grapples with both myths and realities about men's work and family lives. In addition, the volume includes chapters comparing U.S. men by ethnicity, class, and age as well as studies of Japanese, Swedish, and Hispanic-American men. By looking at men's work and family lives in a variety of contexts using a wide range of methods, this volume helps to "deconstruct" monolithic images of hegemonic masculinity (Carrigan et al., 1987) and uncover the complexity hidden in the intersection of gender, work, and family.

Each chapter in the volume helps us understand some of the many ways in which work and family roles are gendered. In so doing, the authors implicitly contribute to the debate about the utility of "role" as a concept when discussing gendered activities. Although I agree with West and Zimmerman (1991) and others who argue that the concept of "role" is far too narrow to capture anything so pervasive as gender, the contributors to this volume use "role" to denote categories of responsibilities such as providing, nurturing, and housekeeping. However, because all of these roles are gendered, our authors often find that even these more narrowly defined categories function as master identities (West & Zimmerman, 1991, p. 16) that cut across situations. For example, Polly Fassinger illustrates how even though both single-parent men and single-parent women can find themselves responsible for all the housework, men define that responsibility differently than do women. The first section of the volume includes four articles on fathering and providing. In "What Do Fathers Provide?" Theodore Cohen challenges the primacy of the male provider role. Earlier work on men transitioning to parenthood (R. LaRossa & M. LaRossa, 1981) found expectant fathers preoccupied with the provider role. A decade later, all but 2 of the 18 working- and middle-class men Cohen interviewed described parenthood in terms of nurturance rather than financial providing. Although data from small purposive samples such as Cohen's can neither inform us about the pervasiveness of the father-as-nurturer image nor tell us whether that image is a new phenomenon, Cohen's data do allow us to question the hegemony of the father-as-provider image. Only by pulling father and provider roles apart can we begin to examine their influence upon each other.

In their chapter, "Are Men Marginal to the Family," Haya Stier and Marta Tienda look at fatherhood and providing from a different vantage point. Using data from NORC's 1986-1987 Urban Poverty and Family Life Survey of Chicago, the authors debunk the noncustodial-father-as-scoundrel myth. By comparing black, white, Mexican, and Puerto Rican fathers, Stier and Tienda demonstrate that income rather than ethnicity determines the amount of material support noncustodial fathers give their children. The ethnic differences that do surface pertain to patterns of material and emotional support of nonresident children. From Stier and Tienda's careful analysis of data from 811 fathers, we learn, for example, that black men are nearly twice as likely as any other category of men to visit daily with their children.

The first two chapters shatter stereotypes; the third chapter partially supports one. In her qualitative study of 20 middle-class Japanese fathers, Masako Ishii-Kuntz puts a human face on the image of the workaholic Japanese father. Ishii-Kuntz's interviews with 20 Japanese husbands and wives illustrate how fathers retain their authority over their children in absentia. For the fathers in her sample, the provider role almost completely overlapped the father role. By placing her study in historical context, however, the author points out that father absence in Japan is a recent phenomenon that is more the result of labor market structure than of culturally specific gender values.

In the last chapter in this section, Norma Williams looks at links between fathering and providing for 23 elderly Mexican-American men. Among Williams's respondents, the men least likely to be isolated from their adult children were the minority who had to provide for divorced daughters and their offspring. In this case, providing enabled parenting by keeping the lines of communication open.

The second section of the volume includes six studies on role allocation and role change. Although as a category these studies represent the modal type in the men's work and family literature, each contributes important new insights into the relative priority of work versus family for different categories of men. Chapters 5 and 6 examine U.S. young people's attitudes towards family and work. Katherine Dennehy and Jeylan Mortimer examine questionnaire data from an ongoing panel study of Minnesota high school students (1980-1990). By analyzing changes in boys' and girls' responses between the 9th and 11th grades, the researchers illustrate the effects of both gender and maturation on young people's plans for marriage, family, and work. In the following chapter, Beth Willinger uses time series data to look at changes in college men's work and family orientations between 1980 and 1990. Both studies find males more willing to accept an increase in females' responsibilities outside the home than in males' responsibilities inside the home.

Chapters 7 and 8 each challenge conventional wisdom about minority men. In "Ethnicity, Race, and Difference," Beth Anne Shelton and Daphne John use survey data to uncover the joint effects of ethnicity and employment status on men's household labor. Neither they nor Scott Coltrane and Elsa Valdez, in a qualitative study of Chicano dual-worker couples, find any evidence that ethnicity affects the amount of time that married men devote to household labor. Black men do more housework than white men because they earn less, and Hispanic men share housework and child care with their working wives for much the same reasons and to about the same extent as do other husbands of working wives. Shelton and John do find, however, that whereas white and Hispanic men do more housework when they are underemployed, black men do less. And even though the husbands Coltrane and Valdez interviewed are neither more nor less egalitarian than other husbands of working wives, they think that they are more egalitarian than other Chicano men, especially their fathers. Ethnicity shapes these men's images of masculinity far more than it appears to shape their behavior.

Although fathers in dual-worker families negotiate housework and parenting responsibilities with their spouses, single-parent fathers struggle with their children, their employers, and themselves. Chapters 9 and 10 look at single-parent custodial fathers from two different vantage points. Geoffrey Greif, Alfred DeMaris, and I collaborate to explore the work-family links decipherable in Greif's national survey of custodial single-parent dads, and in the following chapter, Polly Fassinger discusses the ways in which gender conditions housework for single-parent men and women. Taken together, these two chapters show that whereas single-parent fathers wish employers and co-workers would respect and support their parenting responsibilities, single fathers are less likely than mothers to identify with the housekeeping role. The last section of the book, "Workplace Organization and Policy," consists of three chapters examining links among policy, workplace organization, and family roles. In his chapter on family-supportive employer policies, Joseph Pleck argues that men may be both spending more time on family work and experiencing more work/family stress than Hochschild (1989) and others suggest. However, even though men want employers to allow them more family time, the time they actually take for their families often masquerades as something else, such as sick time. And even men who are offered parental leave are more apt to use paid vacation and sick time than the more formal unpaid option. Thus, Pleck says, in the United States men's needs for workplace changes are often invisible and therefore unacknowledged.

In the following chapter, Linda Haas offers several explanations for Swedish men's relatively low use of extended paid parental leave benefits. She finds that in spite of Sweden's egalitarian gender attitudes, occupational sex segregation and informal norms at men's workplaces limit men's use of parental benefits. Thus, in both Sweden and the United States the occupational culture of men's work inhibits formal use of family leave benefits.

In the final chapter, Amy Andrews and Lotte Bailyn analyze interview data from a longitudinal study of men and women who received MBAs in 1979. Although at first the women had more difficulty juggling work and family, after 10 years the men suffered more work/family stress than the women. Andrews and Bailyn find that gender affects the ways in which people think about the relationship between work and family. Women adapted better over the long run because they were more likely than men to have a synergistic outlook that allowed them to more effectively juggle work and family. Here again we see that when men and women in dual-career families are confronted with similar work/family conflicts, their responses are gendered. In this case, it appears that men have not learned to juggle as effectively as do women.

Collectively the chapters in this volume provide a great deal of new information as well as useful insights about the ways in which gender conditions men's work and family lives. The picture is indeed one of "resistance and change," as Willinger argues in her chapter. The relationship between parenting and providing is changing for many U.S. men of all social classes and family statuses. However, both structural and cultural barriers continue to prevent gender symmetry in the work/family balancing act. Since 1977, men have begun to make adjustments in their work to accommodate their families, but workplace policy and occupational cultures have been slower to change.

Years ago, Hochschild helped us understand how the "clock work of male careers" (1975) made it difficult for women to combine work and family. It is now time to pay more attention to the ways in which both the culture and structure of men's work affects those men who are now choosing more parenting and household responsibilities.

References

Bailyn, L. (1970). Career and family orientations of husbands and wives in relation to marital happiness. *Human Relations, 23,* 97-113.

Carrigan, T. B., Connell, B., & Lee, J. (1987). Toward a new sociology of masculinity. In H. Brod (Ed.), *The making of masculinities* (pp. 63-100). Boston, MA: Allen & Unwin.

Crosby, F. J. (1991). *Juggling: The unexpected advantages of balancing career and home for women and their families.* New York: The Free Press.

Ehrenreich, B. (1983). *The hearts of men: American dreams and the flight from commitment.* Garden City, NY: Anchor.

Hochschild, A. R. (1975). Inside the clockwork of male careers. In Florence Howe (Ed.), *Women and the power to change* (pp. 47-80). New York: McGraw-Hill.

Hochschild, A. R. (1989). *The second shift: Working parents and the revolution at home.* New York: Viking.

Hood, J. C. (1983). *Becoming a two-job family.* New York: Praeger.

Kanter, R. M. (1977). *Work and family in the United States: A critical review and agenda for research and policy.* New York: Russell Sage.

LaRossa, R., & LaRossa, M. (1981). *Transition to parenthood.* Beverly Hills, CA: Sage.

Lein, L. (1983). *Families without villains.* Lexington, MA: Lexington.

Pleck, J. H. (1977). The work-family role system. *Social Problems, 24,* 417-427.

Rapoport, R., & Rapoport R. (1971). Dual-career families. Middlesex, UK: Penguin.

Rapoport, R., & Rapoport R., with Blumstead, J. (Eds.). (1978). *Working couples.* New York: Harper & Row.

Risman, B. (1987). Intimate relationships from a microstructural perspective: Men who mother. *Gender & Society, 1,* 6-32.

Stacey, J., & Thorne, B. (1985). The missing feminist revolution in sociology. *Social Problems, 32,* 301-316.

Weiss, R. S. (1990). *Staying the course: The emotional and social lives of men who do well at work.* New York: Free Press.

West, C., & Zimmerman, D. H. (1991). In J. Lorber & S. Farrell (Eds.), *The social construction of gender* (pp. 13-37). Newbury Park, CA: Sage.

PART ONE

FATHERING AND PROVIDING

1

What Do Fathers Provide?

Reconsidering the Economic and Nurturant Dimensions of Men as Parents

THEODORE F. COHEN

For much of the 20th century, Americans have associated fathers with the act of working and the responsibility of "providing" for their families. This image of fathers arises more from general assumptions about men and the dominant ideologies of gender than from any empirical evidence. As many scholars have noted, men were long typecast in "instrumental," economically derived positions whereby masculinity, male identity, and male role performance all center around work (Brannon, 1976; Cohen, 1987, 1988; Pleck, 1979, 1983). We have "measured masculinity by the size of the paycheck" (Gould, 1976), assumed that men identified themselves with and derived their self-esteem from performance at work (Goetting, 1982; Rubin, 1979), and acted as if the most meaningful male activity took place outside of the family in pursuit of a wage (Parsons, 1942; Zelditch, 1974). Even men's familial roles and responsibilities were seen as discharged outside and away from the family itself as "good providers" or in the "Husband-Economic-Provider-Role" (Bernard, 1983; Grönseth, 1972; Liebow, 1967; Rubin, 1976). Working from such traditional assumptions, researchers studied men's lives almost exclusively in their more public dimensions, as if men's familial experiences had no bearing on their daily realities. Likewise, social scientists studying families have paid little attention to fathers and husbands. Studies of marriage or parenthood relied, instead, on data drawn primarily from wives and mothers (e.g., Blood & Wolfe, 1960; Miller & Swanson, 1958; Safilios-Rothschild, 1969).

A corollary of this oversight was to narrowly portray women's lives as centered primarily on family and maternal responsibilities. This treatment of women is well critiqued by Ann Oakley (1974) in the following excerpt from *The Sociology of Housework*: "By far the largest segment of sociological literature concerning women is focused on their roles as wives, mothers and housewives. . . . Possibly the family and marriage are areas in which [women's] sociological visibility exceeds social presence" (pp. 17-18).

With such "core assumptions" guiding our thinking about gender and family, the specific formulations of parental roles followed accordingly. "Parenting" was culturally perceived as "mothering," in that it implied nurturance, an activity seen as natural to women but foreign to men (Cancian, 1985). Fathers' connections to their children were portrayed as chiefly financial; good fathers were "good providers" and good providers made good fathers (Bernard, 1983). Numerous cultural and scientific implications followed these emphases. For example, maternal employment was perceived as a potentially serious social problem in that it implied the absence of mothers and a lack of nurturing. Because fathers were inexorably associated with providing, their job-induced absence was normal and their sustained, full-time presence (via unemployment, disability, "role reversals") assumed to be problematic. As Joseph Pleck noted, the dominant, though not exclusive, cultural image of 20th-century fathers has been the "father-breadwinner model" (Pleck, 1987), wherein fathers were the ultimate sources of both morality and discipline, but physically, socially, and emotionally removed from the family by their concentration on work.

Given the overwhelming acceptance of the male economic provider role as the model of what men *ought* to be like, it is difficult to know whether there were many men whose parental roles did not conform to the dominant model. Cultural messages about men's roles in the family discouraged much open deviation, and researchers, guided by earlier ideologies of gender, asked questions that assumed compliance with a traditional division of responsibilities (Pleck, 1979). Because men's daily lives were consumed largely at work, their actions seemed to affirm both the earlier traditional functionalist model and the later critical feminist perspectives of men and families. As a result, many questions about the depth and substance of men's parental attachments went unasked.

Recent years have seen an explosion in research on fathering (Bronstein & Cowan, 1988; R. LaRossa, 1988; Lewis & O'Brien, 1987; McKee & O'Brien, 1982). There are indicators of greater male investments and involvements in parenting and child care. Culturally, we herald the emergence of the "new father," noting an increase in both male involvement in parenting and the meaning of fatherhood to men. Ambiguities remain, however. Even late-20th-century "alternative" and more intimately involved styles of fathering have failed to completely replace the father-breadwinner model or challenge its position of cultural dominance (Pleck, 1987). Further, in pointing to the increasing emphasis on nurturant dimensions of fatherhood, Ralph LaRossa cautions that such expectations may say more about changes in motherhood than about shifts in what is truly desired of and by fathers (R. LaRossa, 1988). Thompson and Walker (1989) support this point in their review of literature on gender in families, asserting "Virtually all men believe being a good father means first and foremost being a good provider" (p. 861). Thus, despite much recent attention to men's experience of fathering, it is unclear what contemporary U.S. fathers do or think they should do beyond providing.

It is also uncertain what fathering does to men. If being a father was reducible to being a stable breadwinner, and being an adult male, married or single, meant likewise, the discontinuity between being childless and being a father should not be great, given that men's role repertoire supposedly remained centered around working. If, however, men are adopting broader conceptualizations of fatherhood, they will experience more discontinuity between their childless and parental statuses.

In the following pages I use data drawn from an exploratory study of men's transitions to marriage and fatherhood and their enactments of their marital, parental, and work roles (Cohen, 1986, 1987) to reveal the inadequacy of the traditional father-as-provider ideology. In addition to the "breadwinning" component, I will assess other, more nurturant components of men's paternal role definitions and performances. I will show that neither the impact of fatherhood on my informants nor the way they perceived and performed their roles as fathers can be fully understood by focusing primarily on their activities as economic providers.

Sampling and Data Collection

The data for this analysis come from semistructured interviews with a nonprobability sample of 30 Boston-area new husbands and fathers. Interviews examined informants' experiences "becoming and being" husbands and fathers, that is, their transitions to marriage and fatherhood and their conceptualizations of and involvements in work, marital, and parental roles. Almost half of the informants were married men without children (14 men), and the rest were married fathers of young children. Because I was interested in both "becoming" and "being" husbands and fathers, I sought informants who were able to speak about their life before marriage or fatherhood and had had time enough to assume their new family roles and speak with some depth about how their life had changed as a result of these role transitions. I therefore restricted the sample to men who were relatively new to each status. The 14 childless men had been married 1 to 3 years (average of 1.9 years); the "new fathers" were married men who had been fathers for 5 years or less (average was 2.1 years of fatherhood and the average length of marriage for fathers was 4.6 years). Of the 14 childless husbands, 4 were "pregnant fathers." They were particularly useful sources of information about the transition to parenthood and the shifts in one's perceptions and expectations of fatherhood as the event grows both nearer and more real.

Because I was interested both in the transitions between statuses and in the way informants experience marriage and fatherhood, I chose to restrict the sample so that most men reported on only one transition to marriage and/or one experience of fatherhood. Ninety percent of the sample were men in first marriages; likewise, 13 of the 16 fathers were first-time parents. These sampling requirements yielded a sample of relatively young men (average age was 29; 26.6 for new husbands, 31.5 for new fathers).

I used a combination of nonprobability sampling strategies to generate my sample of informants. Twelve men were obtained via a variety of agencies and organizations, including church or medical personnel in a working-class community outside of Boston. This group "snowballed," yielding eight more men. The remaining 10 were referred by my own colleagues, friends, or neighbors. To increase the range of variation in my sample, I accepted no more than two referrals from any informant.

I deliberately sought men of varying socioeconomic backgrounds. Informants' occupations ranged from laborer (janitor, warehouseman), through skilled laborer (tool and die maker, mechanic), low-level white-collar worker (computer operator, sales representative) to administrator and professional (architect, college professor). Half of the employed informants worked in traditional blue-collar or low-level white-collar occupations. Four men were not employed; three were full-time students, and one was a househusband. More than two thirds of the sample were husbands of employed women. Of the nine wives who were not employed outside the home, eight were "new mothers" who had recently stopped working upon the birth of their child. Informants' educational backgrounds were more "middle class." Sixty percent of the men, including some of those in blue-collar occupations, had college degrees (nine men) or graduate education (nine men).

Using an interview schedule of more than 100 items, I interviewed each informant once about his experiences becoming and being a husband and/or father as well as about the effects of work on his family life. Men were interviewed alone, in settings convenient to them, for an average of just under 2 hours. I tape-recorded and later transcribed each interview. The transcripts were then analyzed thematically, using the existing literature on men, women, and families as initial sources of themes (Oakley, 1980; R. LaRossa & M. LaRossa, 1981; Rubin, 1976). Other themes emerged from the interview material itself through the "constant comparative method" of qualitative analysis (Glaser & Strauss, 1976). Given the size and nature of this nonprobability sample, the findings presented are offered not for generalization to the population of contemporary U.S. fathers, but rather as suggestions for future research. The findings do, however, indicate the inadequacy of traditional assumptions about the content and meaning of fatherhood. If, as I will show, my informants' experiences extended far beyond their roles as economic providers, then at least some men's experiences as fathers are overlooked or misrepresented by those traditional assumptions.

Findings and Discussion

Becoming a Father

> I think everything in a personal relationship a baby changes. . . . It's just fantastic . . . it knocked me for a loop. Something creeps into your life and then all of a sudden it dominates your life. It changes your relationship to everybody and everything, and you question every value you ever had. . . . And you say to yourself, "This is a miracle . . ."
>
> (33-year-old municipal administrator)

Contrary to what traditional thinking about fatherhood would lead one to expect, becoming fathers had a dramatic impact on informants' lives, extending far beyond the economic implications of this transition. Repeatedly, in interviews with both fathers and fathers-to-be, I was struck by moving accounts of the consequences of becoming a father. Although all the men did not react in the same way, they did find themselves affected in unexpected ways. Because little of the assessed impact was economic, the most important aspects of entering fatherhood may be lost if one assumes that fathering is nearly synonymous with breadwinning.

To examine men's reactions to fatherhood, I began with their reactions to pregnancy and childbirth, the point at which men become aware of the impending transition. During pregnancy, men begin to anticipate fatherhood and attempt to ready themselves for whatever conceptions of fatherhood they possess.

Few men recalled being surprised by the news that they were to become fathers, and few remembered having any opposition to the idea. When the pregnancy was confirmed, most men recalled reacting in very positive ways, with feelings ranging from "happy" to "absolutely fantastic." Those who acknowledged any ambivalence seemed to be weighing their pleasure against their sense of change and responsibility. For example, this comment came from a 28-year-old sales representative who was an expectant father at the time of the interview:

> I was excited. . . . [It] was a very, very exciting time but a nervous time too—no turning back now. . . . It was very early; she was only 2 or 3 weeks pregnant when we found out. It was scary. I'm very excited, okay? But I'm also scared at the same time 'cause it's gonna change things.

Pregnancy quickly triggered feelings and concerns that informants had never before felt. One can see this in their answers to both a general question about their feelings and a series of specific probes into selected areas about which they might have worried during pregnancy. Included among my probes were questions about the pregnancy, the birth process, economic matters, and changes that were expected to accompany parenthood.The two most anxiety-provoking areas for men were the baby's health and the wife's health and safety. Because men have little control over either of these matters, a sense of powerlessness heightened their concern. Thirteen of the 20 fathers and expectant fathers found themselves thinking and worrying about possible birth defects or the pregnancy and birth processes. As a 29-year-old laborer said:

> It was all needless worrying, I guess. I was really worried about taking her to the hospital. . . . I thought for sure that she would have the baby . . . in traffic, in the car. . . . And of course you do worry about how the baby is gonna come out. You hope the baby is gonna be healthy. I worried about that—If he wasn't, was I gonna be able to handle that?

Twelve men described worrying specifically about their wife's health and safety. For some this worry included a concern for the fetus, although for most the preoccupation was solely with their wife. For example, a 37-year-old architect said:

> I worried about my wife, that was all. She had a real concern for the health of the child. I had listened to the child late at night and had seen the ultrasound. I tried, maybe I was blocking that [fear] out. . . . I was just hoping that she wouldn't be knocked around too much.

As a result of these two sets of concerns, many found themselves taking more precautions, even imposing limitations on their wife in an effort to exert some control over the uncontrollable. Occasionally wives experienced these preventive measures as overprotectiveness, and at least one man recalled being unaware of how differently he was treating his wife until she pointed it out to him. Most, however, simply went out of their way to be more conscientious.

The next two most common concerns were also closely interrelated. Would they be good fathers and how would fatherhood affect their life? In both cases, the concerns were exacerbated by men's lack of knowledge. Nine of the 20 fathers and expectant fathers had anxieties about their abilities to be "good enough" fathers as well as doubts about knowing how to father. As they voiced such concerns, it was clear that men's perceptions of fathering extended well beyond providing. The following comments illustrate these worries:

> I worry about being a father 'cause I don't know what it will be like. I know how it was for my father to be a father, I know he was always working his ass off, but I don't know how I'm gonna be with my kids.
>
> (26-year-old material control manager)

> Oh yeah, I definitely worried about being a father. . . . I even kept a journal, trying to figure that out. My worries . . . came down to: "What is it that will qualify me to be a father? What am I going to be able to give to him?"
>
> (30-year-old truck driver)

In a similar vein, eight men talked about not knowing how the presence of a child and the demands of child care might affect their life in general or their relationships with their wife.

> I knew there would be this little person that I didn't know anything about . . . exactly what he or she was going to be like. It was unclear to me. Certainly it was going to take up a lot of time. . . . I worried that my [wife] and I would have a lot less time together.
>
> (36-year-old househusband)

Most surprising was the relatively low level of anxiety expressed about the economic responsibilities associated with being fathers. Only six men recalled thinking about the economic impact of parenthood. They reported worrying about increased expenses associated with children and reduced income due to wives stopping work. Expecting that the "burden will fall more heavily" onto their shoulders led them to worry about having their "financial end together." One man expressed this in the following terms:

> Most of our worries were out of our financial condition. She made significantly more money than I did and it was obvious that she wasn't going to be working for a while. . . . She felt she wanted to stay home with the baby and I felt guilty about not being able to afford her that opportunity.
>
> (31-year-old retail manager)

There are a number of explanations for why more men didn't express greater concern with economic aspects of the transition to fatherhood. Although one might assume that the financial component of the father role was less salient to these men than other components, one should not conclude that it was unimportant. Given that nearly all of the fathers and expectant fathers were stably employed prior to the birth of their children, it is possible that they worried more about those responsibilities that were unknown to them. Work was something they were used to, wage earning something they were already doing. Many may have simply expected to keep doing what they were doing at work while feeling less confident about, and therefore more preoccupied with, those more immediate changes that fatherhood would trigger.

It is also possible that more attention was not paid to the economic dimensions of fathering because of men's perceptions that they would be able to absorb whatever additional costs might follow. Although this was not a particularly affluent sample, the fact that they were dual-earner couples until the birth of the child may have delayed financial concerns. Three fathers, who admitted that they hadn't worried enough about money, support this interpretation. For example:

> I thought about the future but I didn't think about the real important things. I didn't worry about money . . . I still hadn't thought about that. . . . She worked until just about when he was born . . . [and] I didn't think about what I was gonna be doing about money as far as saving for a new apartment or a house or for [son's] education since she wasn't gonna be working anymore. I never thought about saving, just went along. . . . I bought little gifts for her [and] we did a lot of the same things we had before.
>
> (29-year-old laborer)

Even men who claimed not to make "great money" thought that they made enough to afford the expenses that they would incur. As a 33-year-old municipal administrator said:

> I don't think I anticipated them [expenses] correctly. Babies are a very expensive commodity today . . . just his daily upkeep and his care, doctor's bills and stuff like that. . . . It's just unbelievable.

Whatever the reasons behind it, the deemphasis on issues of providing is instructive. I did not hear the deep or frequent expression of concern about providing that would be expected if men did indeed perceive fathering as breadwinning.

The Impact of Fatherhood

Going far beyond increased breadwinning responsibilities, men saw changes in the ways in which they perceived themselves, the relationships they maintained with their wife and others, and the kinds and meaning of activities that they engaged in:

> It's almost like I've been completed in a way . . . like a little candle has been lit inside of me. It's there all the time, you can feel its warmth, you can use it for light if you want. . . . It's almost like I have a focus in life. Before, everything I did really didn't matter much, but now everything I do has bearing for the future.
>
> (25-year-old food handler)

Nicely suggested in the previous quote, the impact of fatherhood was broader and more dramatic than men expected. Beginning with the birth of their children, men were acutely affected by becoming fathers. New priorities, less freedom and free time, restricted relationships with peers, and diminished relationships with wives were common outcomes. As one man put it:

> I had to give up everything I knew and was comfortable with; just open up the drawer, put it all in the drawer, and close the drawer.
>
> (33-year-old municipal administrator)

Many of the most widely expressed effects of the transition to fatherhood are invisible to the outsider. Alterations in men's sense of self and life priorities cannot be observed in behavioral changes after children are born. Even men's continued performance of role behaviors initiated long before fatherhood, such as wage earning, took on new meaning. These roles were redefined within the context of parenthood. If fatherhood were reducible to providing, one would not expect either the extent or depth of change these men reported.

In addition to the intrapersonal and interpersonal adjustments men made, they found that their role obligations were affected through both the addition of new responsibilities and the heightening of others. Those tasks associated with child care were, of course, new to men's round of activities. These responsibilities were broader than men had anticipated and therefore required more adjustments. Their activities covered everything from daily physical care to more long-term responsibilities as teachers or nurturers in their child's socialization:

> It's not like a puppy—great when it's small but now [that] it's starting to chew up things . . . get rid of it. It's not like that . . . type of commitment. . . . In effect, you are a butler or maid for them for the first year or two.
>
> (25-year-old food handler)

> I told someone once that I was a manservant for a midget. . . . At the time I was putting my son's coat on. . . . And then simple things, like crossing the street—I have to teach my son how to cross the street. All those things, there's never a moment's rest. You can't just take it out and unplug it like a TV or a radio.
>
> (33-year-old municipal administrator)

The transition to fatherhood also bound men more tightly to their existing occupational roles. Because most of the fathers in the sample became sole breadwinners for at least a time after the birth of their first child, it is not surprising that many of them found their work-related concerns heightened. Some worried for the first time about how well they were providing or about either losing their job or having to be "stuck" in jobs that they found ungratifying. What is important about these anxieties is that they were activated by men's transitions to fatherhood. With the arrival of children and the wife's at least temporary departure from the labor force, men who had never before given priority to breadwinning began to feel more like "providers." This shift in role priority is a real though easily misunderstood indicator of the impact of fatherhood on men.

It is easy to overlook the role fatherhood plays in causing men to modify or revise their commitments to their jobs. In fact, because they continue to work as they did before becoming parents, men may seem relatively unaffected by becoming fathers. Any changes in their commitment to work may be interpreted as just that: changes in their commitment to work. Yet when one explores the altered meanings men attach to their activities, one sees that they are initiated by fatherhood. This greater than expected impact of fatherhood in men's lives was matched by broader than anticipated definitions and enactments of the male parenting role.

Being a Father

If the traditional depiction of men in families were accurate and complete, then fathers' roles in their children's lives would center around providing rather than around any other dimension of parenting. It would also follow that breadwinning activities would be what made them most feel like fathers because that would represent the fulfillment of their primary obligation as a parent. My interviews with new fathers suggest that neither of these characterizations can be adequately generalized to all fathers. Although a few fathers in the sample saw their roles in more traditional terms, a majority offered role definitions and attachments that emphasized more nurturant dimensions of parenting.

When asked to define a father's main responsibilities to his children, only 5 of the 16 fathers even mentioned "providing." The only one of these five who restricted his answer to traditional notions of fatherhood said:

> I would say mostly financial. . . . Also, I would be the one to put my foot down when he's disobeying; she threatens him—"I'll get Daddy. . . . Wait till I tell Daddy."
>
> (29-year-old laborer)

The other four fathers who included father's economic provider responsibility listed it as one of a number of both instrumental and expressive responsibilities. A 30-year-old truck driver described fatherhood this way:

> To provide the child with the physical means to live and grow, every father should provide that whether in opulence or poverty. . . . [Also] to teach about the things I enjoy . . . give him my sense of morals . . . do the things that help him to be happy.

By far, the most frequent responses dealt with the father as a role model or teacher in his child's socialization:

> Same as a woman's responsibility—show the child the right way to grow up and stuff.
>
> (27-year-old warehouseman)

> Just to be a parent, to be a role model for behaviors that will help your child master things. . . . It's appealing to me to think that I could be worthy of being a role model.
>
> (37-year-old architect)

Also mentioned repeatedly were fathers' roles as nurturers and as companions or playmates for their children. For instance:

> I think the most important responsibility is that of nurturing the child. I think it's important for fathers to be with a child as much as mothers are, if it's at all possible. If it's not, they ought to try and make it possible, even if it means giving up something.
>
> (31-year-old retail manager)

Despite a question that invited reference to the breadwinner-provider role, less than one third of the fathers even included this role among fathers' "major responsibilities." In a similar vein, when asked what they themselves do that most makes them feel like fathers, only one father, this time a 30-year-old truck driver, referred to the meeting of his breadwinning responsibilities:

> Sometimes, the fulfillment of what I feel are my financial responsibilities will make me feel like a father because I will feel like I'm doing this for him.

Much more common were answers about nurturing activities. For some men this nurturance was expressed through teaching their children certain values or necessary skills; for others it was being emotionally supportive, physically affectionate, or playful with their children. Finally, a few fathers stressed moments when they attempt to discipline their children as occasions when they most feel like fathers.

The combination of answers men gave to the questions described above indicate a much greater emphasis on the nurturant dimensions of the father role than on any other aspect. Men also emphasized nurturing activities in their accounts of what they value most about being a father and in the way they considered themselves most unlike their own fathers. Taken together, it was the importance informants placed on their expressive relationships to their children that most separated the fathers I interviewed from what has traditionally been written or thought about men as parents. As others have noted (Cohen, 1991; McKee & O'Brien, 1982; Pleck, 1983), if we want to know how men think about being and becoming fathers, a qualitative analysis of their own descriptions of fatherhood experiences is more useful than quantitative measures of the amount of time spent in child care activities. Although informants did see a connection between being a father and "providing," they had a much broader idea of what it is that fathers ought to provide. Even examining what informants reported doing as fathers, however, revealed an involvement greater than expected.

Informants' Activities With Their Children

Estimates of fathers' actual time spent with their children have varied considerably, depending on whether one measured total time together (which might include mothers and others) or one-to-one time. Estimates have ranged as low as 37.7 seconds a day (Rebelsky & Hanks, 1971), through Fischman's (1986) finding of an average of 8 minutes a day during the week and 14 minutes a day on weekends, to more optimistic measures of "total time" such as Barnett and Baruch's (1988) 29 hours a week. The wide variability in these and other such estimates of fathers' participation in child care results from a number of factors, including how long ago the study was conducted, the age of the children receiving care, and most important, how father participation was operationalized (e.g., sole responsibility vs. time together) and measured (e.g., time diaries, estimates, etc.).

It is important to note that regardless of the sample or measurement strategies used, estimates of fathers' involvement with their children and responsibility for child care indicate that they spend less time with their children than do mothers. Fathers are also more likely than mothers are to concentrate their time with children in passive and less demanding "secondary child care activities" (Barnett & Baruch, 1988; R. LaRossa, 1988; R. LaRossa & M. LaRossa, 1981).

These same differences surfaced in my informants' accounts of their and their partners' parenting. Although the fathers in my sample displayed a greater attachment to and involvement in their parental roles than even they had expected, all but one were still secondary caretakers when compared to their wives. There were, for example, still some men whose activities consisted almost exclusively of "play" and whose involvement with their children consisted of "secondary" passive child care such as watching their child at play or watching television together (R. LaRossa & M. LaRossa, 1981). Men offered no descriptions of wives employing this same style of parenting, and it is not likely that many can or do. With only one exception, even the most active and involved of the fathers were less active and involved parents than their partner. However, it is equally true that most of the fathers were more active and involved in parenting than men have typically been thought to be.

When asked about the amount of time spent with their children, fathers reported spending a range of time, from relatively little to nearly all of the child care given to the children. The latter father, the 36-year-old, full-time househusband, described his primary caretaking responsibilities:

> I don't want to exaggerate my role in the child care. My wife takes care of the kids a lot, she loves taking care of the kids, but she reaches a point where she's got to go do something else. If I reach that point, I don't have a choice. I just have to keep doing it.

The other end of the spectrum was more common. Five fathers, in keeping with traditional notions of fathering, were struggling to maintain even a low level of involvement in daily child care. This comment from a 28-year-old computer technician is typical of these fathers:

> I spend little overall time with them during the week; I'm gone before they wake up and I get home at 5 or 5:30. I spend a little time here in one form or another—playing or eating [together]—Usually my wife and I try and talk too, so I'm not even sure how much time I spend with the kids.

The majority of fathers fell between these two extremes. These men described active daily involvements in day-to-day child care and rather high estimates of actual time spent with their children. When pressed to qualitatively assess their involvements with their children and in child care, these men revealed role relationships that were both active and extensive, encompassing most of the tasks associated with child care. For example:

> I get up early in the morning with him. I'm with him for like an hour and a half in the morning, I make him breakfast every morning, play with him before I go to work. . . . When I come home at night, I get home around 6 so I'm with him for about 3 1/2 hours, four times a week. On the weekends, I have him every other weekend for a whole weekend at a time, from 7 in the morning till 7 at night. . . . I've even taken weeks off, a week off on vacation, so that [my wife] could go away and I took care of [him].
>
> (33-year-old municipal administrator)

> I'd say we spend 40-50 hours a week together. This comes from having 2 days off and every other weekend. [During that time] I'll wash him, feed him, go for a walk. . . . I could [either] just watch TV and bounce him on my knee or I can take him to the park or to a shopping mall. Maybe because I see a return coming back I [choose not to] just sit there and watch the tube. I change him, feed him, bathe him.
>
> (25-year-old food handler)

In analyzing men's comments about fatherhood, I identified the following three factors accounting for their actual levels of involvement in child care: (a) their commitment to fathering, (b) wives' needs for "down time" (R. LaRossa & M. LaRossa, 1981) and most relevant for the present discussion, (c) their work schedules (see Presser & Cain, 1983). Thus, whereas men's work did not form the substance of informants' responsibilities as fathers, the timing of that work was the strongest determinant of the shape of their parenting activities.

As some of the comments above indicated, men's relationships with their children had to be fitted around their jobs. Men who reported the lowest levels of time with their children also described "having to leave" the house before their children even woke, or "not getting home until" an hour in the evening that left little opportunity to spend time together. As was true of their marital relationships (Cohen, 1987, 1988), occupational constraints on involvement was a source of much discontent or guilt. A 31-year-old retail manager described the conflict between work and family time:

> Work eats into our time together. Before, [my wife] worked part-time evenings and I worked part-time days so that we had more time to spend with our daughter and we had weekends to spend all three of us together. Now we have, at most, one day off a week together. . . . I have fantasies about being able to have a livable income off of [business in the home] and spending all day with my daughter. If I could do that, I would like to.

For some fathers, then, attachment to fathering well surpassed the amount of time spent with their children. This being the case, any measure of the former that uses the latter as the sole or major indicator would be suspect.

On the other hand, men's paid work schedules occasionally afforded them unique opportunities to engage in more extensive activity with their children, which itself fostered a greater involvement in parenting. Two fathers who worked nights, a third who as a teacher returned home early from work, and a fourth whose job included two weekdays off all associated their work schedules with higher than expected levels of involvement in child care (Hood & Golden, 1979; Presser & Cain, 1983). Thus, whereas some fathers felt that their jobs restricted their parenting activities, others owed their high levels of involvement to their work schedules. In both directions, work became a dominant influence over the nature of men's relationships with their children.

Retreat From the Provider Role?

> I think if you are going to have kids it is important that you interact with them. That is something I didn't have that much with my father because he was working 10 hours a day. . . . But it doesn't have to be that way.
>
> (29-year-old physicist)

Measuring attachment to and performance of the "provider role" is problematic (Hood, 1986). If one defines the provider role as requiring a single-mindedness about working and an identification of work as one's primary contribution to one's family, then informants deliberately rejected attachment to this role. There were three manifestations of this rejection. First, when I asked about the "most important roles" in their lives, men identified more strongly with being a father and husband than with being a worker (Cohen, 1987, 1988). Second, they staked no ideological claim on working and providing. When they were sole supporters of their family, they described this condition as the result of the practical circumstances of having very young children and a wife who had recently left the labor force. This mostly temporary, parentally induced, shift to sole wage earning may have made some men come to see themselves as breadwinners and worry, for the first time, about their role performance. It was not, however, a role that they performed and protected with any sense of ownership. When I asked informants how they felt about their wives working outside the home, only one man noted that he "was not happy about it." More typically, men claimed to have positive feelings about their wives' employment. Examples of men's responses were, "It's great, I love it"; "I think it's fine"; and "It doesn't bother me." As the following comments reveal, most informants questioned the whole idea of the father as the provider:

> When I was growing up, work was my father's responsibility. That is no longer the case. Everybody works—everybody has to pitch in. It is no longer a husband's position or a wife's position. It's everybody's.
>
> (40-year-old mechanic)

> I think it's great that she works. . . . I knew one guy in high school who, when he got married, gave his wife orders that she was to stay home and make his meals. I thought he was a real jackass; I have no respect for people like that. We supposedly got rid of slavery a hundred years ago.
>
> (29-year-old physicist)

Interestingly, whereas only one informant openly objected to his wife working outside the home, four others recalled objecting to the idea of their wives not working.

Finally, and most notably, men seemed to be consciously attempting to avoid replicating with their children the kinds of relationships they recalled having had with their own father.

When fathers and expectant fathers were asked to compare themselves to their own father, overwhelmingly men described trying, wanting, or expecting to be unlike their own father. They wanted to be "better" parents, "interact more," be "more involved" with their children, and have better father-child relationships. In their accounts it becomes clear that the deficiencies in their early relationships with their father stemmed from what they saw as excessive job-induced father absence from daily life. Without blaming their fathers for the lack of time or attention they received as children, fathers and expectant fathers embraced a more active version of fathering:

> In a certain sense, my approach is a response to my relationship with my father, who—until I was 10—would be gone for work before I woke up, and not until I was 7 or 8, was he back before I went to bed. I spent little time with him. I still feel little emotional echoes from it . . . so I make an effort with my son.
>
> (42-year-old teacher)

> When I was a kid we hardly saw [my father] because he worked two jobs. That's something that I'd rather not do, not 'cause I don't want to work two jobs or we couldn't use the money, it's just that I'd rather see more of my kids. . . . My father never saw us kids.
>
> (29-year-old laborer)

These comments suggest only that men can, and do, articulate a larger, more involved notion of fathering. Actual relationships between informants and their children may ultimately come to resemble what they recall of relationships with their fathers. Because the men's memories came from later stages of childhood than represented in their current families, it is even possible that their fathers started with similar desires and comparable levels of participation when their children were young, but as the children grew older, shifts in the demands of jobs conspired to reduce their involvements in the sons' childhoods.

If, however, one accepts men's disavowal of the kind of fathering they received, then one must accept, too, the implications of this repudiation. As men themselves noted, it was not their fathers that they were rejecting but the life-style their fathers had to live. In seeking to avoid the same outcome with their children, they were advocating less involvement in the provider role.

Absence of Class Differences

Somewhat unexpectedly, there was little socioeconomic variation in the ways in which informants defined fathering and in the impact becoming a father had in their lives. Working-class men were as likely to emphasize the nurturing dimensions of fathering as middle-class men. Further, in both the range and extent of child care involvement, social class influences were not apparent. Where economic variation existed in involvement in child care, it manifested itself indirectly through occupational constraints (e.g., schedules, expected levels of commitment) imposed from without rather than differing class-based ideologies of fathering. Only in the meaning attached to work and its relationship to being fathers did social class make a noticeable difference.

More common for working- than middle-class fathers was a sense that one's work was an expression of family roles. It was their status as husbands and especially fathers that frequently led them to take or keep the jobs they were in. They became "locked into" their jobs because the responsibilities of parenthood made occupational change difficult. Additionally, with little intrinsic gratification derived from their jobs, they were more likely to understand their work as part of what they contributed to their families.

Middle-class informants were more likely to see intrinsic rewards in their jobs. Their work was more deeply a part of how they saw themselves and less immediately seen as something they gave their families. Whereas they recognized the contribution their working made to their wife and children, this familial contribution was neither the sole nor most powerful motivation for working (Cohen, 1988).

Summary and Conclusion

The preceding discussion has suggested that traditional work-centered definitions of "fathering" are inadequate for characterizing either informants' beliefs about fathering or their behavior as parents. Despite inferential limitations imposed by sampling, my informants' experiences show that the traditional father-provider role does not fit all men's lives. Few informants advocated the ideology of the father-provider. For the majority, experiences becoming and being fathers stretched far beyond working. Study participants described attachments to the more nurturant dimensions of "parenting" that sounded like endorsements of contemporary, involved fathering. Ralph LaRossa's cautionary assessment of how much substantial change has really occurred in the substance of fatherhood is an important one, especially lest anyone conclude from the foregoing discussion that I'm suggesting fathers are becoming interchangeable with mothers in the caring for children. However, Pleck (1983) makes a persuasive case that if men already possess high levels of psychological involvement in their family roles, there is a greater likelihood of increasing their familial role performance than there would be if they first had to shift their psychological involvement from work to family. In a similar vein, if men accept the ideology of "involved fathering," and if that filters into and is reinforced through the expectations of their spouses, the fathering they do is more amenable to enlargement than it would be if definitions of fathering centered around "providing."

Accepting men's accounts as sincere expressions of a desire for more involvement in more aspects of parenting than the traditional role of father as provider prescribes may require looking beyond their relative allocation of time to work and parenting. By themselves, such temporal distributions may seem to validate the traditional role, because when fathers are "providers," work is an expression rather than a restriction on fathering. If, however, men are enlarging their attachments to more nurturant dimensions of parenting and pushing for or being pushed into more involvement with their children, work will become increasingly defined as a barrier to parenting. Thus, to maximize what men are available for and encouraged to do as parents will require reducing or restructuring what they are required or expected to do as workers. If informants sincerely wish to avoid "the sins of the fathers" by having greater and deeper involvement with their sons and daughters, they will need the time to do so. This need for time may be met through many of the familiar work-family supports—flextime, parental leave, job-sharing, and so on—typically identified as "women's issues." Coupling these family supports with continued and widened cultural reinforcement of the value of more involved fathering will be the most viable combination for creating broader and more fulfilling styles of fathering.

References

Barnett, R., & Baruch, G. (1988). Correlates of father's participation in family work. In P. Bronstein & C. Cowan (Eds.), *Fatherhood today: Men's changing role in the family* (pp. 66-78). New York: John Wiley.

Bernard, J. (1983). The good provider role: Its rise and fall. In A. Skolnick & J. Skolnick (Eds.), *Family in transition* (3rd ed., pp. 125-144). Boston: Little, Brown.

Blood, R., & Wolfe, D. (1960). *Husbands and wives.* New York: Free Press.

Brannon, R. (1976). The male sex role: Our culture's blueprint of manhood and what it's done for us lately. In D. David & R. Brannon (Eds.), *The forty-nine percent majority: The male sex role* (pp.1-48). Reading, MA: Addison-Wesley.

Bronstein, P., & Cowan, C. (Eds.). (1988). *Fatherhood today: Men's changing role in the family.* New York: John Wiley.

Cancian, F. (1985). Gender politics: Love and power in the private and public spheres. In A. Rossi (Ed.), *Gender and the life course* (pp.253-262). Hawthorne, NY: Aldine.

Cohen, T. F. (1986). *Men's family roles: Becoming and being husbands and fathers.* Doctoral dissertation, Boston University. (University Microfilms No. 86-09272)

Cohen, T. F. (1987). Remaking men: Men's experiences becoming and being husbands and fathers and their implications for reconceptualizing men's lives. *Journal of Family Issues, 8,* 57-77.

Cohen, T. F. (1988). Gender, work and family: The impact and meaning of work in men's family roles. *Family Perspective, 22,* 293-308.

Cohen, T. F. (1991). Speaking with men: Application of a feminist methodology to the study of men's lives. *Men's Studies Review, 8*(4), 4-13.

Fischman, J. (1986, October). The children's hours. *Psychology Today,* pp. 16-18.

Glaser, B., & Strauss, A. (1976). *The discovery of grounded theory.* New York: Aldine.

Goetting, A. (1982). The six stations of remarriage: Developmental tasks of remarriage after divorce. *Family Relations, 31,* 213-222.

Gould, R. (1976). Measuring masculinity by the size of a paycheck. In D. David & R. Brannon (Eds.), *The forty-nine percent majority: The male sex role* (pp.113-117). Reading, MA: Addison-Wesley.

Grönseth, E. (1972). The breadwinner trap. In L. K. Howe (Ed.), *The future of the family* (pp.175-191). New York: Simon & Schuster.

Hood, J. (1986, May). The provider role: Its meaning and measurement. *Journal of Marriage and the Family, 48,* 349-359.

Hood, J., & Golden, S. (1979). Beating time/making time: The impact of work scheduling on men's family roles. *Family Coordinator, 28,* 575-592.

LaRossa, R. (1988). Fatherhood and social change. *Family Relations, 37,* 451-457.

LaRossa, R., & LaRossa, M. (1981). *Transition to parenthood: How infants change families.* Beverly Hills, CA: Sage.

Lewis, C., & O'Brien, M. (1987). *Reassessing fatherhood: New observations on fathers and the modern family.* Beverly Hills, CA: Sage.

Liebow, E. (1967). *Tally's corner: A study of Negro streetcorner men.* Boston: Little, Brown.

McKee, L., & O'Brien, M. (Eds.). (1982). *The father figure.* London: Tavistock.

Miller, D., & Swanson, G. (1958). *The changing American parent.* New York: John Wiley.

Oakley, A. (1974). *The sociology of housework.* New York: Pantheon.

Oakley, A. (1980). *Women confined: Towards a sociology of childbirth.* New York: Schocken.

Parsons, T. (1942). Age and sex in the social structure. *American Sociological Review, 7,* 604-616.

Pleck, J. (1979). Men's family work: Three perspectives and some new data. *Family Coordinator, 28,* 473-480.

Pleck, J. (1983). Husbands paid work and family roles: Current research issues. In H. Lopata & J. Pleck (Eds.), *Research into the interweave of social roles: Families and jobs* (Vol. 3, pp. 251-333). Greenwich, CT: JAI.

Pleck, J. (1987). American fathering in historical perspective. In M. Kimmel (Ed.), *Changing men: New directions in research on men and masculinity* (pp. 83-97). Newbury Park, CA: Sage.

Presser, H. B., & Cain, V. (1983). Shift work among dual-earner couples with children. *Science, 219,* 876-879.

Rebelsky, F., & Hanks, C. (1971). Fathers' verbal interaction with infants in the first three months of life. *Child Development, 42,* 63-68.

Rubin, L. (1976). *Worlds of pain: Life in the working class family.* New York: Basic Books.

Rubin, L. (1979). *Women of a certain age: The search for midlife self.* New York: Harper & Row.

Safilios-Rothschild, C. (1969). Family sociology or wives' family sociology: A cross cultural examination of decision making. *Journal of Marriage and the Family, 31,* 290-301.

Thompson, L., & Walker, A. (1989). Gender in families: Women and men in marriage, work and parenthood. *Journal of Marriage and the Family, 51,* 845-871.

Zelditch, M. (1974). Role differentiation in the nuclear family. In R. Coser (Ed.), *The family: Its structure and functions* (2nd ed., pp. 256-258). New York: St. Martin's.

2

Are Men Marginal to the Family?

Insights From Chicago's Inner City

HAYA STIER
MARTA TIENDA

Introduction

Both the rise in the number of children living in poverty and the deteriorating economic status of households headed by women have been attributed to the absence of a male provider in the household (Eggebeen & Lichter, 1991). Child poverty rates have been aggravated by the minimal child support provided by noncustodial fathers (Garfinkel & McLanahan, 1986; Weitzman, 1985). According to Garfinkel and McLanahan (1986), about 60% of absent white fathers and 80% of blacks pay no child support (p. 24). Moreover, child support payments are generally low and usually comprise a tiny share of household income (10% for whites and 3.5% for blacks). But father absence is more than an economic problem. Because fathers are key agents of socialization, their presence is critical for healthy child development (Garfinkel & McLanahan, 1986; Hetherington, Camara, & Featherman, 1983).

Originally presented at the 1992 annual meetings of the American Sociological Association, Pittsburgh. The writing of this chapter was supported by a grant from ASPE to the Institute for Research on Poverty at the University of Wisconsin, Madison. We wish to thank William Julius Wilson for his permission to analyze the UPFLS and Joan Aldous for providing an incentive to focus on men. Institutional support of the Population Research Center of NORC and the University of Chicago is gratefully acknowledged.

Academic and policy discussion about the linkages between family structure and poverty have generated a picture of poor, unmarried minority women abandoned by irresponsible men who shirk their parental responsibilities (e.g., Murray, 1984). In fact, many noncustodial parents either never married or never lived with their children (Furstenberg, 1991; Hannerz, 1969; Sullivan, 1989). Whereas some men actually deny their fatherhood, others who acknowledge paternity renege on obligations to provide support, despite their best intentions. A third group of noncustodial fathers marry the mother of their children, but like many men who marry before children come, lose contact with the children after subsequent separation. Thus, because of rising divorce rates and high rates of nonmarital fertility, growing numbers of children receive inadequate emotional and financial support from their biological fathers.

Do declining levels of support from noncustodial fathers mean that men, especially minority men, are becoming marginal to the family? This provocative thesis is implicit in many recent accounts about the growth of an urban underclass, but it has not been explicitly posed.[1] We explore this thesis by examining the circumstances underlying father absence for a sample of parents residing in Chicago's inner city. A discussion of the historical trends in fathers' familial roles and the factors that lead to current patterns of fatherhood provides a theoretical backdrop for the empirical analysis based on a unique survey of inner-city parents and a national survey of families and households. In subsequent sections, we describe the data and methods and compare the living arrangements of inner-city fathers with a national sample of fathers. To the extent possible we illustrate racial and ethnic comparisons within and between contexts. Finally, we analyze the marriage behavior and correlates of child support among noncustodial fathers and conclude with a discussion of inner-city fathers' familial roles.

Theoretical Considerations

Men's familial roles have undergone substantial changes since preindustrial times. Although all family members contributed to subsistence activities during preindustrial times, men were the dominant source of authority *within* the household. As family heads, men were considered to be primary providers because they were credited with their wives' and children's work. With the relocation of economic activity outside the household that accompanied modernization, men's family roles acquired an almost exclusive concern with economic support functions (Damos, 1986). Although fathers continued involvement with their children, particularly at an emotional level, mothers became the principals in socialization except in unusual circumstances. For example, Furstenberg (1988) noted that until the middle of the 19th century, fathers usually assumed custody over the children in case of a marital disruption. When rates of female labor force activity were low, this arrangement protected children's economic well-being. The belief that children are better off with their mother, especially during their early years of life, gradually led to changes in this practice so that by the end of the 19th century, mothers usually became custodial parents in the event of marital disruption.

The "good provider" role of fathers dominated family ideology until the 1960s, when according to Ehrenreich (1985) and others, men began to retreat from their instrumental familial roles (Bernard, 1981; Furstenberg, 1988; Rotundo, 1985). This retreat manifested itself in two ways: Men either *increased* their familial responsibilities by taking more active roles in child rearing and household duties, or greatly diminished their involvement in domestic and parenting roles.[2] Thus, changes in the division of labor within families resulted in two extreme styles of modern parenthood. Whereas some fathers have become heavily involved in child rearing and have extended their familial roles beyond that of breadwinners (Marsiglio, 1991; Pleck, 1987), other fathers deny responsibility for their children, refusing to support them altogether (Furstenberg, 1988).[3]

Many researchers have argued that men in general and minority men in particular are retreating from the family. The primary evidence for this claim derives from levels of financial and emotional support provided by noncustodial fathers. Alternative interpretations build on differences in the form and content of child support provided by men of varying economic means and ethnic group membership. These two views of child support patterns undergird our analysis of whether or not men are becoming marginal to the family.

The growing number of fathers who fail to provide child support for noncustodial children and who have minimal contact with them is socially problematic because it results in both economic and emotional deprivation (Furstenberg, Nord, Peterson, & Zill, 1983; Garfinkel & McLanahan, 1986; Weitzman, 1985). But it is unclear whether noncustodial fathers' failure to provide child support reflects their irresponsibility in dealing with familial obligations, denial of access to their children, or economic constraints. To be sure, men who lack steady incomes find it difficult to provide regular support to their noncustodial children (Furstenberg, 1991; Furstenberg et al., 1983). Before judging men's disregard of child support as evidence of their marginality to the family, it is essential to establish why they fail to provide child support. For example, learning that lack of access to jobs is the reason for neglect shifts the locus of policy debate from concerns about how to force "the scoundrels" to pay their due to concerns about the circumstances underlying their precarious labor market position (Wilson, 1987; Wilson & Neckerman, 1986). Such considerations are particularly germane to the recent debates about the growth of an urban underclass.

There is compelling evidence that some men refuse to support children even when they have resources do so. For example, economic explanations for limited child support stress the low potential benefits noncustodial fathers receive from nonresident children with whom they have limited contact (see, for example, Weiss & Willis, 1985). Presumably, restricted access to children reduces incentives for working fathers to invest in their children. Further, when noncustodial fathers establish new families, they usually give primary attention to their co-resident (often adopted) offspring. This circumstance further decreases incentives to provide child support to nonresident children, reinforcing Weitzman's (1985) contention that able fathers provide inadequate support even when they are financially capable.

Aggregate statistics reveal inadequate levels of financial support by noncustodial fathers, but qualitative studies that disclose more subtle forms of child support tell another story (Furstenberg, 1991; Stack, 1974). For example, both Furstenberg (1991) and Stack (1974) found that many fathers provide in-kind support to their children and to the mothers of their children, albeit on an irregular basis. Furstenberg makes a distinction between "daddies" and "fathers" as indicating those who "do" and "don't do" for their children. Doing for one's child includes support ranging from regular financial contributions to purchasing an occasional box of diapers or looking after the child on occasion. Stack showed that when fathers were unable to provide in-kind support themselves, they engaged the services of their close female kin to take an active role in caring for their children. Stack's thick description portrays men as bridges in a broad kin network that functions as a normative extended family. Thus, although the fathers themselves may play a minor role in their children's lives, they often perform a crucial, but indirect support function by ensuring the replacement of functions they are unable to perform.

In sum, with the increasing rates of out-of-wedlock childbirth and divorce, absent fathers are becoming numerous. These men are most likely to lose interest in their nonresident children because many have limited contacts with them and do not provide adequate support. In our judgment these men are marginal to the family because they have lost their traditional roles as providers and are not involved emotionally with the rearing of their children. One consequence of this behavior is a growing number of children, but especially minority children, being reared in poverty (Eggebeen & Lichter, 1991). To date, most empirical work on living arrangements and support patterns of noncustodial fathers has been restricted to blacks or comparisons between blacks and whites. As a result, ethnic differences in parenting styles, living arrangements, and support activities are neither well documented nor understood. In particular, relatively little is known about Hispanic men's roles as fathers and providers.

There are several compelling reasons for examining the parenting behavior of Hispanic men. First, as a group, Hispanic men are more successful in the labor market than black men, although there are marked differences between Mexican and Puerto Rican men (Tienda, 1989). If labor market standing is the key factor predicting whether fathers will provide for their noncustodial children, we would expect higher levels of support from Mexican compared to Puerto Rican men. Second, the marriage behavior of Hispanic men differs markedly from that of black men (Testa, Astone, Krogh, & Neckerman, 1989). Not only are Mexican men more likely to be married at given ages, but their rates of separation are lower than those of black men (Stier & Tienda, 1992). Puerto Rican men are somewhere between these extremes, with high proportions marrying coupled with high rates of disruption, but the patterns of child support exhibited by Puerto Rican men are virtually unknown. Finally, allegations that minority men are marginal to the family require evidence showing that at comparable income levels, men of color are *less* committed to providing child support than their white counterparts.

Short of this information, prevailing stereotypes about noncustodial fathers as "irresponsible scoundrels" must be interpreted as consequences of their weak market position. Our analyses, therefore, compare black, white, Mexican, and Puerto Rican fathers residing in inner-city neighborhoods where father absence is pervasive. In addition to documenting the living arrangements of inner-city fathers and their children, we examine the circumstances that undergird their support patterns.

Data and Methods

Our analyses are based on the Urban Poverty and Family Life Survey of Chicago (UPFLS) conducted by National Opinion Research Center (NORC) in 1986 and 1987. These data were collected under the auspices of a multiyear study of Urban Poverty and Family Structure in the City of Chicago.[4] The UPFLS is based on a multistage, stratified probability sample of parents aged 18-44 who resided in census tracts representing diverse socioeconomic environments.

Of the 125 tracts sampled, 86% reached or exceeded a family poverty rate of 20%. The remaining census tracts in the sample correspond to mixed poverty neighborhoods, with family poverty rates ranging from 5% to 19%. This sampling strategy deliberately overrepresented poor neighborhoods because it was the most cost-efficient way to study social behavior in deprived neighborhoods, but it is important to distinguish between sampling poor places and poor people. Although poor people have a greater probability of selection in areas with the highest poverty rates, respondents were randomly selected within tracts, hence there is appreciable socioeconomic variability among respondents. In fact, the high income and racial segregation of Chicago resulted in the inclusion of highly affluent and desperately poor respondents. Completed interviews were obtained from 2,490 respondents, which include 1,186 blacks, 368 whites, 484 Mexicans, and 453 Puerto Ricans.[5] The current study is based on 811 men, all of whom were fathers at the time of the survey.

We also used the National Survey of Families and Households (NSFH) to generate baseline tabulations against which to compare family behavior and living arrangements of the inner-city sample.[6] From this survey, which is nationally representative of persons residing in families and households, we selected all men who met the age and parent status criteria used to draw the Chicago survey. To maximize comparability between the Chicago and the national sample, we restricted the NSFH sample to fathers who resided in core cities. These sample restrictions resulted in a national sample of 947 fathers.[7]

Ethnic Differentials in Family Behavior and Living Arrangements

Table 2.1 presents selected characteristics of family behavior and living arrangements for fathers residing in Chicago's inner city and a national sample of comparably aged fathers. Marriage behavior clearly differs along ethnic and racial lines. Both nationally and in Chicago, Mexican and white fathers were more likely to be married than their Puerto Rican and black counterparts. Further, black and Puerto Rican fathers were most likely to have never married, but Chicago's black fathers were more than twice as likely as their national counterparts to have never married.[8] Mexican fathers living in Chicago were over 10 percentage points more likely to be married than white fathers, but at the national level, the 7 point advantage was for whites. Although less than half of all black fathers residing in Chicago were married in 1987, the proportion of married black fathers nationally hovered around 60%.

Despite the considerable ethnic and geographic variation in the propensity of men to marry and stay married, there was surprisingly little diversity in the age at first marriage, which ranged between 23 and 24 years for both samples. However, there was much greater variation in the timing of fatherhood, with black men reporting younger ages at the birth of their first child (22 and 24 years, respectively for the Chicago and national samples). White men became fathers later than minority men, with virtually no difference between Chicago and urban men nationally.

The rate of nonmarital fatherhood in poor inner-city neighborhoods also is striking, particularly by comparison to all urban men. Black men are most likely to enter fatherhood prior to marriage; fathering children out of wedlock is particularly common among Chicago's inner-city black men, where nearly three out of four men acknowledged an out-of-wedlock child. Mexican and white men residing in Chicago's inner city were more likely than their national counterparts to father children prior to marriage, but ethnic differences were trivial. That is, among white and Mexican men, approximately 8% and 25%, respectively, of those in the national and the Chicago samples reported fathering children before they married. By contrast, nearly half of all Puerto Rican men reported fathering at least one child out of wedlock. Although several of these men eventually married the mother of their child (Testa et al., 1989; see also Sullivan, 1989), there persist marked ethnic differences in the likelihood of their doing so.

Table 2.1 Assumption of Family Roles: Fathers Aged 18-44 in Chicago's Inner City and U.S. Cities by Ethnicity

	Black		*White*		*Mexican*		*Puerto Rican*	
	Chicago	*U.S. Cities*	*Chicago*	*U.S. Cities*	*Chicago*	*U.S. Cities*	*Chicago*	*U.S. Cities*
Marriage								
% never married	42.1	17.9	4.8	2.7	7.1	10.0	24.1	20.1
% currently married	41.5	60.8	74.7	87.3	85.3	80.8	66.6	52.1
Parenthood								
Age 1st birth	21.8	23.6	25.7	25.4	24.0	23.4	23.1	24.0
(s.d.)	(4.3)	(4.7)	(5.0)	(4.4)	(4.0)	(4.1)	(4.0)	(4.5)
% out of wedlock 1st birth	71.5	32.2	21.1	7.7	22.6	7.7	48.5	15.7
Age at 1st marriage	23.6	23.8	23.9	22.9	23.7	22.0	24.1	22.9
	(4.8)	(4.3)	(4.4)	(3.6)	(4.4)	(3.7)	(4.4)	(4.6)
Current Co-Residence								
% no children present	31.9	33.0	19.1	13.7	5.6	12.3	7.0	21.8
% with own children present	47.3	63.0	75.6	83.3	91.1	84.8	79.5	67.7
% other children present	20.8	3.9	5.3	3.0	3.3	2.9	13.5	10.5
% with at least one child in other HH	59.2	45.8	27.1	18.9	17.5	19.9	32.7	30.5
N	308	213	127	613	228	101	148	20

SOURCE: Data from the Urban Poverty and Family Life Survey of Chicago (1987) and the National Survey of Families and Households (1987).

As shown in the lower section of Table 2.1, the majority of white, Mexican, and Puerto Rican fathers co-reside with their biological children and stepchildren. Specifically, 83% to 84% of white and Mexican fathers nationally live with their own children, compared to 76% and 91% of whites and Mexicans in residing in Chicago. That Mexican men report the highest rates of co-residence with their own children reflects the larger share of fathers who were married at the time of the survey. Puerto Rican fathers are less likely to marry than Mexicans or whites, but nearly 80% of Chicago fathers reported cohabiting with their own children. The incidence of co-residence between black children and their fathers was appreciably lower—less than 50% in Chicago and just over 60% nationally. In fact, as many as one third of all black men (both in Chicago and the United States) live in households with no dependent children present. The comparable figures for all other groups are lower, especially for Mexicans.

Fathers live without children either because their offspring have already left home or because the men left their children. In most cases of divorce, and certainly most instances of out-of-wedlock births, mothers assume custody of children. Thus, half of all black and one third of all Puerto Rican fathers have dependent children who reside elsewhere. This proportion compares with 27% of white fathers in Chicago, and less than 20% of white fathers nationally. Less than one in five Mexican-origin fathers reported having dependent children who did not live with them.[9]

To examine the linkages between marital status and living arrangements, Figure 2.1 compares the living arrangements of fathers according to three marital status groups—those currently married, those ever married, and those never married. As expected, 5% and 6% of currently married fathers residing in Chicago and U.S. cities, respectively, did not live with children compared to 43% and 55% of never-married fathers. At the other extreme, approximately 90% of currently married fathers reside with their own and other (adopted) children. Yet, between 27% and 30% of Chicago's never-married fathers reported co-residing with their own and other children, and an additional 30% of Chicago's never-wed fathers lived with children belonging to someone else—a mate, an older sibling, a friend. Among black men nationally, the latter pattern is typically rare, representing less than 5% of never-married men. However, the tendency of never- married men to reside in complex families consisting of their own and other children is more common: just over 40% of single fathers reported such living arrangements nationally.

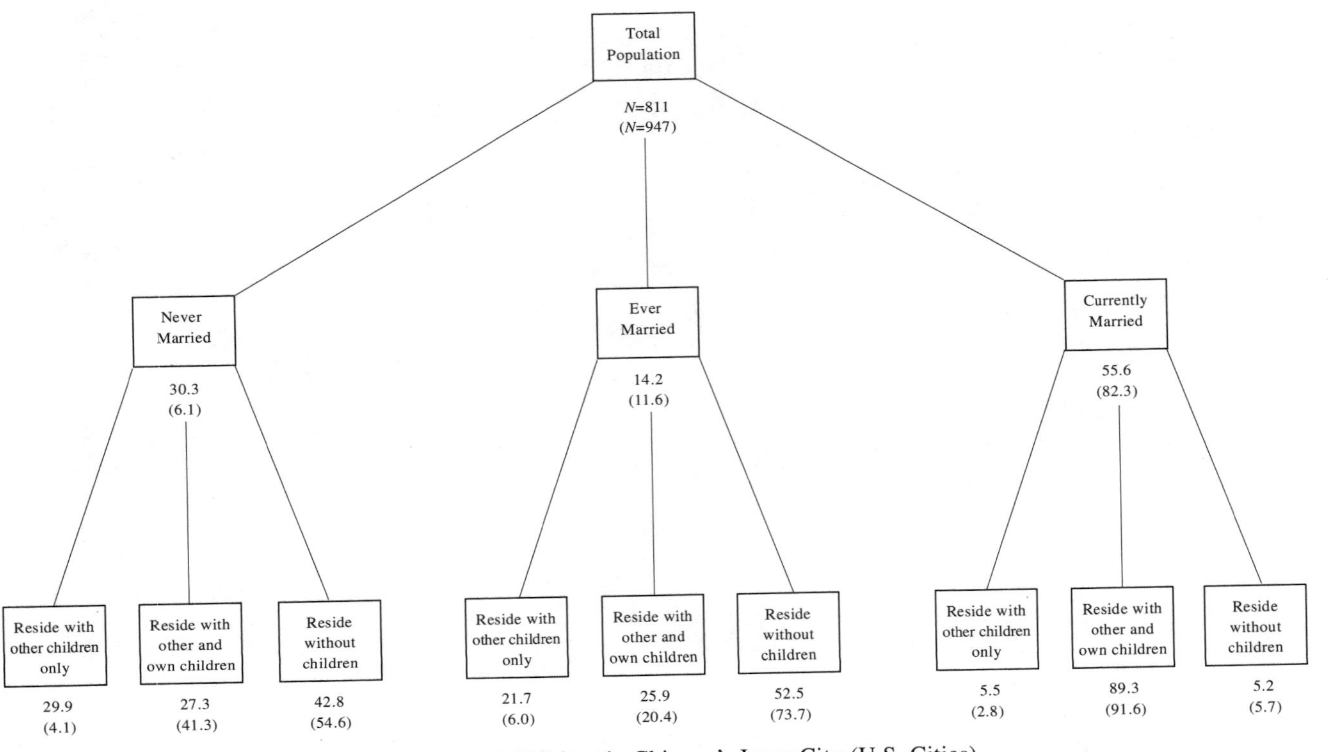

Figure 2.1. Current Co-Residence of Fathers and Children in Chicago's Inner City (U.S. Cities)

These descriptive results raise two questions critical to our concern about men's marginality to the family: first, what circumstances explain the ethnic differences in men's propensity to marry in the first place? And second, what kind and how much support do absent fathers provide to their offspring? Determining whether or not men are deliberately abdicating their family responsibilities requires evidence that decisions to avoid child support are personal *choices* and not merely reflections of material circumstances. In particular, given similar resources, are minority men less likely to provide child support to noncustodial children? To address these questions we turn to a multivariate analysis of marriage and child support. Because of limited information on forms of child support in the National Survey of Families and Households, we restrict these analyses to the Chicago sample.

Fatherhood, Marriage, and Parental Obligations

The previous tabulations show that married fathers are considerably more likely than unmarried fathers to co-reside with their children. Although we lack information about the extent to which co-resident fathers fulfill their paternal obligations, it is reasonable to assume that fathers who live with their own children provide regular emotional and material support. Further, there is ample empirical evidence showing that children residing with both parents enjoy higher economic standing than those who reside with one parent—usually the biological mother (Eggebeen & Lichter, 1991; Garfinkel & McLanahan, 1986). But in light of the high rates of out-of-wedlock fathering, a first major question is: what determines transition into marriage?

Our empirical model draws from current sociological and economic theorizing about marriage behavior. One important finding from this vast literature is that the likelihood of marriage varies directly with improvements in economic standing. Thus, the low marriage rates observed among black men, parents and nonparents alike, are attributed to their weak labor market standing, as reflected by high rates of joblessness and low earnings among those who manage to secure employment. From a social point of view, men reared in broken families may find marriage less compelling when they reach adulthood because experiences with marital discord may dampen interest in permanent commitments to unattractive mates. In other words, parental life-styles may reinforce the acceptability of nonnormative living arrangements.

Our multivariate analysis considers both social and economic factors as determinants of the transition into marriage. To assess the likelihood of marriage, we estimate a proportional hazard model in which the risk of marriage (since age 14) is a function of two categories of variables: (a) background characteristics and (b) economic circumstances. Background characteristics include mother's educational level (whether mother is high school graduate), whether respondents' parents ever received welfare, and whether respondents' parents ever married. These variables capture early socialization experiences as well as the economic status of the family of origin. We expect sons of more educated mothers and those reared in married couple households to exhibit higher marriage propensities. However, experiences of poverty during childhood might depress the probability of marriage, particularly if they were chronic and severe.

The second group of variables captures respondents' economic status, represented by educational level and work status of fathers. We expected higher education (a proxy for earnings prospects) to increase the likelihood of marriage. Similarly, employed men should marry at higher rates than their jobless counterparts. Because employment status changes over time, it is measured as a time-varying covariate. In other words, it reflects respondents' work status for each year after age 14. Education is measured as high school graduation status prior to the marriage (or the survey date in case of never-married individuals) because data limitations precluded an alternative operational specification.[10] A second time-varying covariate included in the marriage model is parental status. Couples who have considered marriage, but have no definite marriage date often decide to marry because of a pregnancy. Testa and his associates (1989) found that many fathers in Chicago poor neighborhoods married the mother of their child *after* the birth. Therefore, a positive effect of birth on marriage can be anticipated. Results of the hazard regressions for the four race/ethnic groups reported in Table 2.2 yield a simple and powerful story.[11] First, no background variable exerted a significant influence on the propensity of inner-city men to marry. Surprisingly, the expected linkage between changes in work status and the propensity to marry was significant only for white men. This might cast doubt on recent arguments about the importance of employment for determining the marriageability of inner-city men. However, as a proxy for labor market status, high school graduation also increased the (log) odds that black and Puerto Rican men would marry. Specifically, the logit coefficients indicate that black high school

Table 2.2 Determinants of Transition Into First Marriage: Fathers Aged 18-45 in Chicago's Inner City by Ethnicity (Asymptotic Standard Error)[a]

	Blacks		*Whites*		*Mexicans*		*Puerto Ricans*	
	β	*Exp* (β)	β	*Exp* (β)	β	*Exp* (β)	β	*Exp* (β)
Background								
Mother H.S. grad.	.007	n.s.	–.006	n.s.	.229	n.s.	.364	n.s.
	(.160)		(.221)		(.365)		(.542)	
If parents married	–.243	n.s.	.370	n.s.	–.390	n.s.	.733	n.s.
	(.233)		(.401)		(.520)		(.389)	
If family on welfare	.085	n.s.	.142	n.s.	–.19	n.s.	.164	n.s.
	(.199)		(1.042)		(.563)		(.230)	
H.S. grad at time of marriage	1.002*	2.724	–.195	n.s.	.812	n.s.	2.373*	10.729
	(.268)		(.412)		(.498)		(.732)	
Time-Varying Covariates								
If birth	.612*	1.844	2.168*	8.740	1.286*	3.618	.715*	2.044
	(.217)		(.291)		(.217)		(.326)	
If work	.181	n.s.	.530*	1.700	.014	n.s.	.335	n.s.
	(.156)		(.201)		(.151)		(.220)	
– 2 log likelihood	–844.3		–397.8		–834.5		–362.6	
% censored		36.6	4.3		1.5		20.3	
N	287		116		203		123	

SOURCE: Data from the Urban Poverty and Family Life Survey of Chicago (1987).
NOTES: a. Model controls for age.
$*p < .05$.

graduates were 2.7 times and Puerto Ricans were nearly 11 times more likely to wed than their counterparts who had not completed secondary school. The birth of a child significantly *increased* the odds of marriage for all groups by roughly a factor of two for blacks and Puerto Ricans. Among whites and Mexicans the risk of marriage increased even more when a child was born—8.7 and 3.6 times, respectively.

On balance, our results support Wilson's (1987; Wilson & Neckerman, 1986) premises about the enabling role of economic position—education or work—in raising the propensity of inner-city men to marry. That the act of fathering a child itself propels men into marriage indicates that they are inclined to accept their parental obligations when they have the means to support their children. These results also corroborate with Stack's (1974) finding that couples often do not formalize their marriage until the advent of a birth. Finally, our results show that there exist alternative pathways into adult roles in the inner city. In other words, marriage often follows rather than precedes parenting in impoverished environments. The sequencing of these two life course events differs markedly by race and Hispanic origins.

Yet, marriage is not a sufficient condition to ensure the economic well-being of children. Divorce can reverse this status, and marriage per se does not guarantee that fathers will be stably employed. Further, the advent of a marriage following a birth does not necessarily result in legitimation of the child in question. In fact, the living arrangements of men in our sample reveal that many fathers live apart from their own children. These children experience the highest risk of poverty and long-term problems with intellectual and social development (Garfinkel & McLanahan, 1986). Therefore it is important to examine directly whether and how noncustodial fathers support their children.

Absent fathers may take an active role in their child's upbringing by showing involvement in either the economic or the emotional needs of the child. As Stack (1974) argued, participation in child support can be done either in person or through female kin. Of course, some absent fathers chose to ignore their children altogether, thus playing only a marginal role in the children's lives. Other fathers face logistical difficulties in providing support. For example, over 80% of Mexican fathers in our sample are foreign born, and if their children reside in Mexico, frequent visits and regular in-kind support are impractical.[12]

Table 2.3 describes the nature and type of support absent fathers provide their noncustodial children. Although sample sizes have been reduced sharply for whites and Mexicans, over 40% of Puerto Rican

Table 2.3 Forms of Child Support: Fathers Not Residing With Own Children in Chicago's Inner City by Ethnicity

	Blacks	*Whites*	*Mexicans*	*Puerto Ricans*
Economic Support				
% who provide financial child support	60.6	60.2	70.1	57.9
% who provide in-kind child support	79.1	76.9	51.9	79.7
% whose relatives provide financial child support	23.2	6.9	15.4	13.1
% whose relatives provide in-kind child support	58.3	60.5	33.1	50.9
Contacts With Child				
Fathers' Visits				
% daily visits	31.4	17.8	8.7	14.8
% monthly visits	32.8	36.6	15.5	33.7
% never visit	35.9	45.6	75.9	51.6
Fathers Care for Child at Least 2 Weeks				
% yes	39.0	21.0	7.9	28.5
N	166	34	39	53

SOURCE: Data from the Urban Poverty and Family Life Survey of Chicago (1987).

fathers and nearly 60% of black fathers reported having one or more children who did not reside with them. This means that the fathers actually recognize these children as their own.[13] Of the population of fathers who reported having nonresident children, most reported providing economic support to their offspring. There is limited ethnic variation in the practice of providing financial support, except that Mexican men, who were less likely to have nonresident children to begin with, were somewhat more likely to provide financial support—probably because they often live far away from their offspring. Puerto Ricans were the least likely to support their children financially. Although there may be limited ethnic variation in the tendency of noncustodial fathers to support their children, the nature and level of support may vary greatly both in its regularity and the amounts provided.

Most fathers also report providing in-kind support (e.g., toys, clothes) to the children. That noncustodial Mexican fathers report a lower incidence of in-kind support reflects practical difficulties: For those who left dependent children in Mexico, monetary transfers are more practical than in-kind support, which often involves services and miscellaneous goods. This interpretation is consistent with other ethnic differences in child support (e.g., the actual contact with the children discussed below).

Not only do noncustodial fathers provide economic contributions to their children, but so do their relatives. This practice is especially evident among black fathers: Nearly one in four report that their noncustodial children receive financial support from other relatives, and over half reported that other relatives provide some in-kind support. Kin-based financial support to children is less common among whites, Mexicans, and Puerto Ricans, but the frequency of in-kind support from other white and Puerto Rican relatives is comparable to that of blacks.

Economic support of any kind is more frequent than direct interaction with children. However, tabulations on visitation behavior reveal that black fathers visit their children more than any other category of men. One third of black fathers reported daily contact with the nonresident children, whereas one third see the child only once or twice a month, and the remainder have no contact at all. This pattern is consistent with Stack's (1974) account of father-child interaction in a poor black community. In comparison, only 18% of the whites, 15% of the Puerto Ricans, and 9% of Mexicans reported daily visits with the children. Half of all Puerto Ricans, three fourths of Mexicans, and nearly half of the whites say they never see their children. On balance, and with the exception of blacks, noncustodial fathers have very limited if any contact with their children.

As a path to separation of fathers from their children, divorce often involves mobility of one parent, thus inhibiting frequent and regular contact with children left behind. For blacks, whose children are conceived out of wedlock at higher rates than the other groups (see Table 2.1), marriage and co-residence seem to play less decisive roles in shaping child-parent interaction. According to Stack (1974), Sullivan (1989), and Hannerz (1969), men (or their close relatives) are expected to take care of the children, regardless of the living arrangements or the marital relationships to the mother. Frequently these obligations are met, as shown by results in Table 2.3.

To shed more light on the circumstances most conducive to the provision of child support by noncustodial fathers, we analyze the probability of providing support in a multivariate framework using logistic regression. The dependent variable is whether the father provided any support—money or in kind. Independent variables capture background and demographic characteristics. The background variables indicate ethnicity of the respondent, whether the father lives in a ghetto poverty neighborhood (neighborhoods with more than 30% families below poverty level), and whether the respondent's father was present in the family of orientation. The demographic characteristics include nativity status (if foreign born), whether the father is currently married, whether the respondent has a high school degree, and his current employment status (currently employed = 1).

The results reported in Table 2.4 clearly show that the only significant predictors of child support are those that reflect the father's economic standing. Fathers who are currently employed are almost three times more likely to support their nonresident children compared to fathers who are not working. Also, high school graduates are 20% more likely to support their children compared to dropouts. That the ethnic differences are not statistically significant conveys an important message about the cultural underpinnings of distinct forms of support for noncustodial children. Stated differently, *ethnicity and race appear to be proxies for economic rather than family marginality.* This is not to dismiss the role of culture in shaping patterns of co-residence and the differential involvement of kin in providing for noncustodial children, but rather to stress that ethnic differences give way to indicators of fathers' economic status as determinants of material support to noncustodial children.

Summary and Discussion

Are inner-city fathers marginal to their families? Our analyses documented the support roles of noncustodial inner-city fathers. That these men have diverse life-styles is evident in their marital behavior and fulfillment of child responsibilities. This diversity, which corresponds to race and ethnic group divisions, results from cultural and normative differences in the way groups define familial responsibility and behavior. On the one hand, Mexican and white fathers represent the traditional mainstream view of men's familial behavior: Most of them are married and they fulfill their roles as providers within their economic means and within normative family settings. Blacks, and to a lesser extent, Puerto Ricans, are considerably less likely to adopt the "normative" path to family and parenthood. Many more bear children out of wedlock, and of these, relatively few live with their own children.

Table 2.4 Multivariate Analysis of Child Support: Fathers Not Residing With Own Children in Chicago's Inner City

	β	*Exp* (β)
Ethnicity		
If black	.606	n.s.
	(.555)	
If Mexican	1.182	n.s.
	(.907)	
If Puerto Rican	1.073	n.s.
	(.690)	
Neighborhood		
If ghetto	–.356	n.s.
	(.362)	
Background		
If raised by father	.488	n.s.
	(.384)	
Demographic Char.		
If foreign birth	.406	n.s.
	(.447)	
If married	–.708	.49
	(.400)	
Education	.177*	1.19
	(.075)	
If currently employed	1.030*	2.80
	(.389)	
Constant	–1.595	
–2 log likelihood	219.2	
% correct predictions	84.0	
N	267	

SOURCE: Data from the Urban Poverty and Family Life Survey of Chicago (1987).
NOTE: *$p < .05$.

Earnings prospects (indexed by educational status) and labor market status appear to be the key determinants of child support activity for all fathers, regardless of ethnicity. Although black fathers are more likely than white or Hispanic men to be noncustodial parents, they compensate for this loss of family responsibility through frequent contact with their offspring and by invoking the financial contributions of their kin. Similar practices, although less prevalent, are reported by white, Mexican, and Puerto Rican fathers. Thus, it appears that through their economic, but especially their social relationships with other relatives, unmarried inner-city fathers provide an alternative family context for their noncustodial children.

Our analyses of inner-city fathers' child support patterns refute the idea that these men are becoming marginal to the family. Despite the severe financial constraints faced by minority men residing in Chicago's inner city, we were most struck by the relatively high proportions of men who reported providing financial and in-kind support to their noncustodial children. Unfortunately, we were unable to assess the regularity of the support provided or to consider whether it covered a reasonable share of their children's living expenses. Given the high rates of joblessness in the inner city (Tienda & Stier, 1991), it is unlikely that child support provided by inner-city fathers was adequate to cover all costs of child rearing. However, it is inappropriate to conclude that these men have retreated from the family, or that they are "irresponsible scoundrels" who neglect their children. Our results show that noncustodial fathers make great efforts to maintain ties with their children. That black fathers report the highest levels of contact with their noncustodial children corroborates Stack's (1974) interpretation about men's interactions with kin. When they lack financial resources, they contribute their own time and solicit support from other kin. We cannot determine whether or not visits compensate for income contributions, but visitation is certainly important for emotional development.

More generally, our study raises questions about the origins of men's marginality in the inner city. There is widespread agreement that minority men, particularly those residing in declining inner cities, have been marginalized from the labor market (Wilson, 1987). Despite their precarious economic position, it is remarkable that inner-city fathers manage to maintain ties with their noncustodial children. However, men's economic marginality, which is clearly reflected in declining rates of labor force participation and higher rates of unemployment, does reverberate in their family roles. Poor labor market standing influences the likelihood of marrying and fathering children, and the sequencing of these major life course events (Testa et al., 1989; Wilson & Neckerman, 1986). The provider roles assumed by inner-city men may not conform to the norms of middle-class whites, but this difference should not be translated as "flight from the family."

Notes

1. We are grateful to Joan Aldous for sharpening our thinking on this issue.

2. The latter circumstance accentuated gender inequities within the family to the extent that men's retreat from the domestic arena was accompanied by an increase in women's labor force activity (Curtis, 1986; Stier, 1991).

3. Of course, there are intermediate variants between these extremes. Our focus on the extremes serves a heuristic function in sharpening our analytic goals.

4. William J. Wilson is the Principal Investigator. The original design called for a sample of census tracts where at least 20% of families had incomes below the 1980 federal poverty line. The final sample included a broader range of socioeconomic contexts.

5. The overall response rate was 79%, and varied from 75% to 83% for the ethnic groups.

6. Larry Bumpass was the Principal Investigator. Also fielded in 1987, this national survey contains sufficient race and ethnic variation for tabular analyses of Mexican, black, and white populations, but the sample of Puerto Ricans is limited for tabular analyses.

7. Both the UPFLS and NSFH surveys were based on cross-sectional designs, but both surveys contain several retrospective sequences on life experiences, including work behavior, marriage and fertility histories, educational histories, and welfare experiences. In addition, both surveys contain information about respondents' family backgrounds and current employment status. Because the principal investigators of both surveys exchanged instruments, many questions are directly comparable. Tabular results for both surveys are weighted to approximate the universes from which they are drawn, but the sample sizes are unweighted to indicate the actual base on which statistics are computed.

8. Among Puerto Rican fathers, the share never married did not differ between the Chicago and national samples, but the national rate is subject to a high degree of sampling variability owing to the small sample size ($N = 20$).

9. Illinois is an AFDC-U state, which means that unemployed fathers are eligible for benefits. Thus, the fact that fathers are not discouraged from living with children requires other explanations for the observed differences in living arrangements.

10. Ideally one would like a time-varying education measure that indicated whether respondent was enrolled in school each year beginning with age 14, but the UPFLS did not collect precise dates on educational outcomes. However, it is possible to ascertain the date of graduation and determine whether it occurred before or after marriage.

11. We report both the coefficients (β) and the corresponding ratios, Exp (β), which have a more intuitive interpretation.

12. We cannot ascertain whether, in fact, the children of Mexican fathers are in Mexico or other parts of the city.

13. We have no indication about how many of these men had children they failed to report as their own, but they would be the most marginal fathers of all.

References

Bernard, J. (1981). The good provider role: Its rise and fall. *American Psychologist, 36*(1), 1-12.

Curtis, R. (1986, April). Family and inequality theory. *American Sociological Review, 51,* 168-183.

Damos, J. (1986). *Past, present, and personal: The family and life course in American history.* New York: Oxford University Press.

Eggebeen, D., & Lichter, D. T. (1991). Race, family structure, and changing poverty among American children. *American Sociological Review, 56*(6), 801-817.

Ehrenreich, B. (1985). *The hearts of men: American dreams and the flight from family commitment.* New York: Anchor.

Furstenberg, F. F. (1988). Good dads—bad dads: Two faces of fatherhood. In A. J. Cherlin (Ed.), *The changing American family and public policy* (pp. 193-218). Washington, DC: Urban Institute.

Furstenberg, F. F. (1991). *Daddies and fathers: Men who do for their children and men who don't.* Unpublished manuscript, University of Pennsylvania.

Furstenberg, F. F., Nord, C. W., Peterson, J. L., & Zill, N. (1983). The life course of children of divorce: Marital disruption and parental contact. *American Sociological Review, 48,* 656-668.

Garfinkel, I., & McLanahan, S. S. (1986). *Single mothers and their children: A new American dilemma.* Washington, DC: Urban Institute.

Hannerz, U. (1969). *Soulside: Inquiring into ghetto culture and community.* New York: Columbia University Press.

Hetherington, M. E., Camara, K. A., & Featherman, D. L. (1983). Achievement and intellectual functioning of children in one-parent households. In J. Spence (Ed.), *Achievement and achievement motives* (pp. 205-284). San Francisco: W. H. Freeman.

Marsiglio, W. (1991). Parental engagement activities with minor children. *Journal of Marriage and the Family, 53,* 973-986.

Murray, C. (1984). *Losing ground: American social policy, 1950-1980.* New York: Basic Books.

Pleck, J. H. (1987). American fathering in historical perspective. In M. S. Kimmel (Ed.), *Changing men: New directions in research on men and masculinity* (pp. 83-97). Newbury Park, CA: Sage.

Rotundo, E. A. (1985). American fatherhood: A historical perspective. *American Behavioral Scientist, 29*(1), 7-25.

Stack, C. B. (1974). *All our kin: Strategies for survival in the black community.* New York: Harper & Row.

Stier, H. (1991). Immigrant women go to work: The labor supply of immigrant wives for six Asian groups. *Social Science Quarterly, 72*(1), 67-82.

Stier, H., & Tienda, M. (1992). *Love and lifestyles: Ethnic variation in marriage behavior among inner city parents.* Unpublished manuscript, University of Chicago.

Sullivan, M. L. (1989, January). Absent fathers in the inner city. *Annals of the American Academy of Political and Social Sciences, 501,* 48-58.

Testa, M., Astone, N. M., Krogh, M., & Neckerman, K. M. (1989, January). Employment and marriage among inner city fathers. *Annals of the American Academy of Political and Social Sciences, 501,* 79-91.

Tienda, M. (1989, January). Puerto Ricans and the underclass debate. *Annals of the American Academy of Political and Social Sciences, 501,* 105-119.

Tienda, M., & Stier, H. (1991). Joblessness and shiftlessness: Labor force activity in Chicago's inner city. In C. Jencks & P. Peterson (Eds.), *The urban underclass* (pp. 135-154). Washington, DC: Brookings Institution.

Weiss, Y., & Willis, R. (1985, July). Children as collective goods and divorce settlements. *Journal of Labor Economics, 3,* 268-292.

Weitzman, L. J. (1985). *The divorce revolution: The unexpected social and economic consequences for women and children in America.* New York: Free Press.

Wilson, W. J. (1987). *The truly disadvantaged: The inner city, the underclass, and public policy.* Chicago: University of Chicago Press.

Wilson, W. J., & Neckerman, K. M. (1986). Poverty and family structure: The widening gap between evidence and public issues. In S. H. Danziger & D. H. Weinberg (Eds.), *Fighting poverty: What works and what doesn't* (pp. 232-259). Cambridge, MA: Harvard University Press.

3

Japanese Fathers

Work Demands and Family Roles

MASAKO ISHII-KUNTZ

Introduction

Post-World War II families in Japan are frequently characterized as "fatherless" (Doi, 1973) due to the lack of interaction between fathers and children. This father absence is caused primarily by overtime work and other work-related demands that keep men away from home. Although mothering in Japan has been studied extensively (e.g., Schooler & Smith, 1978; Smith & Schooler, 1978; White, 1987), many issues concerning Japanese fathers remain unexplored. In this chapter, I focus on how Japanese fathers' work-related absence from home affects their family roles.

First, I present a brief history of the Japanese paternal role. Then I review past surveys and literature and present the evidence of Japanese fathers' psychological involvement in the family. The second half of the chapter will draw from in-depth interviews and observations of a sample of 20 couples in Japan. Using the parents' accounts, I illustrate how Japanese children learn about their fathers through everyday parent-child interaction. More specifically, I explore (a) the extent of father absence in Japanese families and its impact on fathers' interaction with

I would like to acknowledge the helpful comments contributed by Jane Hood. I also thank Hiroshi Ishii, Noriko Onodera, Kyoko Sagawa, and Neil Hickman for research assistance. I am grateful to the 20 couples who participated in this study.

children, (b) how mothers "make up" for the fathers' absence from home, and (c) the impact of father absence on the maintenance of gender inequality in the home.

The History of Japanese Fatherhood

In the prewar era, the Japanese were taught to fear "earthquakes, thunder, fire, and fathers." As this saying suggests, the Japanese father was traditionally defined as an awe-inspiring authority. Under the patriarchal family system, the father was the legal, economic, and moral leader of the family. Japanese fathers' authority began to decline in the late 1800s after the Meiji Restoration introduced compulsory education, and schools assumed the educational function of fathers (Yamazaki, 1979). However, in the absence of major legal and structural transformation, there were no substantial changes in the patriarchal family form. The major transition in legal definitions of fathers and families occurred at the end of World War II. Occupying Americans viewed paternal dominance and the Confucianist family system as obstacles to the democratization of Japanese society (Kawai, 1960). Therefore, the "New Constitution," promulgated in 1946, guaranteed equality among family members, reducing the Japanese father's position to equal status with his wife and grown children. Yamane (1976) describes several effects of this legal transformation on fathers. First, individual development is emphasized more than family lineage. Consequently, fathers lost their status as heads of the family responsible to continue successive generations. Second, equality between husbands and wives as defined in the law allows mothers to exercise more power over disciplining children, thus weakening paternal authority. Finally, the exclusive control and rights over inheritance and its distribution were taken away from the modern father. The new inheritance law states that property left by the deceased family head must be divided equally among the children.

Because of the postwar legal changes and their impact on the modern family, contemporary Japanese fathers are generally assumed to have lost considerable status within the family. This assumption, however, may not be entirely correct. Wagatsuma (1977), for instance, downplays the stereotypical comparison of the prewar "authoritarian" versus the postwar "shadowy" fathers. His criticisms are based on the absence of evidence concerning the actual behavior of prewar men and on the subjectivity of the self-reports that led to many generalizations regarding the modern father. Wagatsuma concludes that fathers in both periods probably combine both tyrant and friend images, and the social norms of each era distort self-reports, making differences more apparent than real.

Although the loss of fathers' status after the war may have been exaggerated, it is quite plausible that the postwar legal changes had a significant impact on modern fathers' behavior, as what is socially desirable now is different from what was acceptable in prewar years. Fathers in the postwar era are assumed to be democratic rather than autocratic. In addition to these changes of norms surrounding fatherhood in Japan, what distinguishes postwar fathers from their prewar counterparts is the dramatically reduced amount of time contemporary Japanese fathers spend with their family. Although fathers in prewar days were much more authoritarian than the postwar fathers, they were frequently at home to exercise their authority (Reischauer, 1981). Contemporary Japanese fathers, on the other hand, have but limited time to interact with their families. These fathers have successfully contributed to Japan's "economic miracle" (Vogel, 1979), but their intense involvement at work often results in shallow interpersonal relationships at home. I will describe the extent of fathers' absence in contemporary Japanese families by reviewing several studies and surveys in the following section.

The Modern Japanese Father

Despite Japan's impressive postwar economic recovery, there are some detrimental effects of men's heavy involvement at work on their family lives. Fathers' overwork limits the time they can spend with their wives and children. For example, a national survey found that fathers in single-earner households, on the average, spent 3 minutes per day on weekdays and 19 minutes per day on weekends on family work, including feeding, bathing, helping, and playing with their children (Management and Coordination Agency, 1981). The shallow involvement of Japanese fathers at home is also frequently the subject of the mass media. For instance, a popular television commercial portrays a father as most appreciated when he is "healthy and out of the house." Japanese fathers are also described as *sodai gomi* (giant garbage) when they hang around the house on weekends and holidays.

The limited father-child interaction in Japan is clearly evident when compared to data in other countries. As shown in Table 3.1, a cross-national survey found that 37.4% of Japanese children "never" interact with their fathers (e.g., eat meals together or talk to each other) on weekdays compared to 14.7% and 19.5% of American and German children, respectively (Management and Coordination Agency, 1986). Approximately, 2 out of 10 Japanese fathers (17.1%) also "never" spend time with their offspring on weekends. Other cross-cultural studies also report that Japanese fathers play a less prominent role in child rearing than do U.S. fathers (Kumagai, 1978; Shand, 1985).

Although it is clear that contemporary Japanese fathers spend less time with their children than their Western counterparts, the recent Japanese data are similar to the U.S. data in the 1960s and 1970s. According to time use studies, for example, U.S. fathers spent about 2 minutes per day with their children in 1965 and about 2 hours per week (or 17 minutes per day) on family work in 1975 (Robinson, 1975). Therefore, although modern U.S. fathers spend more time with children than Japanese fathers, the data show that U.S. fathers' more active involvement is a relatively recent phenomenon. At the same time, however, R. LaRossa (1988) argues that the idea that U.S. fathers now are intimately involved in raising their children is a myth. That is, U.S. men are less active in child care than the popular culture would have us believe. Although the gap between "culture" and "conduct" of fatherhood exists, U.S. fathers seem to be, at least, more involved parents than their Japanese counterparts. Whether we read mass media portrayals or time use surveys, Japanese fathers do appear to play a more peripheral role at home.

The superficial involvement of Japanese fathers, however, does not mean that they are completely ignored and isolated in their families. Wagatsuma (1977), for example, noted that the "shadowy" father of postwar Japan could be an overstatement. He wrote, "While both the husband and wife think, or like to think, that the wife is doing all the scolding, she is actually using her husband as the final authority when she deals with her children . . ." (p. 204). Wagatsuma also pointed out that unless we base answers on more systematic data, we will not be able to discuss very meaningfully the question of "fatherlessness" in Japanese society.

In contrast to the media image of an insignificant father at home, research and survey findings indicate that the authoritative power of the father may still be psychologically present in the Japanese family (e.g.,

Table 3.1 Father-Child Interaction and Children's Views on Fathers in Japan, the United States, and Germany (in percentages)

	Japan *(N = 1,149)*	*United States* *(N = 1,000)*	*Germany* *(N = 1,003)*
Father-Child Interaction			
Weekdays			
Never	37.4	14.7	19.5
About 15 minutes	13.5	22.9	18.5
About 30 minutes	20.3	22.1	23.3
About 1 hour	15.0	18.3	20.7
About 2 hours or more	13.8	22.0	18.0
Weekends			
Never	17.1	5.1	5.7
About 15 minutes	10.6	15.1	7.0
About 30 minutes	15.8	16.2	14.3
About 1 hour	22.5	21.4	25.2
About 2 hours or more	34.0	42.2	47.8
My father has the final authority at home			
Yes	45.0	35.1	23.4
My father is the center of the family			
Yes	62.4	22.8	12.9
My father is the one I can rely on the most			
Yes	34.7	12.0	7.7

SOURCE: Management and Coordination Agency (1986).

Ishii-Kuntz, 1992; Vogel, 1963). When asked about the images of mothers and fathers in a national survey of adolescents and college students (Office of the Prime Minister, 1981), most Japanese youths emphasized understanding as the ideal maternal disciplinary style and authority as the ideal for fathers' disciplinary style. These findings imply that despite the frequent absence of fathers at home, Japanese children expect their fathers to be authority figures and believe that they in fact are.

This image of the father as a central figure also coincides with children's preferences for actual behavior of the parents. In the Prime

Minister's survey noted above, most youths preferred their fathers to be strongly work oriented. These data confirm that the children make a clear distinction between the father's and mother's roles. In another survey of a sample of 7th and 12th graders, fathers were given strong positive ratings for their knowledge in politics and social issues, and for their sense of right and wrong (Kashiwaguma, 1981). These positive ratings indicate that in addition to respecting their fathers as a worker, children respect them as men of society and models of moral judgment.

In contrast, children assess their mother's image and behavior on the basis of more day-to-day interaction and see mothers as a source of emotional assistance. According to a 1980 survey of Japanese adolescents (Management and Coordination Agency, 1980), 60% of youths aged 10 to 15 listed the mother as the one to whom they talked about their troubles as compared to 30% listing the father. Another study found, however, that children's perceptions of mothers were generally less idealistic and positive than were their perceptions of fathers (C. P. Bankart & B. M. Bankart, 1985). Despite many decisions Japanese mothers make at home, only 11% of the children in the above study said that their mother was the boss in their family. Additionally, in a six-nation survey on mothers and children conducted in Japan, the United States, Great Britain, France, Thailand, and Korea, the proportion of children who "respect" their mothers was the lowest in Japan (Management and Coordination Agency, 1980). These findings suggest that there is a contradiction between mothers' total amount of daily responsibility and the respect they receive from children.

If Japanese fathers spend little time with their children as the national surveys indicate, how then is the father's authoritative image transmitted and maintained in the home? How do children learn to respect their fathers? Despite their physical absence, Japanese fathers may be involved in a child's socialization process as a symbol of authority. This symbolic involvement of Japanese fathers may be accomplished by Japanese mothers, who play an important mediating role in transmitting the fathers' values to children and teaching them to respect their fathers. This aspect of mothers' role was first described by Vogel (1963), who surveyed middle-class urban homes and found that Japanese mothers built up an artificial image of the absentee father as an authoritarian figure. These mothers then frequently used this ideal image to gain compliance from their children. Therefore, mothers' use of indirect "power" of fathers is a mechanism for disciplining their own children. Some argue that this practice reflects the mothers' own insecurity in being solely responsible for rearing children. Indeed, a recent longitudinal study found that the less responsible husbands are for child care, the more insecure Japanese wives are about their mothering role (Makino, 1988).

Interestingly, the authoritative image of fathers that mothers portray to their children may not be based on fact. Vogel (1963), for instance, observed that fathers seldom exercised much direct authority. A more recent survey of fathers, mothers, and children also indicates that fathers are not themselves strict in their own behavior. When a sample of fathers was asked who was responsible for disciplining in the home, 60.5% named the mother, whereas only 5.6% named the father (Office of the Prime Minister, 1981). When these same men were asked how strict or easygoing they were with their children, the response "just average" was received more often (53.1%) than "strict" (32.5%) or "easygoing" (13.9%), but twice as many said "strict" than "easygoing." In contrast, more U.S. fathers regard themselves as "easy to talk to" and "understanding" when they interact with children (Management and Coordination Agency, 1986).

A general pattern that emerges is that Japanese mothers engage in a somewhat exaggerated portrayal of fathers' authority, and that this symbolic authority may not be consistent with the actual behavior of Japanese fathers. Although this pattern may hold for many Japanese families, we know little about how the fathers' authoritarian images are maintained despite their physical absence. For example, how do fathers and mothers interact with their children in order to preserve the fathers' authoritarian image? In previous studies on Japanese fathers, most researchers have relied on children's verbal reports about their fathers. Japanese fathers' involvement at home has seldom been studied using in-depth interviews and observation of both fathers and mothers. In the following section, I use qualitative data to describe how a sample of 20 Japanese couples talk about their involvement with children, given the frequent absence of fathers.

The Sample

I carefully observed and conducted in-depth interviews in Japan with 20 married couples who have children under 18 years of age living at home. To find the sample, I initially contacted junior high schools, elementary schools, and day care centers in several suburban communities located in central Japan. Using snowball sampling techniques

(Biernacki & Waldorf, 1981), I selected 20 moderate- to upper-middle-income couples who were the biological parents of at least one school-aged child. I observed families in their home and interviewed husbands (n = 20) and wives (n = 20) separately at their home or office at least once and as many as three times. These interviews and observations, conducted in January 1990, took on the average 2 to 3 hours each. I recorded the interviews and transcribed them for coding and constant comparative analysis (Glaser & Strauss, 1967). The interviews were conducted in Japanese and independently translated into English by two persons to ensure the accuracy of the data. Two sets of completed translations were matched with each other. The final transcription presented in this chapter is the translation agreed upon by both translators.

Table 3.2 summarizes the demographic characteristics of the couples. The respondents' ages range from early 20s to early 40s and they have been married for an average of 11 years. The educational level for mothers and fathers ranges from junior high school to college graduate, with 60% completing high school but having no college education. Although all the men in the sample are employed or self-employed, only 12 women report having paid work. Of the employed wives, eight have full-time jobs. Table 3.2 also lists occupations. Median gross annual family income is $36,700, with three families under $25,000 and three over $55,000.

The children's ages range from 2 to 15 with a median age of 9. Half of the families have a youngest child under 6. More than half of the fathers (n = 14) report very limited interaction with their children, averaging less than 1 hour a week. In contrast, two fathers report longer hours of involvement with their children. What follows are fathers' and mothers' accounts of how they are directly or indirectly involved in parenting.

Fathers' Work Involvement and Perception of Parenting

Consistent with the larger surveys, the sample fathers' participation in child care and in socializing their children is extremely limited. Clearly, this is due to their work demands. On the average, these fathers reported spending approximately 54 hours a week at work. This figure does not even include evening hours and weekends, during which many of these men entertain their clients and bosses. In contrast, U.S. fathers

Table 3.2 Sociodemographic Characteristics for Couples in the Sample

Family	*Husband's Age*	*Wife's Age*	*Husband's Occupation*	*Wife's Employment Status*	*Wife's Occupation*	*Length of Marriage*	*Father's Time With Children (per week)*	*Number of Children*	*Age & Sex of Children*
Abe	35	33	Business	None	Homemaker	11 years	30 min.	2	10(F),5(M)
Endo	29	25	Teacher	Full-time	Teacher	3 years	30 min.	1	3(M),2(M)
Furukawa	35	34	Painter	Full-time	Nurse	9 years	20 min.	2	9(F),7(M)
Hasegawa	35	32	Business	None	Homemaker	6 years	45 min.	2	5(M),2(F)
Ishida	35	31	Teacher	Part-time	Receptionist	10 years	35 min.	2	10(F),8(F)
Ito	28	29	Business	None	Homemaker	5 years	50 min.	2	4(M),2(M)
Konishi	40	39	Taxi driver	Full-time	Nurse	18 years	1 hr. 30 min.	1	14(M),10(F)
Kushii	41	35	Business	Part-time	Custodian	16 years	40 min.	3	15(M),12(M),10(M)
Maeda	36	35	Physician	Full-time	Dentist	12 years	5 hrs. 30 min.	1	9(M)
Mikuni	33	35	City clerk	Full-time	City clerk	11 years	8 hrs. 15 min.	3	10(M),7(M),5(F)
Ohtsuka	42	35	City clerk	None	Homemaker	16 years	55 min.	2	15(F),14(F)
Ozawa	35	33	Business	Part-time	Clerk	10 years	45 min.	2	9(F),4(M)
Sato	34	34	Teacher	None	Homemaker	10 years	30 min.	2	9(F),6(M)
Sawada	35	35	Truck driver	Full-time	Nurse	10 years	20 min.	3	9(M),8(M),5(M)
Shiratori	44	43	Teacher	Part-time	Teacher	20 years	45 min.	3	15(M),13(M),13(M)
Tanaka	34	32	Dry cleaning	None	Homemaker	7 years	1 hr. 15 min.	2	5(M),3(F)
Urata	40	42	Coffee shop	Full-time	Clerk	13 years	1 hr. 10 min.	3	15(F),13(F),9(F)
Watanabe	37	37	Business	None	Homemaker	14 years	1 hr.	2	11(F),9(F)
Yamanaka	33	32	Bookstore	None	Homemaker	10 years	50 min.	2	8(F),4(M)
Yato	33	33	Construction	Full-time	Sales Rep.	9 years	2-3 min.	2	8(M),6(F)

NOTE: Respondents listed in an alphabetical order of family names; names were changed to guarantee anonymity. All husbands employed full-time.

spend an average of 42 hours a week in paid employment (Sweet, Bumpass, & Call, 1988).

The following comment made by Mr. Shiratori, a 44-year-old high school teacher, exemplifies how work demands limit a father's interaction with his children:

> Mondays through Saturdays, I work from 8 in the morning to 9 at night. Sometimes, I go to work on Sundays, too. I probably work about 60 to 65 hours a week on the average. I say "Good morning" to my sons but that's about all I see them. When I come home at night, they are busy doing their homework or studying for their exams, and I am usually too tired to have a lively conversation with them.

Further, not only did many fathers spend little time with their children, but the quality of time spent was "noninteractive" and "noncustodial" in nature. For example, more than half of the fathers said that when they are with their children they watch television together or take the children to the movies. Although the fathers are physically present, these activities involve little direct communication between fathers and children, and require less attention than custodial responsibilities. R. LaRossa and M. M. LaRossa (1989) argue that play is "cleaner" and less demanding than other forms of child care activities such as feeding and clothing. Therefore, fathers "may choose play over work because play 'eats' less into their own free time" (p. 141). Noninteractive activities that Japanese fathers frequently engage in are even less demanding than "play" activities.

Only two fathers (Maeda and Mikuni) mentioned that they regularly share with their wife "taking care of" their children. These fathers also frequently play with their children; read books to them; and take them to the park, movies, and shopping. Although these two fathers have two completely different occupations (one is a city clerk and the other is a physician), the wives are employed full-time and at jobs with a similar status. Wives' employment, however, is not necessarily associated with husbands' increased interaction with children. Of eight husbands whose wives are employed full-time, only Mr. Mikuni and Mr. Maeda reported spending considerable time with their children (5 ½ and 8 ¼ hours per week, respectively). The other six husbands of full-time employed wives spend on average only 39 minutes a week, which is even less than the 49 minutes spent by husbands of nonemployed wives.

Interestingly, although most of the fathers interact very little with their children, they do not seem to feel guilty about it. On the contrary, a majority (80%) of fathers seems to think that their hard work is appreciated by their family, and therefore, worth their absences from home. A common sentiment in that regard was expressed by Mr. Abe, a 35-year-old father of two children, who said:

> I am responsible for supporting my family. I leave home early in the morning and usually don't return until my kids are asleep. There is just no time for me to be with my kids. My only free time is on Sundays, but even then I may go play golf with my clients or colleagues. But you know, I don't do this for my own pleasure, but for my family. I think they [wife and children] are grateful for the kind of life I am providing. Although I spend little time with my kids, I basically trust my wife when it comes to raising and educating them.

Men's participation in socializing their children is limited not only by work demands but also by the image the father wants to maintain among his colleagues and children. For example, Mr. Watanabe, a father of two elementary school-aged daughters, talked about how he maintains his image at the workplace as being a devoted work-oriented person so he will not be ostracized by his colleagues:

> I think that if I really wanted to spend a lot of time with my children and play with them, I would probably be able to come home before they go to bed at least a couple of times a week. But I'm hesitant to do it. Please don't misunderstand that I don't love my kids or anything like that. I really do. But if I don't go out drinking with my colleagues after work or spend the weekend golfing, I am afraid that they would tease me for being "My Home Papa" [homebody father] and see me as being less dedicated to my work. After all, when all my colleagues are still working at 9 p.m., how can I alone stand up and say "Good night"! You just can't do that.

Japanese fathers' reluctance to be more involved at home because of work demands is not unique. In other industrialized countries where being a nurturant father has become more normative, work roles have not been redefined to fit the expectations of the new father. For example, Pleck (1979) points out that U.S. men rarely ask for parental leave and instead take "sick leave" when their wives have babies. Pogrebin (1982) describes a Swedish postmaster general who became the center of controversy after taking a month's paternity leave to be with his newborn.

In addition to the work-related constraints, Japanese fathers also feel that they need to maintain a certain distance from their children. Mr. Sato, a schoolteacher whose daughter is a third grader and son is in the first grade, said:

> I would say that it is a shame that there are fewer and fewer *kaminari oyaji* (thunderous fathers) in Japan. I mean that fathers really need to be good role models for their children—especially sons. I don't really think spending a lot of time with the kids does the trick. I think fathers need to teach and show the kids who has the final say. To me, keeping a certain distance from my children is one way to show them my authority. They know that the last spanking comes from me if they don't listen to their mother. Until that final moment, I let my wife do all the disciplining. After all, if I constantly nag my kids, pretty soon, they won't listen to me anymore.

It is clear that fathers' absence is caused not only by overtime work but also by fathers' intention to maintain their authoritative and dedicated-worker image among their colleagues and children. About half of the fathers feared being labeled as a "weak" and "feminine" man at work if they dedicated more time to their families. For these fathers, the longer hours spent with the family can be seen as damaging to their career and job opportunities.

More than three fourths of the fathers who were interviewed did not feel that they were deprived of the opportunities of raising and socializing children. Only four fathers (Endo, Kushii, Tanaka, and Urata) complained about not having "enough" time to spend with their children; the rest felt that they were spending a "sufficient amount of time." Indeed many fathers thought that they were providing appropriate role models for their children by being devoted workers who financially support the family. These values cut across educational level and occupation type.

In summary, fatherhood in Japan is strongly linked to the provider role. Men frequently reaffirm their responsibility as fathers by describing how well they provide for their families. Men whose wives are homemakers feel appreciated by wives and children as sole providers. But even the two-job families in our sample are what Hood (1986) calls main/secondary providers in which wives' incomes are treated only as secondary to those of husbands. All the husbands whose wives are employed acknowledge that the wifes' income can pay for "minor" expenses, but at the same time, men emphasize that they are the main providers in the family. Accepting the idea of wives as equal co-providers (Hood, 1986) would devalue the male role, thus reducing men's authority as fathers. Because Japanese society rewards men for being "masculine" and masculinity is often equated with men's ability to provide financially, we can understand fathers' frequent absence from home as not only the result of overtime work, but perhaps more important, a result of men's efforts to maintain a masculine image. To be masculine in Japan, therefore, men accede to work demands that require physical distance from their families, which in turn encourages mothers to emphasize authoritarian aspects of the father role.

Mothers' Involvement With Children

Whereas only two fathers reported participating regularly in child care, school, and after-school activities, all of the mothers perceived socialization of their children as their major task, regardless of their educational level and employment status. When the employed mothers and fathers are compared, fathers were much more likely than mothers to feel that the limited interaction with children is justified because of their work demands. This is also true for U.S. fathers. Pleck (1977) argues, for instance, that work demands intrude on family life among men more frequently than among women. Further, Pleck and Staines (1985) found that weekend work of husbands significantly reduces time in child care and housework, whereas no such effect was found for wives' weekend work.

In general, women's employment does not seem to reduce time spent with children. Even Mrs. Mikuni, who is a city clerk and works at the same office as her husband, spends considerably more time with the children than her husband. This mother said, "It is okay for my husband to go out drinking with his colleagues at night, but I could not do that because of my responsibility toward the children. Maybe it is not fair, but I guess that's the way it is." Interestingly, her husband spends much more time with the children than do any other fathers. Perhaps, Mrs. Mikuni's perception of "unfairness" encourages her husband to share some child care responsibilities. However, she still is the primary caretaker of the children. Thus, instead of trying to change the situation, she accepts the "double standard" of gender roles. Mrs. Mikuni and other employed mothers work what Hochschild (1989) calls the "second shift," a second job after returning home.

Most of the mothers not only spend more hours with their children but also are more actively involved than fathers. In addition to daily child care, many mothers reported "playing," "playing games," "reading books," "dancing," "singing," "going to parks," and "going for walks" with their children. Among eight nonemployed mothers, three quit their full- or part-time jobs when they married, and five quit their jobs when they had their first child. These women expressed satisfaction in being full-time homemakers and parents. Mrs. Ito, for instance, said:

> In a way I feel sorry for women who need to work because they really miss out on a lot of fun times with children and friends. I am heavily involved in PTA at my daughter's kindergarten. This way, I cannot only be with my daughter but also make lots of friends who are mothers of my daughter's friends. I was happy to quit my low-paying job when my daughter was born. I finally had a "legitimate" reason to quit, you know. [Laughs]

In short, whereas fathers spend little time with their children and feel fine about this, mothers not only spend a considerable amount of time with their children, but also believe that it is their primary responsibility. This is also true for Japanese professional women, who give mothering priority over their careers. It is clear from these interviews that Japanese couples define male and female parent roles very differently. Whereas mothers are directly involved with their children in all ways, fathers are present at home only psychologically. This psychological presence of fathers is further examined in the following section.

Psychological Presence of Fathers

The mothers frequently talked about how they "use" fathers when disciplining their children. From their descriptions, we can understand how fathers can be psychologically present in their homes in spite of very limited physical interaction with children. Many wives portrayed their husbands as a "decision maker," "strict parent," "disciplinarian," and "boss of the house." This pattern—consistent regardless of parental education, occupation, and employment status—is exemplified in the following comment made by Mrs. Abe, a homemaker-mother of a 10-year-old daughter and 5-year-old son:

> When my husband returns home late, which is just about every day, he is most likely to have been at the bar with his colleagues. But I *never ever* tell that to my children. Maybe they suspect something, but I don't want them to know

> that their dad is goofing around at the bar. So I tell them that their father is working late at night or attending important meetings, and he does this just to support us.

A similar sentiment is echoed by two more mothers:

> When my children are misbehaving, I tell them that I have to phone their father at his office to report this [misbehavior]. Sometimes, I even make a fake phone call. [Laughs] Then they usually stop being naughty, because they know that their father can be very strict when it comes to kids who don't obey their parents.

Another mother also described how she made sure that her children understood that an important decision was made by their father:

> When my children wanted to buy some expensive toys or wanted to take some extracurricular class like kendo or judo, I always told them that we needed to seek their father's permission first. I knew that he would agree with whatever I decided to do, but you know, it is important for kids to know that their father is the important decision maker in this family.

Many mothers also talked about the importance of describing fathers' "power" and "authority" to their sons. Mrs. Sato, a homemaker-mother of a 9-year-old daughter and a 6-year-old son, whose husband sees their children on the average of 4 minutes a day, said:

> Since my husband is gone most of the time, my son really needs a role model to be a strong and responsible man. That's why I remind him constantly of what a diligent, dedicated, responsible, and great father he has. I also tell my daughter that it is important for her to find a hard-working man like her father who earns a comfortable living for the family.

More than half of the mothers also seem to enjoy portraying their husbands as superheroes whether or not they actually are. For instance, Mrs. Hasegawa, a homemaker-mother whose children were playing in the same room at the time of the interview whispered:

> To tell you the truth, I don't think my husband is that strong or authoritarian. But because he is gone a lot, it is important for my kids to understand who has the final authority. I like, in a way, building a "thunderous" image of their father because I can use that image to discipline my kids, and believe me, it usually works well. [Laughs]

This type of idealization of fathers occurs not only in families with sons but also in daughters-only families. For example, Mrs. Urata, a full-time clerk, described why she does not want her three daughters to be "too" educated:

> I want my daughters to go to junior college but no more than that. I think it is very difficult for women with 4-year college degrees to have careers, husbands, and children at the same time. Besides, men don't really like those women who are overeducated. Although I tell my daughters to do well at school, they also know that being happily married to a man like their father with a good job is the ultimate goal of their life.

Although fathers' involvement with their children is limited, half of the fathers in the sample reported making an effort to receive respect from their children. Mr. Sawada talked about how he sometimes reminds his children of the importance of being the family breadwinner:

> I have very little time to spend with my sons but I make sure to tell them that I am working hard to give them a good life and it's a man's responsibility to be the breadwinner. I think that they know that is what a "real" man should do for his family.

From the fathers' and mothers' accounts, it is clear that many mothers engage in transmitting an authoritative and diligent-worker image of fathers to children. Mothers seem to come up with more elaborate methods if their husbands are gone more frequently and for a longer period of time. In the Yato family, for instance, the father is absent on a long-term basis (approximately 6 months) due to his construction job. The mother, who is a full-time cosmetic sales representative, talked about her own efforts to teach the children to appreciate their father and feel grateful for his work:

> I think in raising my son (8 years old) and daughter (6 years old), one of the most important things is for them to know that their father is a great person despite his absence. So my job is to constantly remind them of what a nice father they have although he is away a lot. One thing I have done that seems to be working out well is to have children write a short weekly letter to their father. Of course, my husband enjoys hearing from the kids, but he does not have time to write them back. So I usually write them back pretending the letter was written by their father. I tell them about the hard work of their father and remind them to be good, etc.

All of the above mothers' comments demonstrate that mothers frequently portray their husbands as "hard workers" and "decision makers." Children, in turn, learn fathers' "authority" and come to appreciate their fathers for their financial contribution to the family. Therefore, the traditional gender roles, that is, man as breadwinner and a woman as homemaker, seem to be perpetuated both through direct mother-child interaction and through indirect father-child interaction mediated by mothers. I also found that the image portrayed by mothers did not necessarily coincide with the real personality of fathers. Thus, less authoritarian men are deprived of opportunities to show the "warmer" side of their personalities to their children.

What about families in which the husbands are more involved with children? As previously discussed, both Mr. Maeda and Mr. Mikuni report considerably more time spent with their children. In addition, these men actively engaged in reading to, playing with, and helping them with homework. Although Mrs. Maeda and Mrs. Mikuni still accepted the major responsibility of raising children, they did not exaggerate their husbands' authority to their children as often as other wives. Their husbands are also proud of being involved in their children's lives, and do not mind for being "different" from their friends. Mr. Mikuni, who spends a lot of time helping his sons with their Cub Scouts projects, said that he "really enjoyed scouting because it provides many opportunities to be with" his sons. When asked about what his colleagues thought of his active parenting role, he said that they didn't care too much about it as long as he was doing his job and his share of entertaining bosses. Further, he stated that some men at work are even "envious" about his involvement with his children. This does not mean that Mr. Mikuni and Mr. Maeda are completely different from the rest of the fathers. Although they spend considerably more time with their children than other fathers, their wives remain as major caretakers of the children. For example, my observation of the Mikuni family's dinnertime reveals that while Mrs. Mikuni was busy serving the children's food and making sure they ate all the food, Mr. Mikuni engaged in conversation with the children about their school and friends. This suggests that although Mr. Mikuni interacts with his children more frequently and actively than other fathers, the "physical" part of child care is still his wife's responsibility.

As previously discussed, the position of women in the traditional family in Japan was a lowly one under the patriarchal system. Today's Japanese wives enjoy more "free" time and are given more time to cultivate personal interests. This fact, however, cannot be interpreted as an indication of gender equality in Japanese families. It has been almost half a century since Japanese husbands and wives were legally given equal status. But the weak cultural support for fathers' increased involvement and the lack of structural opportunities for men to spend time with their children indicate that legislative changes, no matter who imposes them, are not likely to encourage men to become more involved fathers.

Summary and Conclusions

The image of postwar Japanese fathers is that of "weak," "insignificant," and "ineffective" figures who have a minimal psychological involvement with their wives and children. However, this thesis is not supported by the evidence reported in this qualitative study. Although Japanese fathers are frequently absent from home, they are psychologically present. The fathers' authority is frequently reinforced by daily mother-child interaction.

In the context of growing affluence in Japanese society, expectations for fathers have centered on their ability to meet the material needs of their families. In this sense, the Japanese father role is inseparable from the provider role. Mothers frequently portray the importance of their husbands, without whom the family could not maintain a decent standard of living. Children, therefore, respect their fathers as a dedicated providers. The potential impact of this strong relationship between father and worker roles is twofold.

First, because the paternal role is virtually synonymous with the provider role, Japanese men who might choose to reduce work hours in order to be more involved with their children may not be appreciated by co-workers or family members. Therefore, potentially active fathers in Japan may remain providers, staying peripheral to the mother-child bond. At the same time, mothers are placed in precarious positions. They are held responsible for the child's behavior, but yet they do not have clear authority for laying down rules. The techniques mothers use to build an authoritarian image of fathers are an adaptation to the problem of managing the children without clear authority. This unique situation is found to cause anxiety and insecurity among Japanese mothers (Makino, 1988).

Second, a strong relationship between worker and father roles perpetuates traditional gender socialization at home. Japanese mothers frequently emphasize the importance of boys being "diligent" and "responsible" workers, and girls being "happy homemakers." According to a poll on attitudes toward education (Office of the Prime Minister, 1982), although 45% of all parents want to see their sons get a university education, fewer than half of that, 19% of all parents, have the same aspiration for their daughters.

These gender-differentiated messages later result in gender differences in education and employment. Because education is compulsory through the ninth grade, girls receive as much education as boys through secondary school, but then go in different directions. Women are, for instance, heavily concentrated in junior colleges (Ministry of Education, 1985). These colleges are looked upon as finishing schools that prepare women with polite accomplishments for marriage. Employment conditions for women are also still considerably inferior to those for men. In addition to the wage gap between men and women, female employees have fewer chances to be promoted to managerial posts or become high-ranking specialists in companies, fewer opportunities for training, and little hope of finding employment in major corporations in high-paying areas of industry (Bando, 1986). Women, who often leave the work force upon their marriage or birth of the first baby, are at a disadvantage in a system that rewards longer continuous service.

In summary, gender discrimination in Japan is maintained in a cyclic manner. Children are raised learning the importance of men's provider roles and women's homemaker roles. Women are often discouraged from pursuing higher level of education, thus limiting their opportunities to pursue careers. This, in turn, reinforces existing gender stratification in the economy. Finally, gender inequality in the economy and workplace also sends a message to Japanese parents to socialize their children in gender-segregated manners. Japanese families still maintain and reinforce traditional gender roles. Japanese women are also frequently discriminated against in the workplace. Consequently, the prospects for gender equality in Japan do not seem to be as promising as in Western countries. Japan, however, has been undergoing many structural and demographic changes that could help to decrease gender segregation in the family.

In addition to the impact of absentee fathers discussed above, there are several reasons for couples' sharing parenting and provider roles. First, Japanese labor statistics show an increase of working mothers, 48.2% in 1979 to 59.6% in 1989 (Ministry of Finance, 1990). But at the same time, the Japanese government is slow in implementing child care policies to meet the needs of working parents. Sharing child care is thus becoming more important in Japanese families. Second, the sex ratio of younger Japanese is highly imbalanced; there is a surplus of 2 million young men who are competing for marriageable women. Because of this demographic change, today's Japanese women demand more from men, including sharing housework and child care (Itoi & Powell, 1992). Japanese men's traditional values are thus challenged by the demands of younger Japanese women. Finally, children's problems, such as refusal to attend school and suicide, are attributed to Japanese youths growing up without emotional support from fathers.

The feudal family system of Japan was abolished with the enactment of the new Civil Code after World War II. Exposure to Western culture has apparently contributed to people's willingness to adopt the modern family system and life-styles in Japan. The Japanese family today, however, is best described as externally modern but internally traditional. At the superficial level, there is an increase of nuclear families resembling Western counterparts. But the stem family households consisting of two nuclear families in adjacent generations are still pervasive (Kumagai, 1986). At the internal level, Japanese families still retain traditional elements, including gender-segregated ideology.

The postwar structural changes imposed on Japanese economic and family systems increased the number of absentee fathers, which in turn acts to preserve traditional gender roles in modern Japanese families. Therefore, the definition of fatherhood has changed little. This does not mean, however, that Japanese families will continue to perpetuate gender-differentiated messages. In fact, there are several factors, such as *karoshi* (death from fatigue) among salaried men and the imbalanced sex ratio, that may cause enough concern to enable reconsideration of men's provider and family roles.

The history of fatherhood in the United States shows that it has taken many decades to replace the image of "distant breadwinner" with that of "nurturant father" (Pleck, 1987). The history in Japan differs greatly from that of the United States; thus, a direct comparison is not possible. However, recent social and demographic changes suggest that Japanese fatherhood may be undergoing a transition. For one thing, the Japanese government has become increasingly concerned with fathers' absence, and it has shown more interest in increasing men's involvement with their children (Management and Coordination Agency, 1990). The government's concern about the lack of fathers' involvement at home coincides with the increasing rate of truancy and suicide among youth, for which absentee fathers are often blamed. Additionally, an increase of employed mothers in Japan necessitates discussion of how to and who will care for children. Given the limited funding for child care facilities, fathers' roles as parents are being considered as a valid option. For example, in April 1985, male city employees of Tanashi, located in a Tokyo suburb, were granted child care leave (*Asahi Shimbun,* February 8, 1985). This "innovative" law is the first allowing fathers to take paternity leave in Japan. Educational programs that appeal to the importance of fathers' participation in raising children have also been implemented in other cities. At a more individual level, an increasing number of younger men is now interested in their family lives, and report more active involvement with their children (Ishii-Kuntz, 1989). Therefore, in recent years, local and national governments as well as younger fathers themselves are taking "small" steps to strengthen the role of the father in the Japanese family.

In summary, Japanese men's work and family roles are beginning to respond to some societal and demographic changes. It is unrealistic to assume that these changes will quickly result in men's greater sharing of child care at home. My findings suggest that it is not only work demands but also men's efforts to maintain an authoritarian image that keep fathers away from home. Giving fathers more time to spend with children may be the first step, but that step alone will not produce a more gender-neutral environment in Japanese homes.

References

Asahi Shimbun. (1985, February 8). A male employee granted child care leave.

Bando, M. S. (1986). *Japanese women yesterday and today.* Tokyo: Foreign Press Center.

Bankart, C. P., & Bankart, B. M. (1985). Japanese children's perceptions of their parents. *Sex Roles, 13,* 679-690.

Biernacki, P., & Waldorf, D. (1981). Snowball sampling. *Sociological Methods and Research, 10,* 141-163.

Doi, T. (1973). *The anatomy of dependence.* Tokyo: Kodansha International.

Glaser, B., & Strauss, A. (1967). *The discovery of grounded theory.* New York: Aldine.

Hochschild, A. (1989). *The second shift.* New York: Avon.

Hood, J. (1986). The provider role: Its meaning and measurement. *Journal of Marriage and the Family, 48,* 349-359.

Ishii-Kuntz, M. (1989). Collectivism or individualism? Changing patterns of Japanese attitudes. *Sociology and Social Research, 73,* 174-179.

Ishii-Kuntz, M. (1992). Are Japanese families "fatherless"? *Sociology and Social Research, 76,* 105-110.

Itoi, K., & Powell, B. (1992, August 10). Take a hike, Hiroshi. *Newsweek.*

Kashiwaguma, Z. (1981). The father in relation to the mother. In H. Katsura (Ed.), *The paternal role* (Vol. 5, Home Education Series, pp. 77-98). Tokyo: Kaneko Shobo.

Kawai, K. (1960). *Japan's American interlude.* Chicago: University of Chicago Press.

Kumagai, F. (1978). Socialization of youth in Japan and the United States. *Journal of Comparative Family Studies, 9,* 335-346.

Kumagai, F. (1986). Modernization and the family in Japan. *Journal of Family History, 11,* 371-382.

LaRossa, R. (1988). Fatherhood and social change. *Family Relations, 37,* 451-457.

LaRossa, R., & LaRossa, M. M. (1989). Baby care: Fathers vs. mothers. In B. Risman & P. Schwartz (Eds.), *Gender in intimate relationships* (pp. 138-154). Belmont, CA: Wadsworth.

Makino, K. (1988). Ikuji fuan: Gainen to sono eikyo yoin ni tsuiteno saikento. [Child care anxiety: Reconsideration of definitions and influential factors]. *Katei Kyoiku Kenkyujo* [Family Research Institute], Vol. 10, pp. 52-55.

Management and Coordination Agency. (1980). *Kodomo to hahaoya chosa* [Survey on children and mothers]. Tokyo: Author.

Management and Coordination Agency. (1981). *Shakai seikatsu kihon chosa* [Basic survey on life in society]. Tokyo: Author.

Management and Coordination Agency. (1986). *Kodomo to chichioya ni kansuru kokusai hikaku chosa* [International comparative survey on children and fathers]. Tokyo: Author.

Management and Coordination Agency. (1990). *Nihon no chichioya to kodomo* [Report on Japanese fathers and children]. Tokyo: Author.

Ministry of Education. (1985). *Gakko kihon chosa* [Survey on schools]. Tokyo: Author.

Ministry of Finance. (1990). *Fujin rodo hakusho* [White Reports on women's labor]. Tokyo: Author.

Office of the Prime Minister, Japan. (1981). *Gendai no wakamono: Junen mae to no hikaku* [Today's youth: A comparison with those ten years ago]. Tokyo: Author.

Office of the Prime Minister, Japan. (1982). *Kyoiku ni kansuru ishiki chosa* [Attitudes toward education]. Tokyo: Author.

Pleck, J. H. (1977). The work-family role system. *Social Problems, 24,* 417-427.

Pleck, J. H. (1979). Men's family work: Three perspectives and some new data. *Family Coordinator, 28,* 481-488.

Pleck, J. H. (1987). American fathering in historical perspective. In M. S. Kimmel (Ed.), *Changing men: New directions in research on men and masculinity* (pp. 83-97). Beverly Hills, CA: Sage.

Pleck, J. H., & Staines, G. L. (1985). Work schedules and family life in two-earner couples. *Journal of Family Issues, 6,* 61-82.

Pogrebin, L. C. (1982, February). Are men discovering the joys of fatherhood? *Ms.,* pp. 41-46.

Reischauer, E. O. (1981). *The Japanese.* Cambridge, MA: Harvard University Press.

Robinson, J. P. (1975). *Americans' use of time project.* Ann Arbor: University of Michigan, Survey Research Center.

Schooler, C., & Smith, K. C. (1978). ". . . And a Japanese wife": Social structural antecedents of women's role values in Japan. *Sex Roles, 4,* 23-41.

Shand, N. (1985). Culture's influence in Japanese and American maternal role perception and confidence. *Psychiatry, 48,* 52-67.

Smith, K. C., & Schooler, C. (1978). Women as mothers in Japan: The effects of social structure and culture on values and behavior. *Journal of Marriage and the Family, 40,* 613-620.

Sweet, J., Bumpass, L., & Call, V. (1988). *National survey of families and households.* Madison: University of Wisconsin, Center for Demography and Ecology.

Vogel, E. F. (1963). *Japan's new middle class: The salary man and his family in a Tokyo suburb.* Berkeley and Los Angeles: University of California Press.

Vogel, E. F. (1979). *Japan as number one: Lessons for America.* Cambridge, MA: Harvard University Press.

Wagatsuma, H. (1977). Some aspects of the contemporary Japanese family: Once Confucian, now fatherless? *Daedalus, 106,* 181-210.

White, M. (1987). The virtue of Japanese mothers: Cultural definitions of women's lives. *Daedalus, 116,* 149-163.

Yamane, T. (1976). Changes in the Japanese family. In K. Morioka & T. Yamane (Eds.), *"Ie" and the contemporary family* (pp. 112-135). Tokyo: Baifukan.

Yamazaki, K. (1979). Transition of the father's role in the Japanese family. *Annual Report of the RCCCD,* Sapporo, Japan: Hokkaido University Faculty of Education, pp. 43-53.

4

Elderly Mexican American Men

Work and Family Patterns

NORMA WILLIAMS

This chapter focuses on the role of elderly Mexican American men in relation to their work histories, their families, and their community settings. Although Facio (1988) has written about Mexican American elderly women, elderly men have been neglected in the social science literature. The current literature on Mexican American men focuses on their masculinity (N. Williams, 1990; Zinn, 1982), but this focus represents only one aspect of Mexican American men's family and community roles (Gordon, 1961; Lewis & Salt, 1986). Because of the fragmentary nature of data on Mexican American elderly men, I shall not survey the

I thank the University of North Texas for financial support (1989-1990) for preliminary work on this research project. I am especially grateful to the Gerontological Society of America for the Postdoctoral Fellowship of the 1991 Technical Assistance Program (TAP), funded in part by award number 90AM037802 from the Administration on Aging, Department of Health and Human Services, Washington, D.C., and by the American Association of Retired Persons (AARP), Area 7 Office, Dallas, Texas; this award made it possible for me to carry out fieldwork in Dallas in summer 1991. I especially want to thank John P. Luby and Michael Donnelly for their support and assistance throughout the research project. The views set forth in this chapter do not necessarily represent those of the aforementioned agencies or organizations.

The helpfulness and support of Joan Mahon and Felicitas Hernandez, La Voz del Anciano (The Voice of the Elderly), Dallas, Texas, have been crucial in carrying out my research.

I also sincerely thank Jane Hood for her constructive editorial criticism and for helping me clarify my analysis.

existing literature, but instead shall weave, when feasible, the relevant materials into the body of the text.

Here I examine several interrelated issues. After briefly considering some of the problems relating to the definition of the ethnic group "Mexican Americans," I outline the main sources of data for this chapter and consider the restructuring (or breakdown) of the Mexican American extended family. Then, in light of this background, I examine two ways in which the work (and educational) histories of these elderly men are related to their family lives. First, the parents of the men in my sample were poor and this, along with other social constraints, made it nearly impossible for the men to acquire the skills necessary as to obtain stable, relatively high paying jobs. Second, the respondents' own work histories and present poverty typically contribute to a set of unstable relationships with their children and grandchildren.

Who Are the Mexican Americans?

Most official government reports use the terms "Hispanic" or "Latino." However, these administrative categories fail to distinguish among distinct cultural groups. The term "Hispanic" encompasses Mexican Americans, Puerto Ricans, Cubans, Central and South Americans, and Other Hispanics. The Hispanic population is growing very rapidly, and some scholars believe that this group will be the largest ethnic minority in the United States by the early part of the next century. Chelimsky (1991) cited a U.S. Census Bureau projection that "the Hispanic population is expected to increase by an additional 200 percent (40 million persons) between 1990 and 2080" (p. 76).

As Aponte (1991) documents, the concept of Hispanic glosses over significant social, cultural, and historical differences that exist among the subgroups noted above. In my research I have focused on Mexican Americans, who are by far the largest group within the Hispanic category. But even the term "Mexican American" is often misinterpreted. As I have discussed elsewhere (N. Williams, 1990), we must not confuse Mexican Americans with Mexican nationals or with recent immigrants from Mexico. A number of Mexican Americans, for instance, trace their ancestry back prior to the Treaty of Guadalupe Hidalgo in 1848. Moreover, the Mexican Americans I studied have few if any ties with Mexico. Mexican Americans today have a rather distinctive culture within the United States. They should be distinguished from both

Anglos and Mexican nationals (and from recent immigrants from Mexico). After examining the problem of "Mexican Americans" in an historical perspective, Limerick (1987) stated, "In New Mexico, Texas, California, and Arizona, Hispanic ways had been changed by distinctive circumstances, and the resulting way of life was neither solely Mexican nor solely American—but Mexican-American" (p. 255). As the second largest minority group in the United States, Mexican Americans should be accorded far more attention than they have received (e.g., Hayes-Bautista, 1992).

Although Mexican Americans can be distinguished from other major Hispanic groups as well as Anglos, there are also important regional and class differences within the Mexican American population. In general, however, Mexican Americans are an economically disadvantaged group within the United States (cf. Maril, 1989), and unfortunately, many of the Mexican American elderly live in impoverished conditions.

Sources of Data

This chapter is a by-product of a larger study on elderly Mexican Americans in Dallas, Texas. Outsiders typically view Dallas as not having a significant Hispanic (mainly Mexican American) population. However, during the decade of the 1980s the Hispanic population in Dallas County grew faster than in any other metropolitan area in Texas, except for Harris County, in which Houston is located (Murdock & Ellis, 1991).

I conducted most of the research in summer 1991, but have collected additional data since that time. The larger project includes both men and women. I collected most of the data through in-depth interviews with Mexican Americans who were 60 years or older. Because I used snowball sampling (Bailey, 1987), I entered the elderly Mexican American population in Dallas through different contact persons; this increased representativeness. Although my efforts were time consuming, I also interviewed persons who lived in different areas of the city in order to include a wider range of respondents in my sample. Nonetheless, I did not interview any elderly men whose children are members of the professional class.

My research suggests that elderly Mexican Americans are likely to be underrepresented in social surveys for a variety of reasons, including lack of telephones, use of only a limited amount of English, and a suspicion of "outsiders." Because I am bilingual and bicultural, I was able to interview a segment of the elderly who are otherwise often bypassed in social surveys.

I have data on 23 males, all 60 years of age or older, most over 65. In conducting the in-depth interviews, I used an interview guide and asked one set of questions regarding demographic characteristics of each respondent. Another set of questions was intended to elicit information regarding the personal and social issues that the elderly defined as of primary importance to them. Throughout the interviews, I probed for the respondents' definitions of the situation (Snow, Zurcher, & G. Sjoberg, 1982).

The Restructuring of the Extended Family

To understand some of the problems confronting elderly Mexican American men, particularly their isolation from family and social environment, we need to understand ongoing changes in the Mexican American family. On the basis of past research by anthropologists such as Rubel (1966) and Madsen (1964) as well as the work of Sena-Rivera (1979) and Keefe and Padilla (1987), many social scientists still assume that the extended family continues to be an integral part of the Mexican American community. For example, Queen, Habenstein, and Quadagno (1985) accept this premise without qualification (Vega, 1991).

In my research on the Mexican American family, however, I discovered that the extended family has undergone fundamental change. My research findings challenge prevailing generalizations about the Mexican American extended family (N. Williams, 1990). My conclusions regarding the extended family are based on understanding fundamental changes in the life cycle rituals relating to birth (*compadrazgo*), marriage, and death. These rituals were once a central integrating element for extended family relationships. The data from in-depth interviews as well as participant observation indicated that funerals are the last remaining life cycle ritual that brings the extended family members together. At funerals many persons meet aunts, uncles, and cousins they have not seen in years. A number of Mexican Americans have never met some members of the extended family who attend funerals. If funerals are the last vestige of social interaction with members of the extended family, then we should not expect the extended family to provide social and economic support for persons in their everyday activities.

The data from Dallas strongly support my previous findings. The extended family does not play a significant role in the lives of the elderly Mexican American men and women I interviewed. This research lends support to Trevino's (1988) contention that "a common misconception about the Hispanic elderly is that they are taken care of by their extended family" (p. 67). The elderly men in Dallas had little, if any, social interaction with their brothers and sisters (cf. Townsend, 1967) and almost no ties with their nieces or nephews. None of the elderly men (and only one elderly woman) mentioned the role of nephews and nieces in providing them with support in daily life.

Educational and Work Histories

The elderly I studied in Dallas were poor and often very poor. Markides and Mindel (1987) argue that the minority elderly have always had a lower standard of living than the white aged. Only 1 of the 23 men I interviewed might be classified as having been a white-collar worker.

Data on Mexican Americans living in Texas show that the elderly are likely to have low educational levels and to live in poverty. Prior to 1940 (or even 1945), the number of high school graduates in the United States was still relatively small, and we can assume that the percentage of Mexican Americans who graduated from high school was considerably smaller than it was for Anglos. A report by the National Council of La Raza (1991) documents the limited education of the Hispanic elderly: "According to the Census Bureau's *Statistical Abstract of the United States, 1990*, only about one in five Hispanics 65 and over had graduated from high school, and more than one third have less than five years of schooling, compared to one in 20 of all elderly" (p. 5).

Even today, there is a high dropout rate among Mexican Americans in middle grade levels and high schools. Moore and Pachon (1985) contend that "Hispanics' drop out rates are nearly double those of blacks and Anglos between the ages of 14 and 25 years" (p. 68) (cf. Carter & Segura, 1979).

In the past the educational opportunities for Mexican Americans were even more limited than they are today. In the 1930s and 1940s, when my respondents were in their teens, they suffered greatly from racial discrimination (San Miguel, 1987). According to Grebler, Moore, and Guzman (1970), "The larger society began to show an increasing awareness of the schooling gap in the early 1930s" (p. 142). However,

Moore (1976) indicates that there was "no special effort to educate Mexicans" in the 1930s (p. 79). In fact, San Miguel (1987), in discussing this era, states:

> If provided an education, they were usually given a shorter school year than Anglos and segregated educational facilities. In most cases, the segregated Mexican schools lacked proper school equipment, had poorly trained teachers, and contained a curriculum that did not reflect the heritage and interests of Spanish-speaking children. (p. 24)

Although discrimination against Mexican Americans exists today, the patterns are not as overt as they were when these men were young.

My respondents not only had limited educational opportunities, but also had to go to work at an early age in order to help their parents provide food and shelter for the family. The majority of the respondents spoke Spanish only. This pattern is in keeping with data on the poor Hispanic elderly (Andrews, 1989). Given their limited education and English skills these Mexican American men generally worked as unskilled or, at best, semiskilled laborers. They worked extremely hard at jobs that the middle class consider "dirty work."

Reflecting on his hard life, one man in his late 70s noted:

> El principal me dijo "Get out of here" porque no tenía zapatos. Fui descalzo. Eramos pobres. Esta es la razon que no tengo escuela.
>
> (The principal told me to "Get out of here" because I did not have any shoes. I went barefoot. We were poor. This is the reason why I do not have an education.)

Another respondent, who was in his 90s, was born in Mexico. His parents were very poor and had many children. This man became teary eyed when he said that his mother died while giving birth to him. Thus, when his aunt (his mother's sister) offered to take him as her own and rear him, his father agreed. After his aunt died in the early 1900s, he became homeless and moved to South Texas, spending his teens and adult years in the United States. As he reflected on his life he noted:

> Tuve muchos trabajos. Hago todo. Y todavía hago todo. Yo aprendí solo. Carpentería, electricidad, limpiar pisos, todo. Ni quiero acordarme. Mi vida ha sido muy triste.

> (I had a lot of jobs. I do everything. And I still do everything. I learned alone. Carpentry, electricity, cleaning floors, everything. I don't want to remember. My life has been very sad.)

In light of these kinds of life histories, it is not surprising that most of these men had worked in unstable jobs that paid low wages and provided little job security. These jobs also provided inadequate old-age and disability benefits (Santos, 1981). Before retiring, three of my respondents had been maintenance workers—one in a school, one at a department store, and one at a golf club. Still another respondent had been a dishwasher in a restaurant; one had worked in a semiskilled position in a printing shop, and another worked in a hardware store; another had been a handyman who was an unskilled laborer; and another had worked in a shop where automotive and airplane parts were assembled and repaired.

Some men had at times worked for employers who did not contribute to the Social Security system. Some expressed resentment against their employers. For example, one man who worked for a golf club complained that he had not received tips, as had some of the Anglos. He was sensitive to his low status and to the patterns of discrimination he experienced as part of his work history.

A minority of these elderly men had held stable jobs. One had worked for a company for 19 years, and just 1 year before he was to retire, the company folded. Instead of receiving a pension, this man received a few thousand dollars in severance pay. Another man saw the company for which he had worked for a number of years close its operations in Dallas. He was so uncertain about the future of the company that he decided not to leave his children and their families. He did not transfer with the company and retired instead. Thus, even among the minority of respondents who had held stable jobs, some could rely only on Social Security benefits. These job and income patterns, in turn, have direct relevance for present-day family relationships.

My data are in keeping with the findings of a report by the National Council of La Raza (1991) regarding the lack of the Hispanic elderly's financial resources during retirement. According to this report,

> Hispanic elderly are also less likely than Whites to receive private pensions or to have incomes from interest and other assets, and less likely than either Blacks or Whites to receive Social Security. As of 1988, only 77% of Hispanic elderly received Social Security, compared to 93% of White elderly and 89% of Black elderly. (p. ii)

Present Social Circumstances

My data indicate that elderly men's living conditions, lack of knowledge about the organizational structure of social service agencies, and especially their family relationships make old age a difficult period of life for Mexican Americans.

These men, for the most part, live in substandard housing in the poorer sections of the city. Their apartments or homes are in very poor condition, and many do not have adequate heating and cooling.

But living conditions are only one aspect of the men's current social circumstances. Although the respondents treated me with great courtesy, many were suspicious of strangers. One elderly man whom I interviewed with his wife, commented:

> No podemos sentarnos afuera. Nos gritan palabras malas. Nos pueden golpear. (We cannot sit outside. They yell obscenities at us. They could beat us.)

In another instance, I had been informed by a contact person that one man would not let me in his living quarters. His wife had died, and he wanted no one in his apartment. Thus, the interview was conducted outside his apartment. Why did this man react in this manner? His neighbors told me that he was afraid that someone might steal the few possessions he owned. This neighborhood was an unsafe area. Like many other elderly men—and elderly women—he lived in considerable fear of being mugged or robbed.

The social backgrounds of the elderly men in Dallas affected them in still other ways. Because they had not acquired basic knowledge of the programs and benefits available to the elderly, they had difficulty securing services to which they were entitled.

I briefly elaborate on two cases to clarify these generalizations and then relate these issues back to family life. One man, who suffered from problems with his vision, heard that the government was no longer going to pay Medicare benefits. Upon obtaining this information, he went to a medical center where he had an operation on his eyes. The surgery was not successful, and he has lost most of his vision in one eye. He now regrets having had the surgery. He recognized that the information leading him to have the operation was based on a false rumor. Another elderly Mexican American man had heard of elderly persons losing their Social Security benefits if they worked. The respondent did not have knowledge of the bureaucratic rules regarding Social Security benefits, and he did not have anyone (especially family members) who could provide him with adequate information about the regulations. Thus, he feared that if he worked to supplement his income he would face the possible loss of his Social Security benefits. If his Social Security benefits were taken away from him, he would be unable to fulfill his role as the provider for the family.

Limited knowledge reduces access to social service agencies and further undermines the quality of life among the elderly. For example, some elderly men are unable to take advantage of the Food Stamps program. The public transportation facilities in Dallas are inadequate for the elderly, and thus a number of these men suffered from health impairments that made it difficult for them to ride buses to various agencies if multiple transfers were required. The cost of taxi fare to the welfare agency to get food stamps often exceeded the value of any stamps they could get (only $11 of food stamps per month for the majority of elderly in this study).

If these elderly men had not been so isolated from family, they might have known more about and had better access to social services. However, the restructuring (or breakdown) of the extended family has limited the respondents' relationships with their family. These men could not rely on their nephews or nieces, who because they are likely to have somewhat more formal education, could have provided them with much-needed assistance (Korte, 1981), and other social support from extended family members was not available. More important, the tenuous nature of social bonds between the men and their own children and grandchildren made it impossible for them to rely on the latter for knowledge or assistance in acquiring social services. In one instance, a stepdaughter helped her elderly father fill out the proper forms because he did not know the names or locations of the social service agencies. A number of these men did not read and write English, and without support from their children or grandchildren they were totally dependent on English-speaking agency personnel for assistance. Therefore the lack of either a strong family support system or English-speaking personal advocates further undermined the quality of life for many elderly men.

The role of children as, for example, mediators between the family and community agencies comes into sharper focus when I contrast the Dallas research with my earlier work on the Mexican American family (N. Williams, 1990). The adult children of some of the members of the working class served as mediators or "constructive brokers" (Zurcher, 1986) between their parents and community organizations. These particular children helped interpret the bureaucratic rules for their parents. Few, if any, elderly men in Dallas had this kind of social support.

I have emphasized that the elderly Mexican American men had few meaningful ties with their extended family. They did not mention their brothers and sisters or nephews and nieces as providing them with emotional or other kinds of social support. My data, therefore, support Korte's (1981) call for research on the relation of the elderly to their middle-aged children and grandchildren.

Relationships With Family Members

On the basis of this exploratory study, I delineate two main types of family patterns. In one type the elderly man is neglected and isolated from his own family. In another type the elderly man plays a provider role. After describing these types and their variations, I discuss some exceptions to these patterns.

Only a minority of elderly men have close interpersonal relationships with their children (cf. U.S. Senate, 1991). In some instances in my sample, the children did not live within the Dallas metropolitan area. In other cases, there was tension between the men and their children. For example, one respondent whose daughter married an Anglo believed that the daughter had distanced herself from the family, and this belief limited his interaction with his grandchildren. In a number of other cases, the children of the elderly had married and had families, but because the children also were poor and struggling to survive, they were unable to assist their father and seemed to have little time to spend with him.

The Neglected-and-Isolated Role

One indicator of the social distance from their children is the fact that the men could not identify where their children lived. Even when their children lived in Dallas, they did not know the exact location of their residences. Although some respondents could identify their children's residences with a particular section of Dallas such as Oak Cliff, it was apparent that typically the men had not visited their children's homes on any regular basis. Again, poverty was a contributing factor. These men either did not own cars or were unable to drive, and the public transportation system is highly inadequate. Their social isolation was heightened because many suffered from health problems that limited their mobility. Further, their children often had limited transportation because they either did not own cars or had automobiles in poor working condition. For example, one respondent was deeply troubled because his son had recently asked him to co-sign for a car. He reported:

> Mi hijo quería que le firmara para un carro. No podemos. El no tiene trabajo seguro, y nosotros no tenemos dinero. Nosotros no podemos hacer los pagos. Es mucha responsibilidad para nosotros.
>
> (My son wanted me to co-sign for a car. We can't. He does not have a secure job, and we do not have any money. We cannot make the payments. It's too much responsibility for us.)

In this case, in addition to contributing to his physical isolation from his children, poverty has caused special stress and tension in the father's relationship with his son.

Another respondent described his efforts to assist his daughter despite the fact that his actions created special difficulties for him. His daughter asked to borrow his car because her car was being repaired and her son needed transportation to the university. The father lent the daughter the car. But the respondent had forgotten that he had a doctor's appointment 2 days later. He called a social service agency for a ride to the doctor's office. After he explained why he did not have a car a volunteer agreed to take him to the doctor. Yet technically the personnel of the agency were not supposed to provide transportation for their clients.

The respondent experienced considerable personal tension and stress because his own responsibilities conflicted with his efforts to reduce the social distance between himself and his daughter. Because she lived in a suburb on the other side of town, he saw her very infrequently. As a father he felt obligated to assist his daughter because she was without an automobile and was experiencing family problems of her own. However, the daughter provided little social support for him.

The next two cases illustrate the pattern of social isolation. One man in his 70s had been a widower for over two decades. His five children lived in the Dallas metropolitan area; however, they seldom visited him. One son came to see him periodically, but stayed only for a short time. This Mexican American man did not know his children's occupations. When I probed regarding his ties to his children, he stated:

> Están ocupados con sus familias. No les importa de mí, no los necesito.
>
> (They are busy with their families. They don't care about me; I don't need them.)

Although this man had rationalized his children's neglect of him, his comments and my observations revealed that because of his physical disabilities, he required financial and other kinds of social support. He depended on the Senior Citizen's Center to pick him up for lunch twice a week, which appeared to be his sole contact with the "outside world."

Another man was married, had heart problems, and did not drive because he was afraid of wrecking the car. He did not have a good relationship with his only son, who had been divorced and remarried. The son on occasion helped with grocery shopping, but the father was estranged from his son's ex-wife as well as his daughter-in-law. The grandchildren are adults, and one granddaughter has twin daughters. In speaking about his grandchildren he observed:

> Yo les doy consejos pero no quieren escucharme. Les digo que se eduquen. Que trabajen y alcen dinero. El tiempo se va poner muy duro. Yo tengo experiencia pero ellos no quieren aprender.
>
> (I give them advice but they don't want to listen to me. I tell them to get educated. To work and save money. Times are going to get hard. I am experienced but they don't want to learn.)

His complaints about his grandchildren not listening to him should be interpreted in the context of an estrangement from his son and from his grandchildren. Although the respondent and his wife were proud of their grandchildren, they emphasized that they had been unable to communicate with them. The respondents believed that their life experiences could contribute positively to their grandchildren's quality of life if the young people would listen to their advice. However, the children did not seem interested. The grandparents attributed the lack of meaningful social interaction with their grandchildren to their inability to help them. The grandparent role, as Korte (1981) suggests, is being undermined by a growing generation gap—a gap that has resulted from rapid industrialization and urbanization.

The Provider Role

Although the neglect and isolation of elderly Mexican American men is a dominant pattern, one important subpattern also exists. Some men were providers for at least some of their children (and grandchildren). In one instance, a divorced daughter had moved back in with her father and mother. In another instance, the man was a widower. In these cases the respondents found themselves helping to rear their grandchildren, and they worried about what would happen to their daughters and the grandchildren after their death. They defined themselves as "providers" rather than as "grandparents." Another case points to the complexities that arise among some of the elderly in coping with the provider role. An elderly couple was at one time living in a house provided by their son when a daughter divorced and moved back with her parents. Although the divorce settlement awarded her house to her ex-husband, the ex-husband could not keep up with the maintenance of the home, and after a short time, gave it to his ex-wife and children. The elderly parents then moved out of their residence (over the objections of their son) to join their single-parent daughter because she needed their assistance and support. The grandparents took care of the grandchildren while the daughter worked. But now the grandchildren were teenagers and tensions existed in the family. The grandfather wanted to move out but was unable to return to the son's house because his son's feelings were hurt.

In another case, the divorced daughter and her children moved in with her elderly father after the divorce. The grandfather took care of the children while their mother worked 5 hours a day. He was very concerned about his daughter's present economic situation because she did not earn sufficient money to support herself and the children and could not afford to pay for day care services. He feared that she would be unable to care for her family if something should happen to him. He, too, felt that he was still in the provider rather than the grandfather role.

Another elderly man (and his wife) reported that they had taken care of their grandchildren at times when their son had experienced financial problems. However, the son had recently found a steady job, and his wife had hired a baby-sitter for the children. When the respondents called their son to ask if they could continue to take care of the grandchildren, they were shocked by his response. He informed them that he did not want them to take care of the children because their car did not have an infant's seat and was in poor condition and thus not reliable in case of an emergency. In addition, the children could not communicate with their grandparents because the former did not understand Spanish. The respondents' feelings were hurt because the son had sought their assistance only in times of family crises and need.

One elderly man (and his wife) had, in comparison to other respondents, adequate resources that permitted him to carry out the provider role in a meaningful way. He was in good health and had a pension in addition to his Social Security benefits. Nevertheless, the couple's concern about their children's future demonstrated the emotional toll of their children's problems.

In sum, I discovered two types of elderly men. First, the most common type is the isolated or neglected man who lived in unstable communities and had unstable ties with his children and grandchildren. This is not what he wanted. However, the social changes accompanied by modernity (along with poverty) made it almost impossible for him to sustain stable family bonds with his children or grandchildren. Second, a significant minority of men performed provider roles with very meager resources.

Only two men did not conform to either of these two types, and they were exceptions that proved the rule. Both were in good health. One was a widower who had no children, but was very active within certain community organizations. The other man, who was married, had a pension in addition to Social Security and thus had social resources that permitted him to carry out what the broader society might view as a typical grandfather role.

After having delineated these two main types, I attended a small meeting of elderly Mexican American men and women. I discussed the patterns outlined above with a group of four men and women and with two other elderly persons on an individual basis. All agreed that the patterns I have described reflected the lives of Mexican American elderly they knew or had heard about. Moreover, because of changing economic conditions in the society at large, they assumed that the patterns discussed above will be exaggerated in the future. They believed that there will be greater isolation for many elderly as well as increased demands placed on others to help provide for adult children and grandchildren. They were pessimistic about the society providing for the basic needs of the elderly Mexican Americans. They were also pessimistic about the younger generation being willing to care for their elderly parents. The recent reactions of the privileged sector of the United States to the poor, as well as the divisions among generations in the society as a whole, suggest that the concerns of these elderly Mexican Americans are realistic.

Conclusions

In this exploratory study, which is based on field research carried out in Dallas, Texas, I have shown how the work and educational histories of elderly Mexican American men are interwoven with their family patterns.

The work histories of the elderly men I interviewed have led to limited resources in their old age. With rare exceptions, because they have worked in low-paying unstable jobs, they must rely solely on minimum or near-minimum Social Security benefits.

Typically these elderly Mexican American men live in poverty. Their quality of life is undermined because of their lack of knowledge of, as well as access to, the social service organizations in the community.

The men's two main family patterns—isolated and neglected versus struggling provider—are a result of these men's life histories. They have worked very hard, but had limited education and had to work in low-status jobs that provided limited retirement benefits. In addition to their poverty, the processes of urbanization, industrialization, and bureaucratization have fostered the isolation and neglect by members of their immediate family or have placed these men in a position to help care for some of their adult children (and grandchildren) with meager resources. Further, the decisions by the privileged sector of society restrict the resources or other support systems that might otherwise alleviate the suffering and difficulties these men experience in old age.

For future research and policy implications of my research, I move beyond the data at hand. Because of our exceedingly limited data on Mexican American elderly men (and women), the need for more systematic research should be self-evident. In carrying out this kind of research, we first need to know more about how social changes on the national level (particularly social policies on aging) are affecting the Mexican American elderly. Social policies instituted during the 1980s in the United States have meant that the very rich have become richer and the poor have become poorer (e.g., Bartlett & Steele, 1992). It is therefore not surprising that a number of the Mexican American elderly in my study perceive the future as becoming bleaker for them. Priority should be given to understanding how national (as well as state) policies affect the daily lives of the Mexican American elderly. Social scientists thus can fill an important gap in our knowledge about the impact of social policies on the minority elderly.

Within the context of the larger social and cultural changes that adversely affect the poor in the United States, we must then recognize that—as social scientists (e.g., M. D. Williams, 1992) have emphasized—the poor can be highly resourceful and creative. Although we must be careful not to glamorize the harsh life of the poor, my observations indicate that the Mexican American elderly men are unable to cope effectively with local community agencies not because they lack initiative but because they lack basic knowledge of the rules and regulations of the community agencies on which they depend. Therefore we require systematic information about how the economically disadvantaged elderly, in this instance Mexican Americans, relate to community organizational structures (e.g., Starret & Decker, 1986). Yet we need to go farther and design pilot programs that will help the Mexican American elderly help themselves, particularly in securing services to which they are rightfully entitled as citizens.

In addition to focusing on the elderly, we need to find ways of improving the manner in which social services are delivered (Starret & Decker, 1986). Many social service agency personnel, who are typically underpaid, but well intentioned, lack knowledge about Mexican American culture. For example, my case materials suggest that some agency personnel assume that because the Mexican American extended family provides assistance to elderly men and women, older Mexican Americans are not in need of the kind of assistance offered to other groups. However, the evidence I have collected indicates that the extended family among Mexican Americans is in a state of restructuring (or breakdown). Therefore, the service personnel require basic knowledge about the nature of Mexican American social and cultural patterns if they are to properly assist the men and women who are poor and elderly.

Embedded in the aforementioned discussion is another issue that should be made explicit. Data from various sources indicate that people in privileged positions do not necessarily define situations in the same way as do people in less privileged positions (e.g., N. Williams, 1989; G. Sjoberg, N. Williams, Vaughan, & A. F. Sjoberg, 1991). If we are to design effective pilot programs for improving services to the Mexican American elderly, we must be aware of their situation and should consider measures by which potential misunderstandings between the privileged and nonprivileged can be bridged or overcome.

In general, then, it is striking how little systematic research we have on Mexican American elderly men. At the very least, this research report should highlight the lack of information on Mexican American elderly men—or women—and should point the way toward new directions for future research.

References

Andrews, J. (1989, September). *Poverty and poor health among elderly Hispanic Americans.* Baltimore, MD: Commonwealth Fund Commission on Elderly People Living Alone.

Aponte, R. (1991). Urban Hispanic poverty: Disaggregations and explanations. *Social Problems, 38,* 516-528.

Bailey, K. D. (1987). *Methods of social research* (3rd ed.). New York: Free Press.

Bartlett, D. L., & Steele, J. B. (1992). *America: What went wrong?* Kansas City: Andrews & McMeel.

Carter, T. P., & Segura, R. D. (1979). *Mexican-Americans in school.* New York: College Entrance Examination Board.

Chelimsky, E. (1991). *Hispanic access to health care: Significant gaps exist in Hispanic health care: Today's shame, tomorrow's crisis* (Joint Hearing before the Select Committee on Aging and the Congressional Hispanic Caucus, U.S. House of Representatives Comm. Pub. No. 102-842). Washington, DC: U. S. Government Printing Office.

Facio, E. L. (1988). The interaction of age and gender in Chicana older lives: A case study of Chicana elderly in a senior citizen center. *Renato Rosaldo Lecture Series Monograph, 4* (Series 1986-87), 21-38.

Gordon, M. S. (1961). Work and patterns of retirement. In R. W. Kleemeier (Ed.), *Aging and leisure* (pp. 15-53). New York: Oxford University Press.

Grebler, L., Moore, J. W., & Guzman, R. O. (1970). *The Mexican-American people.* New York: Free Press.

Hayes-Bautista, D. E. (1992). Latino health indicators and the underclass model: From paradox to new policy models. In A. Furino (Ed.), *Health policy and the Hispanic* (pp. 32-47). Boulder, CO: Westview.

Keefe, S., & Padilla, A. (1987). *Chicano ethnicity.* Albuquerque: University of New Mexico Press.

Korte, A. O. (1981). Theoretical perspectives in mental health and the Mexicano elders. In M. Miranda & R. Ruiz (Eds.), *Chicano aging and mental health* (pp. 156-184). San Francisco: Human Resources Corporation. (U.S. Department of Health and Human Services, DDH Adm. 81-952)

Lewis, R., & Salt, R. (Eds.). (1986). *Men in families.* Newbury Park, CA: Sage.

Limerick, P. N. (1987). *The legacy of conquest.* New York: Norton.

Madsen, R. (1964). *The Mexican-Americans of south Texas.* New York: Holt, Rinehart & Winston.

Maril, R. L. (1989). *Poorest of Americans.* Notre Dame, IN: University of Notre Dame Press.

Markides, K. S., & Mindel, C. H. (1987). *Aging and ethnicity.* Newbury Park, CA: Sage.

Moore, J. W. (1976). *Mexican Americans.* Englewood Cliffs, NJ: Prentice-Hall.

Moore, J. W., & Pachon, H. (1985). *Hispanics in the United States.* Englewood Cliffs, NJ: Prentice-Hall.

Murdock, S., & Ellis, R. (1991). *Patterns of ethnic change 1980 to 1990: The 1990 census* (1990 Census Series No. 2, Departmental Technical Report 91-2). College Station: Texas A&M University.

National Council of La Raza. (1991, February). *Becoming involved in the aging network: A planning and resource guide for Hispanic community-based organizations* (Prepared by C. Lopez with E. Aguilera). Washington, DC: Policy Analysis Center and Office of Institutional Development.

Queen, S. A., Habenstein, R. W., & Quadagno, J. S. (1985). *The family in various cultures.* New York: Harper & Row.

Rubel, A. (1966). *Across the tracks: Mexican-Americans in a Texas city.* Austin: University of Texas Press.

San Miguel, G., Jr. (1987). *"Let all of them take heed": Mexican Americans and the campaign for educational equality in Texas, 1910-1981.* Austin: University of Texas Press.

Santos, R. (1981). Aging and Chicano mental health: An economic perspective. In M. Miranda & R. Ruiz (Eds.), *Chicano aging and mental health* (pp. 156-184). San Francisco: Human Resources Corporation. (U.S. Department of Health and Human Services, DDH Adm. 81-952)

Sena-Rivera, J. (1979). Extended kinship in the United States: Competing models and the case of la familia Chicana. *Journal of Marriage and the Family, 41,* 121-129.

Sjoberg, G., Williams, N., Vaughan, T. R., & Sjoberg, A. F. (1991). The case study approach in social research: Basic methodological issues. In J. R. Feagin, A. M. Orum, & G. Sjoberg (Eds.), *A case for the case study* (pp. 27-79). Chapel Hill: University of North Carolina Press.

Snow, D., Zurcher, L. A., & Sjoberg, G. (1982). Interviewing by comment: An adjunct to the direct question. *Qualitative Sociology, 5,* 385-411.

Starret, R. A., & Decker, J. T. (1986, Spring). The utilization of social services by the Mexican-American elderly. *Ethnicity and Gerontological Social Work* (Special Issue—Ethnicity), pp. 87-100.

Townsend, P. (1967). *The family life of old people.* London: Routledge & Kegan Paul.

Trevino, M. C. (1988). A comparative analysis of need, access, and utilization of health and human services. In S. R. Applewhite (Ed.), *Hispanic elderly in transition* (pp. 61-71). New York: Greenwood.

U.S. Senate. (1991). *An advocate's guide to laws and programs addressing elder abuse* (Special Committee on Aging, Serial No. 102-1). Washington, DC: U.S. Government Printing Office.

Vega, W. A. (1991). Hispanic families in the 1980s: A decade of research. In A. Booth (Ed.), *Contemporary families: Looking forward, looking back* (pp. 297-306). Minneapolis, MN: National Council on Family Relations.

Williams, M. D. (1992). *The human dilemma: A decade in Belmar* (2nd ed.). Orlando, FL: Harcourt Brace Jovanovich.

Williams, N. (1989). Role taking and the study of majority/minority relationships. *Journal of Applied Behavioral Science, 25,* 175-186.

Williams, N. (1990). *The Mexican American family: Tradition and change.* Dix Hills, NY: General Hall.

Zinn, M. (1982). Chicano men and masculinity. *Journal of Ethnic Studies, 10,* 29-44.

Zurcher, L. A. (1986). The future of the reservist: A case of constructive brokering. In L. A. Zurcher, M. Boykin, & H. Merritt (Eds.), *Citizen-sailors in a changing society: Policy issues for manning the United States naval reserve* (pp. 221-253). New York: Greenwood.

PART TWO

ROLE ALLOCATION AND ROLE CHANGE

5

Work and Family Orientations of Contemporary Adolescent Boys and Girls

KATHERINE DENNEHY
JEYLAN T. MORTIMER

Introduction

The current generation of youth has grown up in a rapidly changing sociohistorical context. Given major alterations in the work and family roles of adult men and women, it is important to know whether boys' and girls' attitudes toward educational attainment and work and family roles have converged in recent years or if boys and girls continue to hold divergent attitudes reflecting more traditional gender role norms. We first present a brief description of changes in gender roles regarding work and family responsibilities and review prior studies on youth orientations toward achievement and family life. Drawing on data obtained from a representative sample of contemporary Midwestern adolescents, we then examine youth attitudes and plans with respect to education, work, family, and friendship, indicating how young persons anticipate their future. Finally, we assess the implications of these patterns for the life-styles of men and women in the years ahead.

The research was supported by the National Center for Research on Vocational Education and the National Institute of Mental Health (MH42843, "Work Experience and Adolescent Well-Being"). Special thanks to Carol Zierman for bibliographic assistance.

The Historical Context

During the past century, work, family, and the gender roles structured by these institutions have undergone considerable change. In recent decades, women have pursued higher levels of education, delaying marriage, remaining employed after marriage and after the birth of children, and divorcing at high rates (McLaughlin et al., 1988). Because the majority of mothers in two-parent households are now employed, and one fourth of U.S. children under the age of 18 now live in single-parent households (Barringer, 1991), the 1950s "traditional" family model (with the husband as sole breadwinner and the mother as full-time homemaker) is becoming increasingly anachronistic.

Family Roles

Although the breadwinner/homemaker family model remains culturally dominant, some researchers allege that a new ideal of fatherhood is emerging (Bronstein, 1988; Pleck, 1985, 1987). This new ideal not only emphasizes a more egalitarian sharing of household and child care responsibilities, it also advocates that fathers practice greater intimacy, expressiveness, and nurturance in their parental role. Some researchers claim that men are now spending more time with the family (Daniels & Weingarten, 1982; Lewis, 1986) and contributing more time to household labor and child care (Gershuny & Robinson, 1988; Pleck, 1985).

Other researchers, however, are doubtful about such change (Furstenberg, 1988; LaRossa, 1988). Males are widely considered (by both men and women) to be the main family providers even though both spouses contribute to the financial support of the family (Thompson & Walker, 1991). Contemporary adult men are also less egalitarian in their views about family roles than women (Thornton, 1989), and contemporary women, despite their high levels of employment, still have primary responsibility for children and household tasks (Berardo, Shehan, & Leslie, 1987; Coverman & Sheley, 1986; Hochschild & Machung, 1989). Several studies report no change in the division of labor or continued unequal allocations of family labor (Cohen, 1987; Hiller & Philliber, 1986; Ross, Mirowsky, & Huber, 1983; see Ferree, 1991, and Thompson & Walker, 1991, for reviews). There is evidence of reversion to a more traditional division of household labor between couples after children are born (Entwisle & Doering, 1981; Weiss, 1990). LaRossa's (1988) assessment is appropriate: Although the ideal about men's participation in family life may have changed, the actual behavior of men has changed relatively little.

Adult women tend to organize their paid labor force participation (i.e., movements in and out of the labor force, number of hours, and time of day worked) in response to family demands (McLaughlin et al., 1988; Moen, 1985; Thompson & Walker, 1991). Moen (1985) finds that the presence of small children is associated with women's reduced labor force participation. In comparison to men, women's employment is more often interrupted by demands to care for ill, aged, or young family members (Menaghan & Parcel, 1991). In view of these trends, the continued gender differences in status attainment and the large disparities in the earnings of men and women (Marini, Shin, & Raymond, 1989) are not surprising.

It should be noted that fathers face institutional and normative constraints that lessen their family involvement. Pleck (1985) argues that men face structural barriers, such as inflexible and demanding work schedules, which make it difficult to meet family obligations. Male parents may face impeded careers and lower incomes when they devote more time to family responsibilities (Greif, 1990).

Personal Relationships

Although scholarship has focused on the implications of recent social and cultural trends for the division of family labor, it is also important to consider their effects on men's life-styles and well-being. Several studies show that men benefit greatly from family life. Gove and Hughes (1980) find increased longevity among married men in comparison to divorced or single males. Both Weiss (1990) and Nordstrom (1986) find that men obtain a sense of security, attachment, and companionship from their marriages. However, census data reveal that over the decade from 1970 to 1980 men experienced increasing singlehood, divorce, and childlessness (Cooney & Uhlenberg, 1991). If men are living alone for longer time periods, as a result of delayed marriage and divorce, their emotional well-being could suffer.

Men also rely heavily on their wives to foster and maintain friendships and extended family networks (Weiss, 1990). In interviews with more than 200 men and women, Rubin (1983) found that women were more likely than men to name friends, in addition to the spouse, that could be relied upon in troubled times. In contrast, the men more frequently named only the spouse as a trusted friend. Some men regret later in life that they did not develop more friendships with other men (Lewis & Salt, 1986). Men's reliance upon women for social intimacy and for maintaining familial and social ties could place them at greater risk of loneliness and isolation in the absence of spouses.

But there is some controversy about the quality of men's friendship. Past research found that same-sex male friendships were less intimate than same-sex female friendships (Douvan & Adelson, 1966). However, Swain (1989) argues that males do develop strong bonds with other men and that intimacy is fostered through shared activity rather than shared self-disclosure through talk as it is for women.

Youth Orientations to Work, Family, and Achievement

Given changing patterns of family life and broadening occupational opportunities for women, it is reasonable to expect that adolescent boys' and girls' orientations to education, work, family, and friendship would converge. Since the 1960s, sociologists have given much attention to the educational and occupational aspirations of youth, given the important role of these values in the status attainment process (Sewell & Hauser, 1975). Although boys had higher occupational aspirations than girls in the late 1960s (Marini & Greenberger, 1978), studies in the 1980s have not found gender differences in the occupational and educational aspirations of youth (Crowley & Shapiro, 1982; Danziger, 1983). Some research even shows that girls have higher occupational aspirations than boys (Farmer, 1983).

However, it appears that males and females differ in how they plan to coordinate their work and family responsibilities (Maines & Hardesty, 1987). Some researchers (Aneshensel & Rosen, 1980; Waite & Berryman, 1985) argue that young women's occupational expectations are influenced by their expectations or beliefs about their domestic roles. Thus, whereas males plan to have an uninterrupted work or career trajectory (Maines & Hardesty, 1987; Tittle, 1981), young women's educational, work, and career plans are contingent upon family demands (Maines & Hardesty, 1987; McLaughlin et al., 1988). Spade and Reese (1991) found that male and female college students have equal commitments toward work roles and family life, yet both men and women expect women to assume a more prominent role in the family. Machung (1989) reports that college men plan to rely on their wives to care for the home and family as they pursue their own careers.

Although there has been considerable research on adolescent educational and occupational aspirations, little is known about the development of other work and family orientations in adolescence. Keeping in mind that there are structural bases of inequality and—despite affirmative action programs—continued discrimination against women in the workplace, it is still important to consider whether differences in the work and family orientations of adolescent boys and girls might at least partially influence socioeconomic outcomes. Moreover, given the changing work and family roles of adult men and women and the changing nature of parenthood in recent decades, it is necessary to continually monitor adolescent work and family orientations to obtain a fuller understanding of the changing social-psychological concomitants of the transition to adulthood.

The present chapter draws on an ongoing longitudinal study of high school students to address gender differences in orientations to achievement, work, family, and friendship that could influence the processes of status attainment and family formation, the division of family work, and the development of friendship in early adulthood. We examine adolescent boys' and girls' plans to marry and to have children, boys' expectations about their future wives' employment outside the home, and girls' expectations about the continuity of their careers. We also assess whether adolescent boys and girls are equally confident about their abilities to achieve their work and family goals.

Further, we consider whether variations in life circumstances influence adolescents' plans for the future. Given the high divorce rates of the 1970s, many contemporary adolescents have spent at least part of their life in single-parent households. It is plausible that the composition of the family of origin (i.e., whether they are growing up in single- or dual-parent families) and the mother's employment status would influence adolescent attitudes. We also investigate differences by socioeconomic background and race.

We acknowledge that young people's orientations may be stage specific, with girls' earlier maturity prompting them to become more oriented toward boys and dating, and perhaps leading them to think seriously about marriage and parenthood at a younger age (Eder, 1985). Moreover, given the discrimination that employed women face and their difficulty in balancing work and family, adolescent girls may find work and family decision making more problematic and therefore more salient preoccupations.

Further, preferences are often changed by circumstances encountered later in life. Rindfuss, Cooksey, and Sutterlin (1990) find numerous changes in occupational choices as young people move from adolescence into early adulthood. Gerson (1985) illustrates how changing circumstances in women's lives influence their attitudes toward family and work roles. For example, a woman may initially desire to be a full-time homemaker, but a divorce and financial necessity may propel her into the labor force. Former housewives who experience promotions into rewarding and satisfying positions may find that work has become an important part of their identity. Similarly, men who expect their future wives to be homemakers may alter their opinions when their own spouses wish to enter the work force or family economic need necessitates two incomes.

Still, there is reason to systematically study young people's aspirations and plans. Adolescent orientations to the future are reflective of the way contemporary youth see the world ahead, their choices and dilemmas in making decisions that will importantly structure their futures. The relationship between adolescent educational and occupational aspirations and plans and early adult socioeconomic attainments is well established (Spenner & Featherman, 1978). Occupational value orientations in the final years of schooling are significantly predictive of early adult occupational experiences (Lindsay & Knox, 1984; Mortimer & Lorence, 1979). Early marriage and childbearing can be quite detrimental to the economic attainments of both sexes, but especially for women (Marini et al., 1989). Thus, adolescent attitudes and plans with respect to the future may establish a framework for decision making that can have important implications for future life choices, opportunities, and outcomes.

Data Source

The data were collected as part of the Youth Development Study in 1988, 1989, and 1990. The sample was chosen randomly from a list of enrolled ninth-grade students in St. Paul, Minnesota. We gathered questionnaire data from 1,001 ninth graders in 1988; from 962 of these students in the 10th grade (1989); and from 958 in the 11th grade (1990), yielding a retention rate of 95.4% across the three waves. (For more information about the sample, see Mortimer, Finch, Shanahan, & Ryu, 1992.) Approximately three quarters (79.4%) of the ninth graders' mothers were employed outside the home. Slightly more than one fourth (27.6%) of the students reported living with only one parent.

Findings

Educational and Occupational Aspirations and Plans

Consistent with other recent studies, our findings indicate that boys, on the average, do *not* have higher educational aspirations and plans than girls. In fact, throughout the high school years (grades 9, 10, 11), boys consistently have lower educational aspirations than girls. By the 11th grade, boys aspire, on average, to obtain a bachelor's degree, whereas girls report higher aspirations. When asked to report the highest level of schooling that they realistically expect to finish, both boys and girls report slightly lower levels of educational attainment. Both boys' and girls' educational aspirations and plans decline slightly as they move through high school, perhaps indicating growing realism with respect to future educational achievement. Although in absolute terms both boys and girls aim high, in all years, the boys' aspirations and plans are significantly ($p < .05$) lower than those of girls.

Similarly, boys consistently have lower occupational aspirations than girls ($p < .05$ in Waves 1 and 2, $p = .104$ in Wave 3). For both boys and girls, occupational aspirations decline somewhat after the 10th grade, which may also indicate greater realism in occupational goals as awareness of labor market realities increases. Further, contemporary adolescent girls are as likely as boys to report that having a career or occupation will be important to them in adulthood.

Family Plans

Although most adolescents plan to marry and have children, a small minority do not. Roughly 6% of the 11th graders do not plan to marry and about 11% do not plan to have children. This group may reflect growing acceptance of a childfree life-style.[1] These plans differ slightly by gender, with a larger percentage of the boys planning not to marry or to have children (see Table 5.1). For example, 8% of 11th-grade boys, but only 3% of girls, plan to remain single; 15% of boys and 8% of girls do not plan to have children.

These data are consistent with previous surveys monitoring adolescent plans for marriage and children. About 4% of the high school

Table 5.1 Family Plans of Adolescent Boys and Girls

Family Plans		*9th Grade*		*10th Grade*		*11th Grade*	
		Boys	*Girls*	*Boys*	*Girls*	*Boys*	*Girls*
Plans for Marriage	Yes	76.6%	85.2%	73.0%	79.9%	73.2%	84.8%
	Don't Know	11.9%	8.8%	19.8%	14.6%	18.6%	12.0%
	No	11.5%	6.0%	7.3%	5.5%	8.2%	3.2%
	N	470	513	440	493	441	501
	Chi-square	13.00		6.30		21.27	
	p <	.01		.05		.001	
	df	2		2		2	
Plans for Children	Yes	84.4%	91.3%	87.4%	91.6%	85.3%	92.5%
	No	15.6%	8.7%	12.6%	8.4%	14.7%	7.5%
	N	461	515	427	500	434	504
	Chi-square	10.95		4.46		12.52	
	p <	.001		.05		.001	
	df	1		1		1	

seniors from the 1986 Monitoring the Future survey (Bachman, Johnston, & O'Malley, 1986) expressed a preference for remaining single throughout most of their life. Thornton and Freedman (1982), using data from Project TALENT and High School and Beyond studies, show a small increase from 1960 to 1980 in the percentage of high school seniors expecting to remain single throughout their life: For males the figures increased from 8% to 10%; the percentage of females who did not expect to marry rose from 3% to 5%. Buchmann (1989), in her analysis of the same data sets, reports that the percentage of high school seniors not planning to have children rose from 6.3% in 1960 to 10.3% in 1980 (see also Thornton, 1989).

With respect to the anticipated age at marriage, our data are comparable with national trends. According to the March 1990 census survey (Barringer, 1991), men and women are marrying later than ever before in this century (on the average, at age 23.9 for women's and 26.1 for men's first marriage). In our study, girls plan to marry, on the average, at 24.6 years of age; boys anticipate marriage at 25.9 years of age ($p < .001$).

In all years, boys think that marriage and parenthood will be less important to them in the future than do girls ($p < .001$). Whereas there is little change in boys' evaluation of the family sphere across time, the importance of family life for girls increases somewhat during high school.

The girls in this study overwhelmingly plan to work after marriage. In fact, there is almost total rejection of the full-time homemaker role; only 3.4% of the 11th-grade girls plan not to be employed after marriage. With few exceptions, the girls also plan to work after having children; only 4% of the 11th-grade girls plan not to do so. Still, most girls plan to stay out of the labor force until their children are at least 1 or 2 years of age, or until the end of their children's nursery school (see Table 5.2). As girls progress through high school, the length of time that they plan to remain with their children out of the labor force declines (see Table 5.2A). Still, even short interruptions may have deleterious career consequences, as temporary removal from the labor force is often looked upon unfavorably by employers.

In contrast to the girls' almost unanimous desire to join the labor force and work after their children are born, many of the boys are uncertain about whether or not their spouses should return to work after they have children (see Table 5.2B). Across all three waves, from 33% to 42% of the boys said their spouses would work outside the home after having children. Approximately half of the boys in the 11th grade were not sure if their wives would work after having children, and another 10% said

Table 5.2 Plans to Return to Work After Childbearing, 11th-Grade Boys and Girls

Response Options: When my youngest child is . . .	*Boys* %	*N*	*Girls* %	*N*
(1) less than a year old	75.4	288	25.1	115
(2) one or two years of age	14.1	54	39.2	180
(3) in nursery school	4.5	17	15.7	72
(4) in kindergarten	4.2	16	12.2	56
(5) in elementary school	1.6	6	7.0	32
(6) in junior high	0	0	0.7	3
(7) in high school	0	0	0.2	1
(8) in college	0	0	0	0
(9) gone from home	0.3	1	0	0

Table 5.2A Mean Comparison of Plans to Work After Childbearing, Boys and Girls, Grades 9, 10, 11

When Do You Plan to Return to Work?	*Boys* *Mean*	*N*	*Girls* *Mean*	*N*	$p <$[a]
9th grade	1.91	391	2.77	457	.001
10th grade	1.65	381	2.53	448	.001
11th grade	1.44	382	2.40	459	.001

a. t-test of signficance

Table 5.2B Boys' Attitudes About Spouse Working After Childbearing, Grades 9, 10, 11

Spouse Work After Childbearing?	*9th Grade*	*10th Grade*	*11th Grade*
Yes	32.9%	39.6%	42.2%
Don't Know	54.7%	49.6%	48.0%
No	12.4%	10.8%	9.8%
N	371	389	379

that their wives would not be employed after having children. In a study of 600 urban youth, Tittle (1981) found a similar disparity between boys' expectations for their future wives and girls' expectations for themselves: Boys anticipated for their wives a longer delay in returning to work after bearing children than girls predicted for themselves.

It is interesting to note, however, that a minority of the boys in the Youth Development Study did plan to interrupt their careers in order to care for their young children (see Table 5.2). When asked when they would return to work after having a child, 75% of the boys checked the option, "Less than a year old." We may interpret these responses as indicating taking minimal leave to care for the newborn (perhaps none). However, almost 25% of 11th-grade boys told us that they would have a substantial delay (1 year or more) before returning to work after having children.

This finding may support several authors' (Daniels & Weingarten, 1982; Gershuny & Robinson, 1988; Lewis, 1986; Pleck, 1985) contention that men are increasingly choosing to play a more nurturing role in family life. However, as they go through high school, boys may become increasingly aware of the costs that career interruptions entail. It is noteworthy that boys' anticipated average length of time out of the work force to care for children, like that of girls, declines over time (see Table 5.2A).

Self-Efficacy

We asked 10th and 11th graders about their chances for achieving a variety of desirable objectives with respect to work, family, and community. Students rated their chances for achieving each goal on a 5-point scale (a value of 5 meant they thought it was "highly likely" that they would achieve the goal, whereas a value of 1 indicated they felt their chances were "very low").

Even though boys have lower aspirations and plans than girls, we found that boys feel more efficacious than girls in the occupational and economic realms (see Table 5.3). In comparison to the girls, boys were significantly more optimistic about being able to obtain a well-paying job and about owning their own homes in the future. Girls, by observing their employed mothers and other female relatives, may be aware of the difficulties they will face in coordinating their work and family roles; they may also anticipate gender discrimination in the labor market.

Table 5.3 Mean Self-Efficacy by Gender for 10th and 11th Graders

	10th Grade			11th Grade		
Efficacy Variables	*Boys*	*Girls*	$p <$[a]	*Boys*	*Girls*	$p <$
You will have a job that pays well.	3.90	3.73	.001	3.94	3.79	.004
You will be able to own your own home.	4.01	3.76	.001	3.96	3.76	.001
You will have a happy family life.	4.00	3.98	.734	3.93	4.03	.097
Your children will have a better life than you've had.	3.63	3.78	.020	3.64	3.76	.064
You will have good friends you can count on.	4.08	4.20	.024	4.03	4.17	.012
N (range)						
Boys		450-452			446-448	
Girls		500-510			504-506	

a. t-test of significance

Girls, however, had a stronger belief that their own children would have a better life than they themselves; this may indicate that boys feel less efficacious than girls in the family realm. There was an additional tendency in the 11th grade for boys to feel less efficacious than girls with respect to achievement of a happy family life ($p < .10$). Further, consistent with literature (discussed earlier) indicating deficit in male adult friendship, adolescent boys were less likely than girls to believe that they would have good friends in the future. Tenth and 11th grade boys also placed less importance than girls on the role of friendships in their lives ($p < .001$ and $p < .05$; not shown).

Life Situations Influencing Work and Family Orientations

To determine whether adolescents' life situations influence their work and family orientations, we regressed 11th-grade educational plans and occupational aspirations (using ordinary least squares regression) on parental education, family composition (coded 1 if two-parent, 0 if another family arrangement), race (see Table 5.4 for coding), mother's employment (coded 1 if employed, 0 if not), and family income. We used logistic regression to ascertain the effects of the same social background attributes on three dichotomous variables representing family plans: the expectation to marry (coded 1 if yes and 0 if no; "don't knows" were dropped from the analysis), plans to have children (coded 1 if the number of children planned was one or more, 0 otherwise), and for the boys, whether the spouse should work after having children (coded 1 if yes or "don't know," 0 if no). In order to compare gender differences in effects, separate regression analyses were performed for boys and girls.

Few of the background variables significantly predicted boys' and girls' orientations to the future; those representing socioeconomic status tended to be the most powerful. For boys, parental education was the only variable that had a significant effect on educational plans (see Table 5.4) and occupational aspirations (not shown). Surprisingly, family income was not significantly related to boys' educational plans. In contrast, both parental education and family income had significant positive effects on the educational plans (see Table 5.4) and occupational aspirations (not shown) of girls. It thus appears that the educational plans and occupational aspirations of girls are influenced more by differences in family income than are those of boys, which is consistent

Table 5.4 Effect of Social Background on Educational Plans of 11th-Grade Boys and Girls, OLS Regression

	Boys		*Girls*	
Independent Variables	*B*	*Beta*	*B*	*Beta*
Parent education	.300	.444***	.213	.284***
Family composition (1=two-parent, 0=other)	.151	.062	.162	.063
Race—other[a]	.037	.011	.282	.079
Race—black[b]	–.019	–.000	.318	.078
Mother's employment (1=employ, 0=not employed)	.042	.015	.250	.080
Family income	.022	.045	.079	.156**
R^2	.226		.169	
N	376		411	

NOTES: a. Dummy variable coded 1 if other race (reference category is white). This residual category consisted largely of Asians, Hispanics, and adolescents who indicated mixed-race parentage.
b. Dummy variable coded 1 if black (reference category is white).
$**p < .01$; $***p < .001$.

with previous research (Alexander & Eckland, 1974; Danziger, 1983; but see also Marini & Greenberger, 1978).

Boys from single-parent families were less likely to want to marry ($p < .01$) and less likely to plan to have children ($p < .05$) than those from dual-parent families (not shown). However, family composition had no significant effect on planned singlehood or childlessness among girls. It may be that boys who live with a single parent (usually their mother), observing their own father, believe that they themselves will also be less invested in family life. According to Wallerstein (1983), many adolescent children of divorced parents claim that they will never marry because they are afraid that, like their parents, their own marriages will fail.[2]

Not surprisingly, given the importance of economic resources for the support of children, both boys and girls from lower income households are less likely to plan to have children ($p < .05$ for both). Girls from lower income households are also less likely than girls from more advantaged homes to plan to marry ($p < .05$). Girls whose mothers work are more likely than girls whose mothers do not to plan to have children ($p < .05$). Whereas employment may lead to role conflict in balancing the demands of work and motherhood, it is also an important source of family income.

Boys living in two-parent households expected to marry at earlier ages than boys living in other family arrangements ($p < .05$, not shown)[3]; girls from higher income families planned to marry later ($p < .01$). Black girls planned to marry later than white girls ($p < .01$).

Finally, we investigated influences upon boys' attitudes toward their spouses working after having children. Controlling the social background variables, boys whose mothers worked outside the home were much more likely (3.67 times more, $p < .001$, see Table 5.5) to have positive or uncertain views (answering "yes or "don't know") about their future wives' employment after having children, whereas those whose mothers were not employed were more likely to have a negative attitude toward this prospect. Boys from more highly educated families also had more nontraditional orientations.

Conclusion

This research has revealed that girls are quite similar to boys in their plans to work outside the home and in the anticipated importance of their careers. Girls were found to exceed boys in their aspirations and plans for future educational and occupational attainments. If these girls are typical of young women across the country, they foretell high female postsecondary educational attainment and continued high rates of female labor force participation.

Nevertheless, most gender differences in orientations are still to the advantage of boys' socioeconomic attainment. Boys are clearly advantaged with respect to their feelings of efficacy regarding future work. Previous research (Mainquist & Eichorn, 1989) demonstrates that it is not so much one's aspirations or desires to achieve that are important for actual attainment: of far greater significance is the individual's sense of actually being able to attain personal goals. So even though boys do not have aspirations and plans that are as high as girls', their stronger sense of self-efficacy with respect to having a job that pays well (and consistently, being able to own their own homes) may serve them well in the status attainment process.

A small percentage of boys and girls in this study did not plan to marry and to have children. This pattern suggests a continuation of slowly increasing rates of singlehood and childlessness in the population. However, these data must be viewed with caution, as these preferences may simply reflect the respondents' life stage, with issues of

Table 5.5 Effects of Social Background on Boys' Attitudes Toward Wife Working After Childbearing, Logistic Regression

Independent Variables	*Odds Ratio*
Parent education	1.46**
	[1.12 - 1.89][a]
Family composition	1.53
(1=two-parent, 0=other)	[0.30 - 1.42]
Race—other[b]	3.40
	[0.98 - 11.76]
Race—black[c]	2.26
	[0.49 - 10.48]
Mother's employment	
(1=employ, 0=not employed)	3.67***
	[1.82 - 7.40]
Family income	1.01
	[0.86 - 1.19]

NOTES: a. 95% confidence interval.
b. Dummy variable coded 1 if other race (reference category is white). This residual category consisted largely of Asians, Hispanics, and adolescents who indicated mixed-race parentage.
c. Dummy variable coded 1 if black (reference category is white).
$^{**}p < .01$; $^{***}p < .001$.

marriage and parenthood not being pertinent to the immediate life events of teenagers.

We also found gender differences in family plans. Boys are less likely than girls to plan to marry and to have children. Boys also place less importance on marriage and parenthood in their future lives. These orientations may lead adolescent boys to plan careers with little thought about their consequences for family life. Most boys do not plan to interrupt their careers to care for their children, whereas most girls do. The stronger emphasis that girls place on their family roles may direct them to choose jobs in adulthood that allow flexibility in balancing work and family obligations. Maines and Hardesty (1987) find that some women modify their career goals because they anticipate difficulty meeting the demands of both work and family. If young women still place greater emphasis on their family roles than men, they may be more likely to forego higher occupational attainment if job demands conflict with family responsibilities.

There are indications in the data that boys may be disadvantaged, in comparison with girls, when it comes to developing a strong social support network, which is important to mental health and personal well-being. In addition to their weaker emphasis on the importance of family, boys were significantly less optimistic than girls about having good friends in the future. They also attached less importance to friendship. If men are spending longer portions of their lives outside of families (given later marriage), or if they are increasingly less likely to marry at all, they may suffer more than women from feelings of loneliness and social isolation. Because previous research has indicated the importance of marriage and family ties for men's personal well-being, young men may need to learn how to develop and foster friendships. In the absence of marriage and children, these personal bonds could prove vitally important to men's well-being.

In addition to describing gender differences in orientations to the future, we examined variation in these attitudes within each gender group. As many other studies have shown, boys and girls with more highly educated parents have higher educational plans and occupational aspirations. Moreover, it appears that girls' aspirations are still more closely determined by their parents' economic resources than those of boys.

It is especially noteworthy that boys from single-parent households more often plan to remain single than boys from dual-parent families. When they do plan to marry, they anticipate later marriage than other boys. As single-parent families increase in prevalence, we may find that even more adolescents plan to forego marriage or to delay entry into marriage. Finally, boys whose mothers were employed manifested more "liberal" attitudes regarding their future wives' employment following marriage and children.

In general, the work and family orientations of St. Paul youth are consistent with contemporary trends in work and family institutions. Adult men are now considerably advantaged in both spheres, and the preponderance of our findings indicate that this situation is likely to continue. But the attitudes of these adolescents would seem to support the continuation of "nontraditional" life-styles, including delayed marriage, childlessness, and dual-worker families. Moreover, boys' uncertainty about their future wives' employment, coupled with the girls' near-universal interest in working outside the home, presages marital discord as men and women enter marriage with different gender role expectations regarding work and family. If girls almost universally anticipate returning to work after childbearing, but many boys expect their spouses to remain at home, conflict over the sharing of parenting duties is likely to occur.

In one respect, however, our findings suggest greater equality in the future division of family work. Maines and Hardesty (1987) found most male undergraduates do not plan to adjust their career and work behavior to meet family obligations. In contrast, almost 25% of the 11th-grade adolescent males in our study plan substantial "time out" to care for children. These adolescent boys may represent the vanguard of the future. However, if present trends continue, those boys who want to engage in more active parenting may face impeded careers and lower incomes as they devote more time to family responsibilities (see Greif, 1990; Rossi, 1984). It appears that until men and women are willing to assume equal responsibility for child care, and workplace organizations recognize parenting duties of all employees regardless of gender, the careers of those who have primary responsibility for the rearing of children will be hindered.

Still, it remains to be seen whether the work and family orientations monitored in this longitudinal study will influence boys' and girls' actual behavior. Drawing upon data from a national longitudinal study of high school seniors, Rindfuss et al. (1990) report that the expectations of adolescents about their adult life are highly unstable and undergo many changes as they grow older. We will be able to ascertain their predictive power as we continue to follow this cohort of adolescents into the 12th grade of high school and the early years of adulthood.

Notes

1. Huber and Spitze (1983) find that negative attitudes toward childlessness have declined in the 1980s: 70% of the women surveyed thought childlessness was selfish in 1978 compared to only 21% in 1983.

2. Despite their expressed hesitancy toward marriage in adolescence, Glenn and Kramer (1987) point out that children of divorce are just as likely to marry as children from two-parent households.

3. Glenn and Kramer (1987), however, find that children of divorce actually marry at younger ages than children from two-parent households. Consistent with our findings, Glenn and Kramer point out that the clinical evidence reveals that children of divorce are apprehensive about marriage during adolescence, though their behavior indicates they are "strongly impelled" toward marriage.

References

Alexander, K., & Eckland, B. K. (1974). Sex differences in the educational attainment process. *American Sociological Review, 39,* 668-682.

Aneshensel, C. S., & Rosen B. C. (1980). Domestic roles and sex differences in occupational expectations. *Journal of Marriage and the Family, 42,* 121-131.

Bachman, J., Johnston, L. D., & O'Malley, P. M. (1986). *Monitoring the future.* Ann Arbor: Survey Research Center, University of Michigan.

Barringer, F. (1991, June 7). Changes in U.S. households: Single parents amid solitude. *New York Times,* p. A1.

Berardo, D. H., Shehan, C. L., & Leslie, G. R. (1987). A residue of tradition: Jobs, careers, and spouses' time in housework. *Journal of Marriage and the Family, 49,* 381-390.

Bronstein, P. (1988). Father-child interaction: Implications for gender role socialization. In P. Bronstein & C. P. Cowan (Eds.), *Fatherhood today: Men's changing role in the family* (pp. 107-124). New York: John Wiley.

Buchmann, M. (1989). *The script of life in modern society: Entry into adulthood in a changing world.* Chicago: University of Chicago Press.

Cohen, T. F. (1987). Remaking men: Men's experiences becoming and being husbands and fathers and their implications for reconceptualizing men's lives. *Journal of Family Issues, 8,* 57-77.

Cooney, T. M., & Uhlenberg, P. (1991). Changes in work-family connections among highly educated men and women. *Journal of Family Issues, 12,* 69-90.

Coverman, S., & Sheley, J. F. (1986). Changes in men's housework and child care time, 1965-1975. *Journal of Marriage and the Family, 48,* 413-422.

Crowley, J. E., & Shapiro, D. (1982). Aspirations and expectations of youth in the United States: Part 1. Education and fertility. *Youth and Society, 13,* 391-422.

Daniels, P., & Weingarten, K. (1982). *Sooner or later: The timing of parenthood in adult lives.* New York: W. W. Norton.

Danziger, N. (1983). Sex-related differences in the aspirations of high school students. *Sex Roles, 9,* 683-695.

Douvan, E., & Adelson, J. (1966). *The adolescent experience.* New York: John Wiley.

Eder, D. (1985). The cycle of popularity: Interpersonal relations among female adolescents. *Sociology of Education, 58,* 154-165.

Entwisle, D., & Doering, S. (1981). *The first birth: A family turning point.* Baltimore, MD: Johns Hopkins University Press.

Farmer, H. S. (1983). Career and homemaking plans for high school youth. *Journal of Counseling Psychology, 30,* 40-45.

Ferree, M. M. (1991). Feminism and family research. In A. Booth (Ed.), *Contemporary families: Looking forward, looking back* (pp. 103-121). Minneapolis, MN: National Council on Family Relations.

Furstenberg, F. (1988). Good dads, bad dads: Two faces of fatherhood. In A. Cherlin (Ed.), *The changing American family and public policy* (pp. 193-218). Washington, DC: Urban Institute Press.

Gershuny, J., & Robinson, J. P. (1988). Historical changes in the household division of labor. *Demography, 25,* 535-552.

Gerson, K. (1985). *Hard choices: How women decide about work, career, and motherhood.* Berkeley: University of California Press.

Glenn, N. D., & Kramer, K. B. (1987). The marriages and divorces of the children of divorce. *Journal of Marriage and the Family, 49,* 811-825.

Gove, W. R., & Hughes, M. (1980). Reexamining the ecological fallacy: A study in which aggregate data are critical in investigating the pathological effects of living alone. *Social Forces, 57,* 1157-1177.

Greif, G. L. (1990). *The daddy track and the single father.* Lexington, MA: Lexington.

Hiller, D. V., & Philliber, W. W. (1986). The division of labor in contemporary marriage: Expectations, perceptions, and performance. *Social Problems, 33,* 191-201.

Hochschild, A., & Machung, A. (1989). *The second shift: Working parents and the revolution at home.* New York: Viking.

Huber, J., & Spitze, G. (1983). *Sex stratification: Children, housework, and jobs.* New York: Academic Press.

LaRossa, R. (1988). Fatherhood and social change. *Family Relations, 37,* 451-457.

Lewis, R. A. (1986). Introduction: What men get out of marriage and parenthood. In R. A. Lewis & R. E. Salt (Eds.), *Men and Families* (pp. 11-25). Beverly Hills, CA: Sage.

Lewis, R. A., & Salt, R. E. (Eds.). (1986). *Men in families.* Beverly Hills, CA: Sage.

Lindsay, P., & Knox, W. E. (1984). Continuity and change in work values among young adults: A longitudinal study. *American Journal of Sociology, 89,* 918-931.

Machung, A. (1989). Talking career, thinking jobs: Gender differences in career and family expectations of Berkeley seniors. *Feminist Studies, 15,* 35-58.

Maines, D. R., & Hardesty, M. J. (1987). Temporality and gender: Young adults' career and family plans. *Social Forces, 66,* 102-120.

Mainquist, S., & Eichorn, D. (1989). Competence in work settings. In D. Stern & D. Eichorn (Eds.), *Adolescence and work: Influences of social structure, labor markets, and culture* (pp. 327-367). Hillsdale, NJ: Lawrence Erlbaum.

Marini, M. M., & Greenberger, E. (1978). Sex differences in occupational aspirations and expectations. *Sociology of Work and Occupations, 5,* 147-178.

Marini, M. M., Shin, H., & Raymond, J. (1989). Socioeconomic consequences of the process of transition to adulthood. *Social Science Research, 13,* 89-135.

McLaughlin, S. D., Melber, B. D., Billy, J., Zimmerle, D. M., Winges, L. D., & Johnson, T. R. (1988). *The changing lives of American women.* Chapel Hill: University of North Carolina Press.

Menaghan, E. G., & Parcel, T. L. (1991). Parental employment and family life. In A. Booth (Ed.), *Contemporary families: Looking forward, looking back* (pp. 361-380). Minneapolis, MN: National Council on Family Relations.

Moen, P. (1985). Continuities and discontinuities in women's labor force activity. In G. H. Elder (Ed.), *Life course dynamics: Trajectories and transitions, 1968-1980* (pp. 113-155). Ithaca, NY: Cornell University Press.

Mortimer, J. T., Finch, M., Shanahan, M., & Ryu, S. (1992). Work experience, mental health, and behavioral adjustment in adolescence. *Journal of Research on Adolescence, 2,* 25-57.

Mortimer, J. T., & Lorence, J. (1979). Work experience and occupational value socialization: A longitudinal study. *American Journal of Sociology, 84,* 1361-1383.

Nordstrom, B. (1986). Why men get married: More and less traditional men compared. In R. A. Lewis & R. E. Salt (Eds.), *Men in Families* (pp. 31-53). Beverly Hills, CA: Sage.

Pleck, J. (1985). *Working wives/working husbands.* Beverly Hills, CA: Sage.

Pleck, J. (1987). American fathering in historical perspective. In M. S. Kimmel (Ed.), *Changing men* (pp. 83-97). Beverly Hills, CA: Sage.

Rindfuss, R. R., Cooksey, E. C., & Sutterlin, R. L. (1990, July). *Young adult occupational achievement: Early expectations versus behavioral reality.* Paper presented at the World Congress of Sociology, Madrid.

Ross, C., Mirowsky, J., & Huber, J. (1983). Dividing work, sharing work, and in-between: Marriage patterns and depression. *American Sociological Review, 48,* 809-823.

Rossi, A. S. (1984). Gender and parenthood. *American Sociological Review, 49,* 1-19.

Rubin, L. B. (1983). *Intimate strangers: Men and women together.* New York: Harper & Row.

Sewell, W. H., & Hauser, R. (1975). *Education, occupation, and earnings: Achievement in the early career.* New York: Academic Press.

Spade, J. Z., & Reese, C. A. (1991). We've come a long way, maybe: College students' plans for work and family. *Sex Roles, 24,* 309-321.

Spenner, K. I., & Featherman, D. L. (1978). Achievement ambitions. *Annual Review of Sociology, 4,* 373-420

Swain, S. (1989). Covert intimacy: Closeness in men's friendships. In B. J. Risman & P. Schwartz (Eds.), *Gender in intimate relationships* (pp. 71-86). Belmont, CA: Wadsworth.

Thompson, L., & Walker, A. J. (1991). Gender and families. In A. Booth (Ed.), *Contemporary families: Looking forward, looking back* (pp. 76-102). Minneapolis, MN: National Council on Family Relations.

Thornton, A. (1989). Changing attitudes toward family issues in the United States. *Journal of Marriage and the Family, 51,* 873-893.

Thornton, A., & Freedman, D. S. (1982). Changing attitudes toward marriage and single life. *Family Planning Perspectives, 14,* 297-303.

Tittle, C. K. (1981). *Careers and family: Sex roles and adolescent life plans.* Beverly Hills, CA: Sage.

Waite, L. J., & Berryman, S. B. (1985). *Women in nontraditional occupations.* Santa Monica, CA: Rand Publication Series.

Wallerstein, J. S. (1983). Children of divorce: The psychological tasks of the child. *American Journal of Orthopsychiatry, 53,* 230-243.

Weiss, R.S. (1990). *Staying the course: The emotional and social lives of men who do well at work.* New York: Free Press.

6

Resistance and Change

College Men's Attitudes Toward Family and Work in the 1980s

BETH WILLINGER

Over the past several decades, sociologists have come to recognize that work and family are two sides of the same coin. However, this recognition has not always been reflected in the research conducted. Studies concerned with the changing experiences of women and men have focused primarily on the increase in women's labor force participation and its effect on the allocation of child care and housework in the family. Scant attention has been given to changes in men's work and family experiences, and only recently have men's experiences in the family been considered as equally valuable and important as women's (Sweet & Bumpass, 1989). Interest in men's family roles has centered primarily on the question of whether men's participation in child care and household tasks increased as a result of their wives' increased labor force participation. The results of these studies lead to the belief that men's roles have changed little (e.g., Blair & Lichter, 1991; Cooney & Uhlenberg, 1991; Coverman & Sheley, 1986; Kalleberg & Rosenfeld, 1990, to list but a few).

Research directed to what men *say* about their work and family roles has generated even less interest than what men *do* in the family. Studies

The research reported here was supported in part by a grant from the Newcomb Foundation. The author thanks Terry Blankfard for her assistance with the 1985 data and Ellen Kuchta for programming and computer assistance.

examining attitudes toward the changing roles of women and men have focused almost exclusively on women's roles or included only women as respondents (Mason & Bumpass, 1975; Mason, Czajka, & Arber, 1976; Tallichet & Willits, 1986; Thornton & Freedman, 1979). Longitudinal investigations of attitude change have been concerned with men's attitudes largely as they relate to changes in sex roles generally or to the roles of women specifically (Cherlin & Walters, 1981; Davis & Robinson, 1991; Mason & Lu, 1988; McBroom, 1984; Thornton, Alwin, & Camburn, 1983). Men's roles as husbands and fathers have been neglected and only rarely have changes in men's attitudes toward men's work and family roles been considered (Mortimer, Lorence, & Kumka, 1986). Because most attitude studies report that women's attitudes both are more liberal and have changed more rapidly than men's, the work that has been done also lends support to the belief that men have changed little.

Further, the vast majority of the studies concerned with gender role attitude change report on data collected in the 1960s and 1970s. Research mapping gender role attitude change into or through the 1980s is limited (Mason & Lu, 1988; Thornton, 1989). Thus any trends in men's attitudes are little known.

The neglect of men's work-family experiences and expectations seems premised on the belief that women have initiated or welcomed change, as evidenced by the women's movement, whereas men have merely responded to or resisted change altogether (Bernard, 1981; Carrigan, Connell, & Lee, 1987; Ferree, 1990; Goode, 1982; Kimmel, 1987; Polatnick, 1975). Men's resistance to change has been taken for granted. Generally ignored are arguments by men's studies scholars that men have much to gain by changing their patterns of work involvement and interpersonal behavior to develop more fulfilling relationships with women, other men, and children (Brod, 1987; Pleck, 1976). Consequently, there has been little empirical interest in men's attitudes toward men's work and family roles to ascertain if men choose to restructure the work role or choose to participate more fully in family work. The paucity of such data leaves unanswered the question of whether men have been actively resisting change in work and family roles, just dragging their feet, or embracing change in some areas but not others. Also unclear is whether some groups of men resist change more than others.

The analysis presented here attempts to fill these gaps in our understanding by (a) determining men's attitudes toward the restructuring of men's and women's work and family roles, (b) describing the changes in men's attitudes toward women's and men's family and work roles from 1980 to 1990, and (c) identifying the sociodemographic variables associated with men's resistance or willingness to adopt contemporary definitions of equality.

Understanding Men's Resistance

J. G. Hunt and L. L. Hunt (1987) offer three perspectives from which to understand male resistance to changing gender roles: cultural lag, sex stratification, and the politics of domination. The three perspectives situate definitions of masculinity and femininity within specific sociohistorical contexts and consider how these definitions and expectations for gendered behavior become constructed, reconstructed, or altered. Such social constructions of gendered behavior represent a process that might not take into account, or accurately reflect, the day-to-day lived experiences of men and women. As expressed by Carrigan et al. (1987), "An immediate consequence of this is that the culturally exalted form of masculinity . . . may only correspond to the actual characters of a small number of men" (p. 92).

According to the cultural lag perspective, with the beginning of the industrial revolution in the United States, opportunities for employment outside the household economy were created. It was generally agreed that men would assume the jobs in manufacturing while women remained at home to maintain the household and care for the children. Thus, the provider-homemaker role division was created and with it a host of expectations concerning the appropriate behavior, characteristics, and traits of women and men. Both men and women were assumed to be differently, but equally, rewarded and oppressed by gender roles. Yet within this equality of reward and oppression, men and masculinity were valued more highly than women and femininity. In this century, sociotechnological changes rendered the provider-homemaker construction of gender roles obsolete. The definitions of masculinity and femininity now emerging are more symmetrical with regard to work-family responsibilities and more androgynous with regard to characteristics and traits. Because these new definitions deny men their claim to extra privileges solely because of their membership in the male sex-class, men are reluctant to adopt these conceptions of gender roles (Goode, 1982). Hence, according to the cultural lag perspective, men are predicted to discover the advantages of change, but at a much slower rate than women.

The sex stratification perspective of men's resistance to change assumes that the social construction of gender has not oppressed women and men equally, but has limited and constrained women particularly (J. G. Hunt & L. L. Hunt, 1987). According to this perspective, the segregation of work and family provided men with material rewards and access to power and privilege. Men used that power to construct a gendered system that valued the work of men and devalued women and women's work. Changing definitions of gender, particularly of women's roles, present men with a real loss of power and privilege vis-à-vis women. For example, women's assumption of the work role threatens men's power base as sole provider at the same time that it reduces women's services to the household. In contrast, because women's household work is undervalued, the assumption of domestic responsibilities by men is demeaning to their masculine identity. From the sex stratification perspective then, men have much to lose and not much to gain from changing gender roles. They are, therefore, unlikely to change.

The third perspective, politics of domination, expands the sex stratification perspective, but views men's resistance as a symptom of larger forms of oppression. This perspective begins with the premise that very few men actually have social and economic power and those who do, use that power not only to oppress women but also to oppress other men (J. G. Hunt & L. L. Hunt, 1987). Hence, gender role change is thought to reflect the changing imperatives of an industrial and postindustrial society for a labor force ready to serve the interests of the economic and political elite. According to this perspective, industrialization mobilized men to assume jobs outside the home and created a domestic ideology that defined "women's place" as being in the home. However, for postindustrial expansion to occur, increased production and consumption of consumer goods and services were needed. Hence, corporate interests were served by liberating women to enter the labor force at the low end of the wage scale. A woman's wages increased household disposable income for the purchase of new products and for the necessary replacement of her services to home and family. According to the politics of domination perspective, it is the erosion of family life brought about by women's movement out of the home and into the labor force that is at the heart of men's resistance to gender role change. However, the critical factor is not women's employment per se. At issue is the loss of human connectedness, familial support, and caregiving that result when a society requires a family to have two incomes yet provides little, if anything, in the way of support services. The resistance expressed by men then is similar to the disillusionment voiced by women exhausted by holding down two full-time jobs (Mason & Lu, 1988). Because men are more dependent on women for solace and intimacy than vice versa, their resistance is thought to be strong (Goode, 1982). The hypothesis is that men, although recognizing the economic and social benefits of women's labor force participation, will assert their belief in the priority of women's family role for the maintenance of home and family.

In sum, cultural lag theorists would predict that men's attitudes toward both work and family roles will have become less traditional in the 10-year period under study, with increasing support voiced for both the legitimacy of women's work role and men's family roles. In direct contrast, the sex segregation prediction is for men to deny the legitimacy of women's employment, favor men's continued dominance in the work force, and thereby reject any movement toward gender equality. Additionally, it would be predicted that the men most resistant to change would be those who enjoy social and economic privilege. Finally, the politics of domination prediction is that men will recognize the legitimacy of women's employment while simultaneously resisting the restructuring of women's family roles. The men predicted to be most resistant are those who have experienced directly the loss of women's caregiving role as a consequence of their movement into the labor force, such as men whose mother was employed during their childhood or men raised in single-parent families.

Methodology

Sample and Procedures

This study uses data collected in the spring semesters of 1980, 1985, and 1990 from 1,120 senior males enrolled in two southern universities, one a nonsectarian private university and the other a state university enrolling primarily commuter students. The men were selected by systematic random sample to participate and mailed a questionnaire with a cover letter and return envelope.

In 1980, responses were obtained from 58.4% (438) of the sample; in the 1985 and 1990 replications, 45.7% (302) and 47.5% (380) of the men sampled returned completed questionnaires for an average response rate of 51%.[1] Pooling the data from all three sample periods, the

1,120 respondents were predominantly white (87.2%), never married (84.3%), U.S. citizens (95.7%) who ranged in age from 20-66 years old with a mean age of 23.6 years. The majority of the men were Catholic (55.6%) and raised in the South (65%). Although there is considerable variability in the socioeconomic backgrounds of the respondents, the sample is largely middle to upper-middle class. The reported median income for the respondents' fathers was approximately $35,000 with 34% having earnings over $50,000.[2] Over half of the respondents' fathers completed college and almost 29% of the graduates held an advanced degree. Of the respondents' mothers, 40% were described as homemakers with no earned income, 39% had earned a college degree, 11% had completed graduate or professional school.

Analyses of differences between samples indicate that few socio-demographic variables differ statistically among the samples. The differences that did occur pertain to mothers' labor force participation and parental responsibility for the respondents' upbringing. In 1980, 52% of the mothers were described as homemakers and 46.4% had no earned income; in 1990, 32.2% of the mothers were described as homemakers and only 31.3% were reported to have no earned income ($Z = 1.86$, $p < .002$ and $Z = 3.772$, $p < .000$ for work and income, respectively). With regard to the respondents' upbringing, 91% of the respondents in 1980 reported being raised by their mother and their father; in 1985, 84%, and in 1990, 78.5% reported being raised by both parents ($Z = 1.80$, $p < .003$ between 1980 and 1990 samples). The decrease in responsibility for upbringing by both parents resulted in an increase in responsibility "primarily by mother": 4.8%, 10.9%, 12.5% in 1980, 1985, and 1990, respectively.

Measures

Definition of Gender Equality and Measurement of Work and Family Attitudes (WFVI)

Gender equality is defined in this research as the equal access by men and women to participation in the labor force and family work, equal exercise of rights and responsibilities in work and family roles, and the receipt of equal reward for that participation.[3] In a society such as the United States where equality between women and men had been defined previously by their occupation of separate spheres, new definitions of gender equality require a restructuring of society such that participation in family work is valued and rewarded as favorably as participation in the labor force. Although gender equality enables greater access to participation in areas formerly restricted, it also requires the adoption of additional or shared responsibilities and the "letting go" of areas of control. For example, equality requires men to relinquish institutionalized dominance such as that associated with the access, rights, and rewards of the provider role; it requires women to relinquish the unequal access, rights, and rewards of family work, such as caregiving.

Men's attitudes toward equality of men's and women's work and family roles are assessed by their response to eight vignettes from the Work-Family Vignette Index (WFVI). The WFVI is part of a larger 20-item instrument, Attitudes Toward Equality Vignettes (Willinger, 1982), constructed around Ruth Dixon's (1976) conceptualization of equality in six activity areas of the division of labor: sexual relations, reproduction, homemaking and child care, economic production, education, and political decision making. Previous research (Willinger, 1982, 1986) indicated that the greatest barrier to gender equality was located not within the activity areas, but at the point at which work and family roles intertwine and become interdependent, what Pleck (1977) defines as the work-family role system.

Unlike other attitudinal measures of gender role expectations, the WFVI frames the question from the perspective of the male. The respondent is asked to indicate how he would advise the other to respond, or how he thinks he himself would respond, in the given hypothetical situation. For each vignette, three to six statements are provided as possible options. The responses range from a traditional response (polarization and dichotomization of the characteristics and activities of men and women) to a modern response (allocation of role rewards and responsibilities by individual choice and mutual consideration irrespective of sex) (Osmond & Martin, 1975). However, the responses were generated by considering various realistic responses to the situation presented and do not in all instances correspond to a strict theoretical representation of the traditional and modern definitions. For this reason, and because it is unclear whether the traditional and modern definitions of gendered behavior employed in this study represent a single dimension, the responses are considered categorical and not continuous. Therefore, for the multivariate analyses, responses are coded traditional or nontraditional and collapsed into a dichotomy. Traditional responses are identified by bold print in Table 6.1.[4]

The use of vignettes is based on the assumption that the presentation of hypothetical situations of relevance to young adults mitigates a social desirability response by making the question more salient to the respondent than does the more usual Likert-type scale. Vignettes have a further advantage in that respondents select from among the responses the one that best represents what they would do in the situation. Assessing what men say they would do in a situation is thought to moderate the tendency for men to provide a principled or abstract solution to the problem (Gilligan, 1982), thereby reducing the discrepancy between attitudes and behavior, or between what men say they think and what they actually do.

The Work-Family Vignette Index is most easily explained by considering an example from the instrument. The first vignette, based on a true story reported by Brannon (David & Brannon, 1976), pertains to the importance of career advancement:

> Mark is an executive with one of the largest corporations in America. In his early 40s, he is earning over $50,000 a year in an assignment he enjoys and is actually good at. His problem is an impending promotion. Having proven his competence at this level, he is expected to move on to the next. His new assignment means more money but a substantially different kind of work, which he is fairly sure he won't like as well; it would also require him to commute a lot farther. If you were in this position, what would you do?
>
> 1. I'd stay in the job I enjoyed and did well at even if it meant I might not advance any further.
> 2. I'd probably quit the company and look for a job I enjoyed without having the pressure to keep moving up.
> 3. I'd accept the promotion, for I don't think I could resist the urge to move upward or live with a reputation as a guy headed nowhere.

Table 6.1 presents an abbreviated version of the eight vignettes and responses that make up the WFVI. The topics of the vignettes and the dimensions of equality they attempt to assess are as follows: career advancement to measure change in the structure and culture of men's work role (Vignette 1); the priority of work or family (Vignette 2) and acceptance of role reversal (Vignette 3) to assess the legitimacy of men's family work; child care preference (Vignette 4) and the priority for women of work or family (Vignette 5) as measures of change in the structure of women's family roles; woman's income (Vignette 6) and the priority of either the woman's or man's career (Vignettes 7 and 8) to assess the legitimacy of women's employment.

Sociodemographic Variables

The independent variables included in the analysis are primarily sociodemographic: the respondent's age, race/ethnicity, religion, religiosity, academic major, marital status, number of children, the region of the country in which he was raised, and the adult(s) responsible for his upbringing. The socioeconomic status of the respondent is measured by the father's education and income. Mother's labor force participation, considered a better predictor of her children's gender role attitudes than her actual occupational status (Thornton et al., 1983), was assessed by asking the number of years the mother worked full-time and part-time during the first 20 years of the respondent's life.

Results and Discussion

Men's Attitudes Toward Work and Family: Analyses of the WFVI

Table 6.1 shows the percentage of men selecting each response category of the 8-item WFVI by survey year, unadjusted for other sociodemographic variables. The data clearly document a statistically significant change in men's attitudes toward equality in the 1980s. Overall, men in the 1990 survey held less traditional attitudes toward work and family than did men in 1980 ($t = 9.63$, 694 *df,* $p < .000$) and men in 1985 ($t = 4.83$, 598 *df,* $p < .000$). For 7 of the 8 items, men's 1990 scores were significantly less traditional than their 1980 scores. Considerable choice and flexibility in enacting work and family roles is permitted to both men and women by the respondents. Yet within this movement toward gender equality, there is resistance to the restructuring of men's work role and the child care role of women.

A central aim of this research is to ascertain if men are willing to decrease their emphasis on the work role or to relinquish their status as providers and participate more fully in family work. The findings suggest that they are only moderately willing to do so. The only item on which men responded more traditionally in 1990 than in 1980 (Vignette 1) posed the question of how they would respond to an executive's impending but undesirable promotion. Significantly more men in 1990 (36.6%) than in 1980 (27.6%) would accept the promotion, because they could neither "resist the urge to move upward or live with a reputation as a guy headed nowhere." Although half the men in 1990 report that they would stay in the position they enjoyed, men in 1985 and 1990 place more emphasis on the work role, or success within that role, than did men in 1980.

Because of the importance to men of the occupational role and their seeming lack of interest in homemaking and child care, Pleck (1977) predicted that reducing men's work load would not increase men's participation in the family, but rather lead to their greater participation in overtime work, moonlighting, continuing education, or leisure activities. As Pleck's (1985) own research reveals, and the respondents in this study confirm, men place far greater importance on family work than had been predicted (Vignette 2). When presented with the situation of a reduced work week at the same pay, 75% of the men in the 1990 study indicate that they would spend the extra time "helping out and being with my wife and kids at home." Less than 5% of the men in each survey period would respond by getting a second, part-time job.

The legitimacy of men's participation in family work is given additional support by the men's response to Vignette 3. The vignette describes a husband who, when laid off work, "found he really enjoyed being the homemaker and his wife really enjoyed working." The majority of men in all three surveys agreed that the couple should continue this pattern if that's what the couple wanted. However, the respondents indicate some ambivalence about the man abdicating the occupational role. For example, one respondent checked that the man should "continue being the homemaker and [his] wife the money earner" but wrote in the margin, "Although I think he is a wimp for not working." The enjoyment and choice of the homemaker role appear critical factors in role reversal, for as most studies report (Coverman & Sheley, 1986), the respondents express little support for the interchangeability of gender roles in the area of child care. When presented with the situation in which a couple decides to have a child but neither parent wants to quit work to care for it (Vignette 4), the most popular response in each survey period is for the couple not to have the child (57.8% in 1980, 50% in 1985, and 39.2% in 1990). Alternative child care arrangements, such as day care or hiring a housekeeper gained significantly greater acceptance in 1990 (27.1%) over 1980 (11.9%). However, the percentage of men who believe the mother should stay home to care for the child remained about 22% in all three survey periods. The percentage of men who believe the father should stay home to care for the child also remained about the same in all three survey periods—less than 1%. The conclusion is that a man may choose to perform the homemaker role, but few men would consider staying home to raise a child a desirable option.

Table 6.1 Men's Work-Family Role Attitudes: Percentage Selecting Response by Year

	1980	*1985*	*1990*
n	438	302	380
Mean (1a;2a;3a)*	17.65	16.42	15.01
STD DEV	3.65	3.64	3.50
Vignettes**			
Men's Work Role			
1. Decision about promotion to unwanted position (1a;3b)			
1. Stay in present position	59.1	45.7	49.5
2. Quit the company	**12.6**	**13.9**	**10.5**
3. Accept the promotion	**27.6**	**38.4**	**36.6**
Men's Family Role			
2. How to spend leisure time brought about by reduced work week (1b;3a)			
1. More time at home	61.6	77.5	75.5
2. Hobby/time with friends	**12.3**	**9.6**	**8.7**
3. Further education	**14.2**	**9.6**	**8.2**
4. Get a second job	**4.1**	**3.0**	**2.6**
3. Unemployed man has choice to return to work or to reverse roles with wife (2b;3b)			
1. Continue in role reversal	65.8	63.6	72.1
2. Should return to work even if wife works	**26.3**	**30.8**	**24.7**
3. Return to work and wife should stop working	**6.4**	**4.6**	**1.8**
Women's Family Role			
4. Who is to assume responsibility for infant care when both parents work (1b;2a;3a)			
1. Both cut back to half-time	5.5	5.0	9.5
2. Day care or hire housekeeper	11.9	22.2	27.1
3. Father stays home	**0.5**	**0.0**	**0.5**
4. Mother stays home	**22.8**	**21.9**	**21.6**
5. Shouldn't have child if neither parent wants to quit	**57.8**	**50.0**	**39.2**

Table 6.1 Continued

	1980	*1985*	*1990*
5. Preference for wife's approach to child care and employment (1a;3a)			
1. Choice is up to wife	35.8	47.0	51.8
2. Minimum interruption for childbearing	3.2	4.6	4.7
3. Work until birth and return to work when children are in school	**35.2**	**32.8**	**31.6**
4. Work only until birth	**17.8**	**13.2**	**7.6**
5. Prefer wife never work	**5.7**	**1.7**	**2.4**
Women's Work Role			
6. Concern if wife earns more money than husband (1a;3a)			
1. Wouldn't bother man	40.9	52.0	58.7
2. Mildly bothers man	**34.3**	**35.1**	**31.3**
3. Man will eventually earn more	**9.6**	**3.0**	**2.6**
4. Man feels very uncomfortable	**13.7**	**8.9**	**6.8**
7. Consider man's or woman's job more important (1c;3a)			
1. Both equally important	89.5	94.4	96.1
2. Woman's more important	0.7	0.0	0.3
3. Man's more important	8.7	5.3	2.4
8. How to manage woman's promotion to another city (1a;2a;3a)			
1. Both move this time for her, next time for him	19.6	28.5	25.1
2. Woman moves they alternate commuting	12.3	16.6	27.9
3. Woman moves commutes home	4.3	3.6	3.9
4. Woman refuses promotion	**62.7**	**51.0**	**30.5**

NOTES: *1. 1980-1985; 2. 1985-1990; 3. 1980-1990; a. $p < .001$; b. $p < .01$; c. $p < .05$.
**Items in bold print identify the responses representing the traditional pole. Column totals may deviate from 100% because of missing data. Actual phrasing of vignettes and responses is available from author upon request.

An alternative hypothesis concerning child care is that men still consider the child care role as one belonging to women. They are therefore less supportive of the restructuring of women's child care roles. This thesis gains some support from a vignette addressing men's preference for their wives' employment pattern (Vignette 5). Although an increasing percentage of men from 1980 to 1990 (35.8%, 47%, 51.8%) consider the wife's decision to work her own, over 40% of the men in 1990 still prefer wives not work during children's preschool years and possibly longer.

If children are not present, men appear more accepting of women's labor force participation and success within that role. When asked how they would feel if their mate were to earn a higher salary than their own (Vignette 6), significantly fewer men in 1990 than in 1980 said they would feel uncomfortable or would rationalize their lower income if their mate were to earn the higher salary. Almost 60% of the men in 1990, an increase of about 18% from 1980, report, "It wouldn't bother me at all since it really doesn't matter which mate earns more money."

Similarly, when asked if they consider the man's or woman's career to be more important (Vignette 7), the majority of respondents in all three survey periods (89.5%, 94.4%, and 96.1% in 1980, 1985, and 1990, respectively) indicate that the man's and woman's jobs "are of equal importance so that some kind of mutual agreement should be reached" concerning the wife's promotion to another city. Nevertheless, the solution most often selected in response to this dual-career dilemma (Vignette 8) calls for the woman to "turn down the promotion and stay in her present position" (62.7% in 1980; 51% in 1985; 30.5% in 1990). Men in 1990 were more willing to consider alternatives than men in 1980 or 1985, and their preference changed from the couple moving together (19.6% in 1980 vs. 25.1% in 1990) toward some sort of commuter relationship (16.6% in 1980 vs. 31.8% in 1990). The choice of a commuter relationship over relocating may indicate men's greater willingness to accept their wives' careers than to make sacrifices in their own careers in the interest of the relationship. The primacy of men's work role is thus reinforced.

Summarizing the important changes from 1980 to 1990, as predicted by the cultural lag perspective, there has been a significant trend in the past decade for men to recognize the legitimacy of both women's employment and men's family work. However, men remain reluctant to accept the kind of restructuring that would enable men and women to participate equally in both work and family roles. In other words, men grant to women and men a great deal of individual choice and role flexibility, but they fail to support as readily a symmetrical relationship in which women and men share equally in both household and work responsibilities. Rather they continue to perceive the work role as primary to men and the family role as primary to women. This view of men's and women's roles as distinct and nonoverlapping helps to explain some of the apparent incongruities in men's attitudes. For example, men are supportive of wives' employment but uninterested in making a larger investment in the family role; or, they indicate they are unbothered by their wife earning a higher salary even as they accept a promotion they do not want.

The finding that the occupational role retains importance in men's definition of masculinity is reinforced by the respondents' rankings as to which of three roles—career, companion, parent—they anticipate will provide the greatest satisfaction to themselves and their mate in the next 10 years. As can be seen in Table 6.2, men's priority ranking of the career role for Self increased slightly between 1980 and 1990, with a significant increase recorded in 1985. This finding may be consistent with the cultural lag perspective that men are reluctant to give up the privileges and status associated with the male work role because they cannot yet envision similar rewards accruing from adoption of family roles. Or it may be reflective of the sex stratification perspective as explained by Polatnick (1975). That is, men don't want to vacate the work role in order to raise children because doing so would mean giving up power, income, and prestige in exchange for low status, no salary, menial labor, and domestic isolation.

However, if the importance given to the work role by men were a way to maintain power vis-à-vis women or a backlash response to women's equality as predicted by the sex stratification perspective, we would anticipate men voicing opposition to women's employment while advocating their return to family roles. As can be seen in the rankings for Mate in Table 6.2, this is not the case. Men's support for women's career satisfaction increased significantly between 1980 and 1990; their rankings of the Wife-Companion and Mother roles remained high but did not statistically change.

The nonchange in men's rankings of women's family roles between 1980 and 1990 is consistent with the results of the vignette analyses. The seeming contradiction between men's support of women's employment yet resistance to the restructuring of women's family roles is best understood from the politics of domination perspective. It will be remembered that according to this perspective, the benefits of women's employment are acknowledged along with the drawbacks. The particular

Table 6.2 Percentage Ranking Career, Companion, or Parental Role as Providing Greatest Satisfaction for Self and for Mate, 1980, 1985, 1990

Role Priority	*1980*	*1985*	*1990*
n	438	302	380
Self			
Career (1b;2b)*	37.2	47.8	38.9
Husband-Companion	52.1	45.4	46.1
Father (3b)	6.2	9.3	13.7
Mate			
Career (1c)	15.3	22.8	20.0
Wife-Companion	62.8	57.9	55.8
Mother	13.5	19.9	18.7

NOTES: *1. 1980-1985; 2. 1985-1990; 3. 1980-1990; a. $p < .001$; b. $p < .01$; c. $p < .05$.

drawback to men is that they are left without the caregiving and solace they depend on women to provide. Thus men accept women's employment until it infringes on their work and family roles or deprives them of female companionship. For example, men agree that a woman's job is as important as a man's (Vignette 7), yet they are unwilling to share responsibility for infant care (Vignette 4), and unwilling to have her relocate for a better job (Vignette 8). The emphasis given to the companion and mother roles for Mate support this conclusion. In addition, men ranked the companion role first for Self in all instances except in 1985, when a larger percentage ranked the career role first. Consistent with Cohen's findings (1987), the majority of men in this study (58.3% in 1980 and 59.8% in 1990) define their marital and/or parental roles as their most important social roles. Thus we would anticipate their reluctance to have their Mate consider it any less important.

Multivariate Analyses of Men's Attitudes and Sociodemographic Variables

We turn now to the analysis of the sociodemographic variables associated with men's resistance or willingness to adopt attitudes toward equality in the work and family roles of women and men. For this multivariate analysis, data from the three surveys were pooled and the responses to each vignette dichotomized (traditional response = 1; other = 0). Items making up the WFVI were combined or eliminated as indicated below to make up a measure for each of the four dimensions of equality (with multiple items, 2 = traditional; 0, 1 = nontraditional). Logistic regression was then used to investigate the effects of the sociodemographic variables, plus survey year, and the effects of each variable independent of the others, on the four dimensions of equality.

The first dimension of equality, change in the structure and culture of *men's work role* (Vignette 1), is represented at the traditional pole by the responses "I'd accept the promotion, for I don't think I could resist the urge to move upward, or live with a reputation as a guy headed nowhere," and "I'd probably quit the company and look for a job I enjoy without the pressure of having to keep moving up." The recognition of the legitimacy of *men's family role* (Vignettes 2 and 3) is measured by a work-family priority in the ways to spend discretionary time and role reversal. At the traditional pole for Vignette 2 are the statements "I would involve myself with a hobby," "spend the time fishing, hunting or just being with friends," "take a couple of courses at the university," and "get a second, part-time job." For Vignette 3, the traditional responses include the advice "even if your wife wants to continue working, you should go back to work," and "go back to work and have your wife go back to taking care of the house and kids." The third dimension of equality, change in the structure and culture of *women's family roles* (Vignettes 4 and 5), considers traditional responses toward child care in Vignette 4, "[the woman] stays home to take care of the baby until the baby begins nursery school," "[the man] stays home to take care of the baby until it starts nursery school," and "they shouldn't have children if neither of them is willing to quit their job to care for the baby." For Vignette 5 regarding a man's preference for his wife's employment, the traditional response preferences are "work until the babies are born, at which time she would stay home to care for them, and then return to work when they start school," "work outside the home only until the children are born," and "not work outside the home." The last dimension, recognition of the legitimacy of *women's employment* (Vignettes 6 and 8), considers the man's feeling if his wife has the higher salary and ways to handle a woman's promotion and transfer. Traditional statements for Vignette 6 include, "I would feel only mildly bothered by my mate earning more than I do," "I wouldn't be bothered at all since I'll probably be earning more than she does in a few years," and "I would feel very uncomfortable or inadequate if my mate earns more than I do." For

Vignette 8, the statement representing the traditional pole is "[the woman should] turn down the promotion and stay in her present position."

A regression equation was estimated for each of the four dimensions of equality. In a process similar to ordinary least squares regression, backward stepwise elimination was performed with nonsignificant independent variables removed from the statistical model until the final models presented in Table 6.3 were attained. The four dependent variables contrast traditional responses with nontraditional responses.[5]

One of the most interesting findings of the analyses as revealed in Table 6.3 is that factors associated with men's attitudes differ according to the dimension of equality considered. Survey year is the only variable to be significantly associated with the probability of traditionalism on all dimensions. As discussed with respect to the findings on the WFVI presented above, the significant logit coefficient for survey year and men's work role indicates that men became more traditional in the decade regarding their work role, whereas with regard to men's family roles, and women's work and family roles, the probability was for men to be less traditional.

Besides survey year, two additional factors are associated with the probability of traditionalism toward the male work role. Men with highly educated and high-income fathers were more likely to retain traditional attitudes about men's work. The possible interaction effect between father's income and education was examined and found to be nonsignificant—each has a strong and independent effect on producing traditional attitudes among the men. The importance of the father's education and income to men's occupational attitudes underscores the father's influence in the socialization process and is consistent with the expectations of the sex stratification perspective that high-status men will be reluctant to change. The negative relationship between geographic residence and men's work attitudes indicates that there is a greater probability for Southern men to hold less traditional attitudes. It may be that among Southern males, the occupational role holds less importance in defining masculinity.

Attitudes toward men's family roles are associated with the respondent's age, race, and survey year. The significant coefficients for age and race signify that older men are significantly more likely to be traditional than younger men, whereas white males are likely to be less traditional than men of other racial or ethnic groups. The association of traditional attitudes among older men is consistent with research on both college and general population groups (Pascarella & Terenzini, 1991).

Table 6.3 Logistic Regression Coefficients: Social and Demographic Correlates of Men's Attitudes on Four Dimensions of Equality

Dependent Variables *Independent Variables*	*Men's Work*	*Men's Family*	*Women's Work*	*Women's Family*
Year	.03*	–.07***	–.08***	–.11***
	(.02)	(.02)	(.02)	(.02)
Father's education	.13***			
	(.04)			
Father's income	.06**			
	(.02)			
Geographic residence (South)	–.55***			
	(.14)			
Age		.04**		
		(.02)		
Race (White)		–.85***		
		(.20)		
Religion (Catholic)			.29*	
			(.13)	
Religiosity			.29***	
			(.09)	
Mother's full-time employment			–.04***	
			(.01)	
Major (Humanities)			–.91***	–.62*
			(.29)	(.30)
Married			–.38*	–.57*
			(.17)	(.21)
Children				.30*
				(.14)
Constant	3.71**	5.75***	5.96***	8.53***
	(1.32)	(1.39)	(1.33)	(1.42)
N of Cases	1028	1000	1074	1076

NOTES: Vignette responses were dichotomized traditional/nontraditional as described below and attitudes represented by a dummy variable (1 = traditional; 0 = nontraditional) in the logistic regression analysis: Men's Work—Vignette 1 (responses 2, 3 = traditional; 1 = nontraditional); Men's Family—Vignette 2 (responses 2, 3, 4 = traditional; 1 = nontraditional) plus Vignette 3 (responses 2, 3 = traditional; 1 = nontraditional); Women's Family—Vignette 4 (responses 3, 4, 5 = traditional; 1, 2 = nontraditional) plus Vignette 5 (3, 4, 5 = traditional; 1, 2 = nontraditional); Women's Work—Vignettes 6 (responses 2, 3, 4 = traditional; 1 = nontraditional) plus Vignette 8 (4 = traditional; 1, 2, 3 = nontraditional).

With respect to changes in both women's family and work roles, nontraditionalism is associated with marital status and academic major. Single men tend to hold more traditional attitudes toward women's roles than do married men, suggesting that experience in the marital role may bring about an awareness of the difficulties, or even undesirability, of maintaining role segregation. The significant logit regression for academic major indicates that nontraditional men are more likely to be arts and humanities majors than business, architecture, education, engineering, or physical or social science majors. Although the relationship between academic major and gender role attitudes remains relatively unresearched, studies reporting the existence of a relationship between major and college men's attitudes generally support this finding. However, after reviewing 20 years of research on college students, Pascarella and Terenzini (1991) caution that because attitudes toward women become more liberal by the senior year among all majors, the attitudes could be attributed to other factors as much as to any departmental effects. It may also be that men choosing to major in the arts and humanities begin their college careers with less traditional ideas about gender roles.

Traditionalism with respect to changes in women's family roles are associated positively with religion and religiosity. Catholic men and men who consider themselves to be religious are more likely to hold traditional attitudes toward women's child care role. Because most religious organizations tend to be patriarchal and to endorse the role segregation of women and men, this finding was anticipated and consistent with prior research. In contrast, in addition to the arts and humanities majors, married men and men whose mother was employed during their childhood tend to hold less traditional attitudes. Recall that from the politics of domination perspective, it was predicted that traditional men would be those whose mother was employed. Instead, it may well be that mothers who are employed full-time present a different model of women's behavior, hold greater power within the family, or by their employment necessitate more flexibility among family members leading to less rigidly defined gender role attitudes. Similar results are reported among both college and general population samples (Brogan & Kutner, 1976; Mason & Lu, 1988; Tomeh, 1978, but see Kiecolt & Acock, 1988; Thornton et al., 1983).

With regard to women's work role, the only independent variable associated with traditionalism is the presence of children. This finding suggests that the presence of children influences men's attitudes toward accepting a more traditional occupational role for women. It could be that the fathers in this study have very young children and thus find it preferable for the wife's employment to have lesser importance.

In summary, men's attitudes toward men's work and family roles are associated primarily with ascribed characteristics: age, race, geographic residence, and their father's socioeconomic status. In comparison, men's attitudes toward women's work and family roles are influenced more by their experiences within the family and by their involvement in institutional structures that support gender role segregation. However, in the final analysis, men's attitudes appear to be influenced as much by the social and historical period in which we now live as by personal experiences or objective characteristics. Several theories posit that attitudes toward inequality are strongly affected by the historical context in which one is born and grows up (Davis & Robinson, 1991; Mason & Lu, 1988). The majority of men in this study were born and raised in the United States in the 1960s and 1970s. This period is associated with the rise of political movements, including the reemergence of the women's movement in the late 1960s, whose members were committed to eliminating inequalities of race, sex, and class. These findings suggest that the climate of opinion has shifted in favor of gender equality, a finding consistent with the cultural lag perspective predicting change among all subgroups of the population.

Yet the picture that emerges is still one of only partial change. Men showed greater acceptance of women's employment as well as their own involvement in family roles. Men did not change their attitudes toward the importance of the work role for men or the maternal role for women. In fact, in the past decade men reemphasized the importance of both. Some form of the provider role as men's primary family role still exists (Bernard, 1981); the link for women between childbearing and child care remains strong, and the combined opportunities for work and family remain difficult. Change is taking place, but the structure and culture of men's work role and women's family roles have yet to undergo the changes necessary for complete gender equality to occur.

Notes

1. The population size of the state university in 1985 accounts for the smaller number of questionnaires distributed in 1985 than in 1980 or 1990. In 1985, the list of seniors at the state university included only males graduating that semester and hence, 100%, or 285, of the population was sampled. In other years, the population of senior males sampled at the two institutions ranged from 35% to 65%.

Although the response rate is lower than desirable, it is considered adequate for analysis and reporting (Babbie, 1989). The response rate also is within the range predicted by Heberlein and Baumgartner's (1978) model for mailed questionnaires. Based on their equation, the projected response rate would be 55.18% (+26%) for (a) a student population (b) to complete a 13-page questionnaire (c) on a topic of "possible salience" (d) using one follow-up letter. Moreover, the respondents were judged to reflect the university populations from which they were drawn in socioeconomic status, age, religion, and geographic origin. It is important to note that the response rates of men have been found to be lower than those of women in all reported sample surveys (Sweet & Bumpass, 1989). To the extent that the nonresponse rate in this study is associated with traditional masculine attitudes, rather than to factors such as length of questionnaire or lack of interest, bias may be present.

2. Incomes were converted to 1985 dollars using the 1967 consumer price index.

3. The definition of gender equality used in this research is a modification of Dixon's (1976) definition that equality will exist when men and women are "equally *represented* in the aggregate in the various roles, equally *active* in exercising the rights and responsibilities associated with these roles, and equally *rewarded* materially, socially, and psychologically for their performance" (p. 20).

4. Preliminary analyses that investigated the possibility of there being just one underlying construct showed that a scale comprising the 8 items was not reliable across time. Therefore, for these reasons and those indicated above, the analysis focused on the relationships between the sociodemographic variables and the four dimensions of equality.

5. Because of the high degree of skewness, Vignette 7 was omitted from the logistic regression analysis assessing the legitimacy of women's work role. The item-to-total correlations for the two items in each of three dimensions ranged from .72 to .78.

It will be recalled that the samples differed statistically on two variables: parents responsible for upbringing and mother's employment. None of the main effects or interaction effects between family composition, year, and dimensions of equality attained statistical significance in the four analyses. Therefore it is concluded that this factor is not especially important in explaining variation in men's attitudes. The main effects between mother's employment and equality reached significance on the dimension concerned with women's family roles. As none of the other main effects or interaction effects is significant, the differences between samples were not thought to influence the findings.

References

Babbie, E. (1989). *The practice of social research* (5th ed.). Belmont, CA: Wadsworth.

Bernard, J. (1981). The good-provider role: Its rise and fall. *American Psychologist, 36,* 1-12.

Blair, S., & Lichter, D. T. (1991). Measuring the division of household labor: Gender segregation of housework among American couples. *Journal of Family Issues, 12,* 91-113.

Brod, H. (Ed.). (1987). *The making of masculinities: The new men's studies.* Boston: Allen & Unwin.

Brogan, D., & Kutner, N. (1976). Measuring sex-role orientation: A normative approach. *Journal of Marriage and the Family, 38,* 31-40.

Carrigan, T., Connell, B., & Lee, J. (1987). Toward a new sociology of masculinity. In H. Brod (Ed.), *The making of masculinities: The new men's studies* (pp. 63-102). Boston: Allen & Unwin.

Cherlin, A., & Walters, P. B. (1981). Trends in U.S. men's and women's sex-role attitudes: 1972 to 1978. *American Sociological Review, 46,* 453-460.

Cohen, T. (1987). Remaking men: Men's experiences becoming and being husbands and fathers and their implications for reconceptualizing men's lives. *Journal of Family Relations, 8,* 57-77.

Cooney, T. M., & Uhlenberg, P. (1991). Changes in work-family connections among highly educated men and women. *Journal of Family Issues, 12,* 69-90.

Coverman, S., & Sheley, J. (1986). Change in men's housework and child-care time, 1965-1975. *Journal of Marriage and the Family, 48,* 413-422.

David, D., & Brannon, R. (1976). The male sex role: Our culture's blueprint of manhood, and what it's done for us lately. In D. David & R. Brannon (Eds.), *The forty-nine percent majority: The male sex role* (pp. 1-45). Reading, MA: Addison-Wesley.

Davis, N. J., & Robinson, R. V. (1991). Men's and women's consciousness of gender inequality: Austria, West Germany, Great Britain, and the United States. *American Sociological Review, 56,* 72-84.

Dixon, R. (1976). Measuring equality between the sexes. *Journal of Social Issues, 32,* 19-32.

Ferree, M. M. (1990). Beyond separate spheres: Feminism and family research. *Journal of Marriage and the Family, 52,* 866-884.

Gilligan, C. (1982). *In a different voice: Psychological theory and women's development.* Cambridge, MA: Harvard University Press.

Goode, W. J. (1982). Why men resist. In B. Thorne (Ed.) with M. Yalom, *Rethinking the family: Some feminist questions* (pp. 131-150). New York: Longman.

Heberlein, T., & Baumgartner, R. (1978). Factors affecting response rates to mailed questionnaires: A quantitative analysis of the published literature. *American Sociological Review, 43,* 447-462.

Hunt, J. G., & Hunt, L. L. (1987). Male resistance to role symmetry in dual-earner households: Three alternative explanations. In N. Gerstel & H. E. Gross (Eds.), *Families and work* (pp. 192-203). Philadelphia: Temple University Press.

Kalleberg, A. L., & Rosenfeld, R. A. (1990). Work in the family and in the labor market: A cross-national reciprocal analysis. *Journal of Marriage and the Family, 52,* 331-346.

Kiecolt, K. J., & Acock, A. (1988). The long-term effects of family structure on gender-role attitudes. *Journal of Marriage and the Family, 50,* 709-717.

Kimmel, M. (1987). The contemporary "crisis" of masculinity in historical perspective. In H. Brod (Ed.), *The making of masculinities: The new men's studies* (pp. 121-153). Boston: Allen & Unwin.

Mason, K., & Bumpass, L. (1975). U.S. women's sex-role ideology, 1970. *American Journal of Sociology, 80,* 1212-1219.

Mason, K., Czajka, J., & Arber, S. (1976). Change in U.S. women's sex-role attitudes, 1964-1974. *American Sociological Review, 41,* 573-596.

Mason, K., & Lu, Y. (1988). Attitudes toward women's familial roles: Changes in the United States, 1977-1985. *Gender and Society, 2,* 39-57.

McBroom, W. H. (1984). Changes in sex-role orientations: A five-year longitudinal comparison. *Sex Roles, 11,* 583-592.

Mortimer, J., Lorence, J., & Kumka, D. (1986). *Work, family, and personality.* Norwood, NJ: Ablex.

Osmond M., & Martin, P. (1975). Sex and sexism: A comparison of male and female sex-role attitudes. *Journal of Marriage and the Family, 37,* 744-758.

Pascarella, E. T., & Terenzini, P. T. (1991). *How college affects students.* San Francisco: Jossey-Bass.

Pleck, J. (1976). The male sex role: Definitions, problems, and sources of change. *Journal of Social Issues, 32,* 155-164.

Pleck, J. (1977). The work-family role system. *Social Problems, 24,* 417-427.

Pleck, J. (1985). *Working wives, working husbands.* Beverly Hills, CA: Sage.

Polatnick, M. (1975). Why men don't rear children: A power analysis. In J. W. Petras (Ed.), *Sex: Male/Gender: Masculine* (pp. 199-235). Port Washington, NY: Alfred.

Sweet, J. A., & Bumpass, L. (1989). *Conducting a comprehensive survey of American family life: The experience of the National Survey of Families and Households* (NSFH Working Paper No. 12).

Tallichet, S. E., & Willits, F. K. (1986). Gender-role attitude change of young women: Influential factors from a panel study. *Social Psychology Quarterly, 49,* 219-227.

Thornton, A. (1989). Changing attitudes toward family issues in the United States. *Journal of Marriage and the Family, 51,* 873-893.

Thornton, A., Alwin, D. F., & Camburn, D. (1983). Causes and consequences of sex-role attitudes and attitude change. *American Sociological Review, 48,* 211-227.

Thornton, A., & Freedman, D. (1979). Changes in the sex role attitudes of women, 1962-1977: Evidence from a panel study. *American Sociological Review, 44,* 831-842.

Tomeh, A. (1978). Sex-role orientation: An analysis of structural and attitudinal predictors. *Journal of Marriage and the Family, 40,* 341-354.

Willinger, B. (1982). *An analysis of college men's attitudes toward the male role and toward sex-role equality.* Unpublished doctoral dissertation, Tulane University.

Willinger, B. (1986, March). *Men's attitudes toward the changing work and family roles of women and men: 1980-1985.* Paper presented at the annual Women and Work Conference, Arlington, Texas.

7

Ethnicity, Race, and Difference

A Comparison of White, Black, and Hispanic Men's Household Labor Time

BETH ANNE SHELTON
DAPHNE JOHN

Most of the recent research on household labor concerns the impact of women's labor force participation on the allocation of tasks or responsibilities. Researchers routinely recognize that women's household labor time is associated with their employment status, as well as with a variety of other sociodemographic characteristics, including age and education. A great deal has been written about the ways in which time commitments and sex role attitudes affect the division of household labor (Coverman, 1985; Huber & Spitze, 1983; Perrucci, Potter, & Rhoads, 1978; Pleck, 1985; Ross, 1987). Men are by definition included in the analyses that focus on the division of household labor, but these studies typically ignore the relationship between men's work and family roles.

Some researchers have examined the relationship between men's work and family roles (Coverman, 1985; Pleck, 1977, 1985), but the relative scarcity of these studies means that although some questions about men's household roles have been examined, a number of issues remain unexamined. In particular, there has been little research on the impact of men's paid labor time on their household labor time and there

We appreciate the very helpful comments of Jane Hood, Norma Williams, Maxine Baca Zinn, and Marta Tienda..

has been only limited research on racial and ethnic variations in men's household labor time.

In this chapter we begin to examine some of the neglected issues in the study of men's household labor time by focusing on how married men's paid labor time affects their family roles as defined by their household labor time and specific household tasks. Although there is less variation in men's paid labor time than in women's, there is some variation, and just as paid labor time affects women's household labor time, it may also affect men's. Moreover, the amount of time men have available to them may affect the specific household tasks they perform, with men with more time performing more nondiscretionary tasks than men who have less time available to them.

Recently, increased awareness of the need to examine links between gender and race have led many to argue that race and gender cannot, in fact, be discussed separately (Collins, 1990; Reid & Comas-Diaz, 1990; Zinn, 1991). Moreover, "gender studies" should not be limited only to women. Therefore, we assess the impact of selected sociodemographic characteristics on men's household labor time with a special emphasis on race and ethnicity.

Literature Review

The changes in women's labor force participation have resulted in a large number of dual-earner couples. Kimmel (1987) notes that this shift has created not only new role demands for women, but also new demands for men. Just as women have expanded their roles in the paid labor force, men also have expanded their roles in the family. The transition in men's and women's roles may, however, vary by race and ethnicity because of the historically different patterns of black, white, and Hispanic women's labor force participation (Beckett & Smith, 1981; McAdoo, 1990).

Although researchers routinely examine the impact of women's paid labor time on the household division of labor, the impact of men's paid labor time on the household division of labor is generally ignored. The lack of attention to the impact of men's paid work time on their household labor time may reflect the fact that there is less variability in men's paid labor time than in women's. Those studies that have examined the impact of men's paid work time on their household labor time have yielded conflicting results (Barnett & Baruch, 1987; Coverman & Sheley,

1986; Pleck, 1985; Thompson & Walker, 1989). Some find that men's time spent in paid labor is negatively associated with their household labor time (Rexroat & Shehan, 1987; Atkinson & Huston, 1984), whereas others find no association (Kingston & Nock, 1985). Because this research rarely focuses on racial/ethnic variation, we have little information about the ways that paid labor and household labor demands may be related differently for white, black, and Hispanic men.

Research on black and Hispanic households indicates that the images of the egalitarian black household and the gender-stratified Hispanic household may be inaccurate depictions of reality derived from superficial examinations. In the case of black households, egalitarianism is commonly attributed to black women's high rates of labor force participation (McAdoo, 1990). If, however, black women's labor force participation reflects economic pressures rather than egalitarian sex role attitudes (Broman, 1988, 1991), women's employment may be unrelated to the division of labor.

Research on the division of labor in black households does not consistently indicate black and white households differ. Some research on the division of household labor finds that black families have a more egalitarian division of labor than white families (Beckett, 1976; Beckett & Smith, 1981; Broman, 1988, 1991). Other studies by J. A. Ericksen, Yancey, and E. P. Ericksen (1979) and Farkas (1976) also suggest that black men do more household labor than their white counterparts (see also Miller & Garrison, 1982). However, Broman (1991, 1988) argues that although some egalitarian patterns do exist in black households, there is not gender equity. For example, in married couple households the proportions of men who state they do most of the household chores is much smaller than the proportion of women responding that they do all the household chores. Although unemployed men respond that they do more of the household chores more frequently than employed men, they do not make this claim nearly as often as women, regardless of women's employment status. Broman (1988) also notes that women are likely to report being primarily responsible for traditionally female tasks.

Other researchers argue that the image of the egalitarian black family is inaccurate (Cronkite, 1977; Staples, 1978; Wilson, Tolson, Hinton, & Kiernan, 1990). For example, Wilson et al. (1990) point out that black women are likely to be responsible for child care and household labor. Cronkite (1977) says that black men prefer more internal differentiation in the household than do white men. That is, she argues that they prefer a more traditional division of household labor, with women responsible for housework and child care. Others claim that black families are similar to white families in egalitarianism and that the differences that do exist often are based on social class rather than on race per se (McAdoo, 1990; Staples, 1978). Staples (1978) also claims that class differences are consistent across race. McAdoo (1990) argues, in much the same vein, that black and white fathers are similarly nurturant to their children and that black and white middle- and upper-income fathers have similar parenting styles. In contrast to the view that black men are less traditional than white men, Ransford and Miller (1983) find that middle-class black men have more traditional sex role attitudes than white middle-class men.

The literature regarding the division of household labor within Hispanic households is more limited, and much of what is available deals only with Chicanos, excluding other Hispanics. The research on Hispanic households yields conflicting results. Golding (1990) finds that Mexican-American men do less household labor than Anglo men, whereas Mexican-American women do more household labor than Anglo women. Differences between Hispanic and Anglo men's housework and child care time, like the differences between black and white men, may be due to other differences between them (Golding, 1990; McAdoo, 1990; Staples, 1978). Golding (1990) finds that education is correlated with ethnicity and household labor time such that after removing the effects of education, the impact of ethnicity on the division of labor in the household is not significant. Thus, although she finds a more traditional division of labor within Mexican-American households than in Anglo households, this division of labor reflects educational differences rather than solely ethnicity effects. Similarly, Ybarra (1982) finds that although acculturation does not significantly affect who performs the household labor, wives' employment does. She finds that the division of labor in dual-worker households is more equal than in male provider households.

In other research, Mirandé (1979) discusses the patterns of shared responsibility for domestic work in Mexican-American households. Although men's participation in household labor may give the appearance of egalitarianism, it does not necessarily indicate equality. For example, men may participate but spend less time than women. Vega et al. (1986) argue that Mexican-American families are similar to Anglo families but that in terms of their adaptability to change in family roles they appear to be more flexible than Anglo families. Thus, the male provider role may be less firmly entrenched in Mexican-American than in Anglo households, resulting in a less rigid division of household labor. Similarly, Zinn (1980) asserts that Mexican-American women's changing work roles may change their role identification.

There also is research indicating that decision making is not shared in Hispanic households (Williams, 1990). Williams (1990) finds that Mexican-American men continue to have more authority than wives, but that the patterns of decision making are not as traditional as in the past.

Some research suggests that the differences among white, black, and Hispanic men's family roles may reflect differences in the way that they internalize the provider role. Wilkie (1991) argues that black men's ability to fulfill the provider role may be associated with their rates of marriage (see also Tucker & Taylor, 1989). Similarly, Stack (1974) found that when black men are unable to provide financially for their family, they also are less likely to participate in the household (e.g., housework and child care) (Cazenave, 1979; Wilkie, 1991). Although the findings of Wilkie (1991) and Tucker and Taylor (1989) do not directly indicate a relationship between the provider role and men's participation in the household, we can speculate that this association may exist. Thus, to the extent that there are differences among black, white, and Hispanic men's internalization of the provider role, we might also expect to find that the relationship between work and family roles varies by race/ethnicity.

We focus on the definition of egalitarianism based on the division of labor within the household. Hood (1983) notes that there are a number of ways in which an egalitarian marriage is defined. For our purposes, egalitarianism is defined in terms of household labor time. Some studies discuss decision making and role sharing, which are logically associated with the division of household labor, but which are not unproblematically related to it (Blumstein & Schwartz, 1983).

A problem with much of the research on men's household labor time is the failure to incorporate wives' characteristics into the analyses. Just as men's paid labor time may act as a constraint on their household labor time, wives' paid labor time may create a demand for them to spend more time on household labor. The use of couples as the units of analysis in this chapter helps us understand the interaction between spouses' characteristics.

We further examine white, black, and Hispanic men's household labor time to determine the nature of the association between men's paid labor time and household labor time. In addition, we examine racial/ethnic differences in men's household labor time and assess the extent to which any observed differences may reflect differences in paid labor time, education, or other sociodemographic characteristics. We also incorporate wives' paid labor time and attitudes about family roles into our analysis to determine the ways in which husbands' and wives' characteristics interact to affect men's household labor time.

Data and Methods

The data for this study are from the 1987 National Survey of Families and Households (NSFH) (Sweet, Bumpass, & Call, 1988), a national probability sample of 9,643 persons with an oversampling of 3,374 minority respondents, single parents, cohabiting persons, recently married persons, and respondents with stepchildren. One adult per household was selected randomly to be the primary respondent and his or her spouse/partner (if applicable) was also given a questionnaire designed for secondary respondents. Portions of the main interview with the primary respondent were self-administered, as was the entire spouse/partner questionnaire. In this chapter, we include only married respondents with a completed spouse questionnaire. We also employ sample weights to make our sample of married couples comparable to the national distribution of married people by age, sex, and race/ethnicity.

In the analyses to follow we begin by describing black, white, and Hispanic men's and women's household labor time. In addition to comparing household labor time across racial/ethnic groups, we also compare this time by work status.

In the second stage of the analysis, we examine the relationship between ethnicity and men's household labor time after controlling for a variety of other factors, including age, education, sex role attitudes, and both husbands' and wives' paid work. We use multiple regression analysis to determine if there are race/ethnic differences in household labor time or in the impact of paid labor time on household labor time that are independent of sociodemographic differences between white, black, and Hispanic men.

In addition to determining whether or not a race/ethnicity effect on household labor time exists once other characteristics have been taken into account, we look at the relationship between husbands' and wives' paid labor and household labor time. We expect to find that men who spend more time in paid work will spend less time on household labor once other characteristics have been held constant. Moreover, to the extent that wives' market work time may act as a demand on men, we expect to find that the more time wives spend in paid labor the more time husbands will spend on household labor, once other variables have been held constant.

In the final stage of the analysis we use Multiple Classification Analysis (MCA) to examine the patterns of white, black, and Hispanic men's time spent on specific household tasks and assess the impact of work status on specific task time. MCA will provide us with men's household labor time adjusted for sociodemographic characteristics. It also provides a measure of association (beta) that is comparable to a correlation coefficient. Our dependent variable is household labor time and is measured by combining self-reported time spent on each of nine specific tasks. Total household labor time is the sum of time spent in a series of specific tasks by both respondent and spouse. Respondents were asked to estimate their time spent in a week on meal preparation, washing dishes, cleaning house, outdoor tasks, shopping, laundry, paying bills, automobile maintenance, and driving. Our summated measure of total household labor time is more accurate than those measures that are derived from questions that ask respondents to estimate their total household labor time because respondents are better able to estimate time spent on specific tasks than overall time.

Our analyses include separate estimates of white, black, and Hispanic men's and women's household labor time. Hispanics include Mexican-Americans as well as other Hispanic respondents. Paid labor time is measured in hours usually spent per week at work for both respondents and spouses. Education and age are measured in years.

Respondents' and spouses' sex role attitudes are measured by their responses to two attitude items. Each item was scored from 1 to 5. Respondents were asked if they agreed with the following statements:

1. If a husband and a wife both work full-time, they should share household tasks equally.
2. Preschool children are likely to suffer if their mother is employed.

Responses to the two items were summed and divided by two so that the range of the summated measure is 1 to 5. A high score indicates more liberal sex role attitudes and a low score indicates more traditional sex role attitudes.

Presence of children was included as an independent variable in some of the analyses. A score of 0 indicates that the respondent has no children under the age of 18 in the household, whereas a score of 1 indicates that there are children under the age of 18 in the household.

Findings

Findings in Table 7.1 reveal that black and Hispanic men spend significantly more time on household labor than do white men. Women's household labor time also varies by race/ethnicity, but in a different pattern. Hispanic women spend significantly more time on household labor than white women. They also spend more time on household labor than black women, but a t-test of the difference is not significant. Nevertheless, the gap is of substantive interest because the lack of statistical significance is largely a function of inflated standard deviations due to the small number of black and Hispanic respondents. As the results in Table 7.1 indicate, the divergent patterns of variation in household labor time by race and gender combine in such a way that men's proportionate share of household labor also varies by ethnicity.

Black men spend an average of 25 hours per week on household labor compared to 19.6 hours for white men and 23.2 hours for Hispanic men. The absolute size of the gap between black and Hispanic men's household labor time is small, with both groups of men spending significantly more time on household labor than white men. Nevertheless, black men spend more time on household labor than Hispanic men, although the gap is not statistically significant. This pattern both partially confirms and contradicts earlier research. black men's relatively high household labor time is consistent with the view that black households may have a more equal division of labor than other households. The data in Table 7.1 do not, however, allow us to determine the source of black men's household labor time investments. It is possible, for example, that on average, black men spend less time in paid labor and therefore more time on household labor. The pattern also could reflect a number of other possible differences in the sociodemographic characteristics of black and white men that we examine in a later section.

Hispanic men's relatively high time investment in household labor is consistent with previous research finding that Hispanic men participate at least as much as Anglo men in household labor, and contradicts those who argue that Hispanic men participate in household labor less than Anglo men. Of course, much of the research on Hispanic men's family roles examines decision making or the distribution of power, rather than

Table 7.1 Household Labor Time By Gender and Race/Ethnicity

	White	*Black*	*Hispanic*	*T-Test Blk/Wht*	*T-Test Hsp/Wht*	*T-Test Blk/Hsp*
Men	19.6	25.0	23.2	2.3**	2.2*	.6
	(19.3)	(28.7)	(19.2)			
Women	37.3	38.0	41.8	.3	1.9*	1.2
	(21.6)	(26.3)	(24.5)			
Men's % of Household Labor Time	34%	40%	36%			

NOTES: *$p \leq .05$; **$p \leq .01$. Standard deviation in parenthesis.

household labor time. Most of the research on household labor assumes that it is onerous duty and that only someone without the power to avoid it (or without any decision-making authority) will do it (Ferree, 1987). Thus, researchers whose focus is on decision making often assume that egalitarian patterns of decision making are associated with an egalitarian division of household labor.

Women's household labor time also varies by race/ethnicity, with Hispanic women spending significantly more time on household labor than either black or white women. Hispanic women spend an average of 41.8 hours per week on household labor compared to 37.3 hours for white women and 38 hours per week for black women. Thus, Hispanic men and women spend significantly more time on household labor than white men and women, whereas black women's household labor time is not significantly different from white women's household labor time. Women's and men's different investments in household labor time affect men's proportionate share of household labor time. The data on black men and women indicate that black men do 40% of the household labor (done by men and women only) whereas Hispanic and Anglo men do 36% and 34% of the household labor, respectively. Thus, Table 7.1 confirms earlier research reporting that black households have a more equal division of household labor than white households and also confirms research indicating that Anglo and Hispanic households may have few differences in division of labor. In addition, the findings for Hispanic households suggest that there may be even more changes in the traditional patterns of Hispanic households than Williams's (1990) research on decision making indicates.

We begin to examine the source of some of the gap in Table 7.2 where we present white, black, and Hispanic men's household labor time by employment status using Multiple Classification Analysis. We do this in order to determine if black men's relatively high levels of household labor time reflect their lower paid labor time.

With respect to employment status, there are some interesting patterns. For both white and Hispanic men, those who are employed spend less time on household labor than those who are not employed, although the pattern is statistically significant only for white men. For blacks, however, the pattern is quite different. Black men who are not employed spend less time on household labor than black men who are employed, although the difference is not statistically significant.[1] These findings indicate that the relationship between paid labor time and household labor time varies by race/ethnicity and that differences in black, white, and Hispanic men's household labor time are not simply a function of differences in their employment status.

The relationship between black men's employment status and their household labor time may indicate that black men who are not employed are different from nonemployed white and Hispanic men. To the extent that black men are not employed involuntarily, the results in Table 7.2 may reflect the age structure of those who are not employed. It also may indicate the presence of a distinct group of black men characterized by both low time investments in paid labor and low investments in household labor. The argument that the apparent egalitarianism of the black family may be a function of black men's reduced hours in paid labor is not supported by these findings. If anything, these findings indicate that, among blacks, the division of household labor is likely to be more equal in households where the man is employed than in households where he is not. Although this is in some sense counterintuitive, it may indicate that the "breadwinner" role is internalized in such a way that even black men who are not employed may opt out of the family per se, rather than compensating for their reduced paid work with more household labor (Komarovsky, 1940; Stack, 1974). Among the men in this sample, the expression of their "opting out" may be to avoid household labor. (See Cazenave, 1984; Hood, 1986, for more discussion of the importance of subjective perceptions of work and family roles.)

Up to this point we have examined men's household labor time without taking into consideration a variety of sociodemographic characteristics, sex role attitudes, or wives' work status. Thus, some of the observed race/ethnic differences may reflect other differences among

Table 7.2 Men's Household Labor Time by Race/Ethnicity and Employment Status

	White	*Black*	*Hispanic*
Employment Status			
Not employed	23.5	19.5	23.0
Employed PT (1-39 hrs.)	19.1	26.6	22.7
Employed FT	18.2	27.0	22.3
Eta	.12***	.13	.03
N	2798	183	164

NOTES: We use 39 hours as our break between part-time and full-time in order to ensure an adequate *n* for the part-time category. Eta is a measure of association.
***$p \leq .001$.

white, black, and Hispanic households. In Table 7.3 we examine the impact of race/ethnicity on men's household labor time by estimating the direct effect of race/ethnicity on household labor time as well as by estimating the ways that paid labor time may affect white, black, and Hispanic men's household labor time differently, after taking other factors into account. Thus, in Table 7.3 we can determine if the previously observed association between race/ethnicity and household labor time or the race/ethnic differences in the impact of paid labor time on household labor time are artifacts of other differences among white, black, and Hispanic men.

The results in Table 7.3 show that after controlling for respondents' education, age, children, sex role attitudes, wives' sex role attitudes and paid labor time, race/ethnicity is not significantly associated with men's household labor time. Thus, the differences among white, black, and Hispanic men's household labor time that we observed earlier appear to reflect other differences among them. For example, they may reflect differences in social class or education as McAdoo (1990) and Golding (1990) have argued. They may also, however, reflect differences in the presence of children or in wives' paid labor time.

Although we find no direct effects of race/ethnicity on men's household labor time in our multivariate analysis, the differential effect of paid labor time on men's household labor time remains.[2] For white and Hispanic men, each additional hour spent in paid labor is associated with their spending slightly more than 6 fewer minutes per day on

Table 7.3 Regression of Men's Household Labor Time on Paid Labor Time, Race/Ethnicity, Presence of Children, Education, Age, Sex Role Attitudes, Wives' Paid Labor Time, and Wives' Sex Role Attitudes

	b	*s.e.*
Paid labor	−.10***	.02
Black	−3.4	2.4
Hispanic	−.67	3.2
Black/paid	.27***	.07
Hispanic/paid	.08	.08
Children	3.7***	.81
Education	−.15	.12
Age	.02	.03
Men's sex role attitudes	1.5**	.52
Wives' paid labor time .07***		.02
Wives' sex role attitudes	.76	.51
Constant	13.4	3.4
R^2	.033	
N	2782	

NOTES: $^{**}p \leq .01$; $^{***}p \leq .001$.

household labor. For black men, however, each additional hour in paid labor is associated with them spending more time on household labor, even after controlling for sociodemographic and household characteristics. Thus, the pattern we observed in the bivariate analyses is repeated in the multivariate analyses. The more time black men spend in paid labor the more time they spend on household labor, whereas the association between paid labor time and household labor time is negative for Anglo and Hispanic men.

There are a variety of possible explanations for the different association between paid labor time and household labor time for black men than for white or Hispanic men. Black men may define the breadwinner role more narrowly than white or Hispanic men, such that when they are not employed and unable to contribute to their family's financial well-being they may retreat from the family in other ways (Stack, 1974). The race/ethnic variation in the association between men's paid labor time and household labor time may reflect differences in housing patterns. If households with nonemployed black men are more likely to live in apartments, and those with employed black men are more likely to live in single-family houses, the pattern we see may reflect the amount of household labor that must be done. The different association for white and Hispanic men may be the result of different housing patterns. That is, households with nonemployed white or Hispanic men may not be as concentrated in apartments as is the case with black households. Thus there may be variation in the amount of household labor that must be done associated with men's employment status.

The pattern of the effects of some of the control variables is also interesting. For example, men with children spend more time on household labor than men without children, and men with more egalitarian sex role attitudes spend more time on household labor than men with more traditional attitudes. Wives' sex role attitudes are not associated with men's household labor time, but the more time wives spend in paid labor, the more time husbands spend on household labor. Interestingly, after controlling for other variables, men's age is not significantly associated with their household labor time.

In Table 7.4 we further examine the relationship between men's employment status and their household labor time by examining white, black, and Hispanic men's time spent on specific household tasks, after controlling for sociodemographic and household characteristics. Among those men employed full-time, black men spend more time than white and Hispanic men cleaning house, shopping, and repairing automobiles. Cleaning house and shopping are typically "female-typed" tasks indicating that employed black men's household labor time represents less gender stratification rather than simply more time spent on tasks typically done by men. Nevertheless, there are some "female-typed" tasks on which white men spend more time. White men employed full-time spend more time on laundry than black or Hispanic men. Not all of the differences in housework time result from variation in time spent on "female-typed" tasks. White and black men employed full-time spend more time than Hispanic men on outdoor tasks, and black and Hispanic men employed full-time spend more time paying bills than white men.

Among those who are employed part-time or not at all, Hispanic men are most likely to spend more time on specific household tasks than either white or black men, although in a number of cases black and Hispanic men's household task time is similar. Hispanic men employed part-time spend the most time cleaning house, but black men also spend

Table 7.4 Men's Time Spent on Specific Household Tasks by Employment Status and Race/Ethnicity

	Not Employed	*Employed Part-Time*	*Employed Full-Time*
Preparing Meals			
White	3.3	2.9	2.3
Black	4.2	4.9	3.3
Hispanic	5.8	3.2	2.2
beta	.09^{+}	.09	.02
Washing Dishes			
White	2.7	2.2	1.9
Black	1.6	4.5	2.7
Hispanic	4.0	4.1	2.1
beta	.06*	.22**	.05
Cleaning House			
White	2.3	1.8	1.7
Black	2.3	3.2	3.0
Hispanic	4.3	3.9	2.2
beta	.08^{+}	.20**	.11***
Outdoor Tasks			
White	7.5	5.0	5.6
Black	5.8	4.8	5.4
Hispanic	5.2	3.7	3.9
beta	.06	.06	.06*
Shopping			
White	2.9	2.4	2.3
Black	2.7	2.6	4.0
Hispanic	2.5	3.5	3.1
beta	.02	.08	.14***

more time cleaning house than white men. Similarly, black men spend significantly more time washing dishes than other men, although Hispanic men spend almost as much time as black men. Among those who are not employed, Hispanic men spend more time than black or white men preparing meals, washing dishes, and cleaning house; thus among

Table 7.4 Continued

	Not Employed	*Employed Part-Time*	*Employed Full-Time*
Laundry			
White	.7	.8	1.2
Black	.9	1.5	.6
Hispanic	1.3	.4	.6
beta	.06	.11	.08***
Paying Bills			
White	1.6	1.4	1.5
Black	2.5	2.2	2.4
Hispanic	2.1	4.1	2.5
beta	.07	.26***	.09***
Auto Maintenance			
White	1.4	1.6	2.0
Black	1.4	2.5	3.4
Hispanic	2.1	3.2	2.9
beta	.04	.21**	.08***
Driving			
White	1.2	1.3	1.5
Black	1.1	1.7	2.7
Hispanic	1.9	1.4	1.5
beta	.04	.04	.08

NOTES: Controlling for respondents' sex role attitudes, education, age, spouses' paid work time, spouses' sex role attitudes, and number of children. Beta is a partial measure of association.
$^{+}p \leq .10$; $*p \leq .05$; $**p \leq .01$; $***p \leq .001$.

men not employed, Hispanic men are significantly less traditional than white or black men. That is, Hispanic men who are not employed spend more time on "female-typed" tasks than other men.

The patterns observed in Table 7.4 indicate that there is more variation by race/ethnicity among men who are employed full-time than among those who are employed part-time or not at all. Although we should use care when comparing across employment statuses in Table

7.4 (because there may be sociodemographic differences among the groups), we can see that black men's greater household labor time, with respect to white and Hispanic men, appears to be among those who are employed full-time, whereas there are fewer and less definite patterns among those employed fewer hours or not at all.

With respect to specific household tasks, Table 7.4 shows that black men who are employed full-time spend more time on a variety of household tasks, rather than on only a few or male-typed tasks. The pattern of greater involvement in traditionally female tasks among black men employed full-time indicates that among black households there are more egalitarian patterns of family work when the husband is employed than when he is not.

Conclusions

Our findings point to several important patterns. Just as women's paid labor time is associated with their household labor time, we find that men's paid labor time is associated with their household labor time. Thus, although there is less variation in men's paid labor time than in women's, there is enough that it warrants some research attention. Interestingly, the pattern of association between paid labor time and household labor time varies by race/ethnicity. Employed black men do more household labor than those who are not employed, whereas employed white and Hispanic men do less household labor than those who are not employed. These different patterns illustrate the dangers of analyses that fail to examine not only the direct effect of race/ethnicity on household labor time but also the way that race/ethnicity may affect the relationship among other variables. The relationship between men's work and family roles is not such that we can talk about a relationship: the relationship varies by race/ethnicity. This difference in the relationship between work and family suggests that we need to conduct more research on the nature of work and family trade-offs and how they vary by race and ethnicity.

Our analyses also indicate some differences in the family roles (as measured by household labor time) of white, black, and Hispanic men. Our findings from bivariate analyses show that Hispanic and black men spend more time on household labor than white men. Even with Hispanic women's relatively high levels of household labor time, Hispanic men's proportionate share of household labor time is higher than white men's. Black men's relatively high proportionate share of household labor time confirms earlier research indicating that black households may be more egalitarian than white households. Unlike some speculation, however, we find that this pattern is not the result of differences in black men's paid labor time, but that employed black men are the ones who are spending more time on household labor. This somewhat surprising finding indicates the need to examine the relationship between black men's work and family roles in more detail. Given previous findings about black men's attachment to family and work roles (Cazenave, 1979), black men's attachments to the provider role as well as their perceptions of family obligations may be the most fruitful place to begin future studies. In addition, the different patterns observed indicate the complex nature of the work-family linkage for men more generally. Further analyses might also focus on the characteristics of nonemployed black men as compared to nonemployed white and Hispanic men to determine what may account for the different patterns of work and family role trade-offs.

Finally, we find that higher household labor time among black men employed full-time reflects their greater time investments in traditionally female tasks, rather than differences in time investments in "male-typed" tasks. In addition, the pattern of Hispanic men's time spent on specific household tasks indicates that they often spend more time on female-typed tasks than Anglo men. Thus, even though Anglo and Hispanic men's total household labor time is not significantly different once sociodemographic characteristics have been taken into account, Hispanic men may spend more time on typically "female-typed" tasks like meal preparation, washing dishes, and cleaning house than do Anglo men (see also Mirandé, 1985; Zinn, 1980). In addition, our findings indicate that there may be more changes in the Hispanic household than some who have found changing patterns suggest (Mirandé, 1985; Williams, 1990).

In future research we must give more attention to racial/ethnic variation in men's family patterns as well as to the different trade-offs that men may make between work and family. We simply cannot assume that the trade-offs are the same for men as for women, just as we have often argued that we cannot assume that women's labor force experiences can be modeled in the same way that we model men's. At the same time, our findings argue for the systematic inclusion of ethnicity and race in studies of the work-family trade-off for both men and women. We need to examine differences among black, white, and Hispanic men's perceptions of their family responsibilities if we are to understand how they balance work and family responsibilities.

Notes

1. The lack of statistical significance is a result of the relatively small number of black and Hispanic respondents in the survey.

2. To determine the differential effects of paid labor time for white, black, and Hispanic respondents we included interaction terms for race/ethnicity and paid labor time in our analysis. The nonsignificant effect for the interaction term between Hispanic and paid labor time indicates that the impact of paid labor time on Hispanic men's household labor time is not significantly different from the impact of paid labor time on white men's household labor time. The significant interaction term for black men indicates that there is a significant difference in the impact of paid labor time on black and white men's household labor time. By adding the coefficient for paid labor time to the coefficient for the black/paid labor time interaction term, we can see that even after controlling for sociodemographic and household characteristics, paid labor time is positively associated with black men's household labor time. Thus, the more time black men spend in paid labor the more time they spend in household labor, whereas the association between paid labor time and household labor time is negative for Anglo and Hispanic men.

References

Atkinson, J., & Huston, T. L. (1984). Sex role orientation and division of labor early in marriage. *Journal of Personality and Social Psychology, 46*(2), 330-345.

Barnett, R. C., & Baruch, G. K. (1987). Determinants of fathers' participation in family work. *Journal of Marriage and the Family, 49,* 29-40.

Beckett, J. O. (1976, November). Working wives: A racial comparison. *Social Work,* 463-471.

Beckett, J. O., & Smith, A. D. (1981). Work and family roles: Egalitarian marriage in black and white families. *Social Service Review, 55*(2), 314-326.

Blumstein, P., & Schwartz, P. (1983). *American couples.* New York: Pocket Books.

Broman, C. (1988). Household work and family life satisfaction of blacks. *Journal of Marriage and the Family, 50,* 743-748.

Broman, C. (1991). Gender, work-family roles and psychological well-being of blacks. *Journal of Marriage and the Family, 53,* 509-520.

Cazenave, N. (1979). Middle-income black fathers: An analysis of the provider role. *Family Coordinator, 28,* 583-593.

Cazenave, N. (1984). Race, socioeconomic status, and age: The social context of masculinity. *Sex Roles, 11*(7/8), 639-656.

Collins, P. H. (1990). *Black feminist thought: Knowledge, consciousness and the politics of empowerment.* Cambridge, MA: Unwin Hyman.

Coverman, S. (1985). Explaining husbands' participation in domestic labor. *Sociological Quarterly, 26*(1), 81-98.

Coverman, S., & Sheley, J. F. (1986). Change in men's housework and child-care time, 1965-1975. *Journal of Marriage and the Family, 48,* 413-422.

Cronkite, R. C. 1977. The determinants of spouses' normative preferences for family roles. *Journal of Marriage and the Family, 39,* 575-585.

Ericksen, J. A., Yancey, W. L., & Ericksen, E. P. (1979). The division of family roles. *Journal of Marriage and the Family, 41,* 301-313.

Farkas, G. (1976). Education, wage rates, and the division of labor between husband and wife. *Journal of Marriage and the Family, 38,* 473-483.

Ferree, M. M. (1987). Family and job for working-class women: Gender and class systems seen from below. In N. Gerstel & H. E. Gross (Eds.), *Families and work* (pp. 289-301). Philadelphia: Temple University Press.

Golding, J. M. (1990). Division of household labor, strain and depressive symptoms among Mexican Americans and non-Hispanic whites. *Psychology of Women Quarterly, 14,* 103-117.

Hood, J. C. (1983). *Becoming a two-job family.* New York: Praeger.

Hood, J. C. (1986). The provider role: Its meaning and measurement. *Journal of Marriage and the Family, 48,* 349-359.

Huber, J., & G. Spitze. (1983). *Sex stratification: Children, housework and jobs.* New York: Academic Press.

Kimmel, M. S. (1987). Rethinking "masculinity": New directions in research. In M. S. Kimmel (Ed.), *Changing men: New directions of research on men and masculinity* (pp. 9-24). Newbury Park, CA: Sage.

Kingston, P. W., & Nock, S. L. (1985). Consequences of the family work day. *Journal of Marriage and the Family, 47*(3), 619-630.

Komarovsky, M. (1940). *The unemployed man and his family.* New York: Dryden.

McAdoo, H. P. (1990). A portrait of African American families in the United States. In S. E. Rix (Ed.), *The American woman 1990-1991: A status report* (pp. 71-93). New York: W. E. Norton.

Miller, J., & Garrison, H. H. (1982). Sex roles: The division of labor at home and in the workplace. *Annual Review of Sociology, 8,* 237-262.

Mirandé, A. (1979). A reinterpretation of male dominance in the Chicano family. *Family Coordinator, 28*(4), 473-480.

Mirandé, A. (1985). *The Chicano experience: An alternative perspective.* Notre Dame, IN: University of Notre Dame Press.

Perrucci, C. C., Potter, H. R., & Rhoads, D. L. (1978). Determinants of male family-role performance. *Psychology of Women Quarterly, 3*(1), 53-66.

Pleck, J. H. (1977). The work-family role system. *Social Problems, 24,* 417-427.

Pleck, J. H. (1985). *Working wives/working husbands.* Beverly Hills, CA: Sage.

Ransford, E., & Miller, J. (1983). Race, sex and feminist outlooks. *American Sociological Review, 48,* 46-59.

Reid, P. T., & Comas-Diaz, L. (1990). Gender and ethnicity: Perspectives on dual status. *Sex Roles, 22*(7/8), 397-408.

Rexroat, C., & Shehan, C. (1987). The family life cycle and spouses' time in housework. *Journal of Marriage and the Family, 49*(4), 737-750.

Ross, C. E. (1987). The division of labor at home. *Social Forces, 65*(3), 816-834.

Stack, C. B. (1974). *All our kin.* New York: Harper Colophon.

Staples, R. (1978). Masculinity and race: The dual dilemma of black men. *Journal of Social Issues, 34*(1), 169-183.

Sweet, J., Bumpass, L., & Call, V. (1988). *The design and content of the National Survey of Families and Households* (Working Paper NSFH-1). Madison: University of Wisconsin-Madison, Center for Demography and Ecology.

Thompson, L., & Walker, A. J. (1989). Gender in families: Women and men in marriage, work and parenthood. *Journal of Marriage and the Family, 51,* 845-871.

Tucker, M. B., & Taylor, R. J. (1989). Demographic correlates of relationship status among black Americans. *Journal of Marriage and the Family, 51,* 655-665.

Vega, W. A., Patterson, T., Sallis, J., Nader, P., Atkins, C., & Abramson, I. (1986). Cohesion and adaptability in Mexican American and Anglo families. *Journal of Marriage and the Family, 48,* 857-867.

Wilkie, J. R. (1991). The decline in men's labor force participation and income and the changing structure of family economic support. *Journal of Marriage and the Family, 53*(1), 111-122.

Williams, N. (1990). *The Mexican American family: Tradition and change.* Dix Hills, NY: General Hall.

Wilson, M. N., Tolson, T. F. J., Hinton, I. D., & Kiernan, M. (1990). Flexibility and sharing of childcare duties in black families. *Sex Roles, 22*(7/8), 409-425.

Ybarra, L. (1982). When wives work: The impact on the Chicano family. *Journal of Marriage and the Family, 44,* 169-178.

Zinn, M. B. (1980). Gender and ethnic identity among Chicanos. *Frontiers, 2,* 8-24.

Zinn, M. B. (1991). Family, feminism and race in America. In J. Lorber & S. A. Farrell (Eds.), *The social construction of gender* (pp. 110-134). Newbury Park, CA: Sage.

8

Reluctant Compliance

Work-Family Role Allocation in Dual-Earner Chicano Families

SCOTT COLTRANE
ELSA O. VALDEZ

According to popular image and early research, Latino husbands and fathers are authoritarian and uninvolved in the daily routines of family life. Although this stereotypical portrayal has been challenged recently, we still know little about the interplay of Latino men's work and family roles. In this chapter, we draw on interviews with 20 Chicano (Mexican-American) couples to explore how mothers and fathers balance paid and unpaid work. We are especially concerned with whether wives in dual-earner Chicano families assume the role of co-provider and whether women's higher earning power is associated with husbands' assuming more responsibility for child care and housekeeping.

Our everyday experiences, as well as past academic research, show us that housework and child care tend to be divided into separate spheres on the basis of gender. Women usually do most of the indoor tasks, especially cooking, laundry, cleaning house, washing dishes, and caring for young children. Men usually do most of the outdoor tasks such as lawn and car care, perform household repairs, and sometimes play with older children (Berk, 1985). This inside-outside gender dichotomy appears timeless and natural, although it is inaccurate to assume that such divisions of labor are universal or impervious to change (Coltrane, 1988, 1989). Because most studies of household labor have included few minority families, our impressions of task allocation and work-family linkages, like most findings in social science, reflect a white, middle-class bias. This study attempts to redress this shortcoming by focusing on a group of dual-earner Chicano couples. By analyzing the ways in which these couples divide daily chores, we hope to better understand how work and family influence each other in a specific cultural context.

Most theoretical models assume that paid work and family work are interdependent, but we have not yet identified the processes through which they are linked. "New" home economics theories tend to ignore gender and assume that family members allocate responsibility for various tasks based on "tastes" for certain types of work and the underlying desire to maximize benefits for the entire family unit (Becker, 1981). Materialist and conflict theories assume that all family members' needs are not equally served by conventional task allocation, and that responsibility for housework can be seen as a measure of women's powerlessness (Hartmann, 1981). Contemporary role theories suggest that the boundaries between work and family roles are "asymmetrically permeable," buffering men's paid work from their family obligations, but allowing women's family commitments to intrude on their work roles (Pleck, 1977). Underlying most theoretical models is the assumption that changes in paid work will promote shifts in family work, but specific changes have been difficult to predict.

Hood (1986) calls attention to the importance of accurately measuring the provider role if we are to isolate how and why work roles and family roles interpenetrate. In particular, husbands' and wives' perceived responsibility to provide financially for the family and their sense of duty to care for family members and maintain the home can have important impacts on the division of paid and unpaid labor. Accepting the wife as an essential economic provider may be a precursor to the husband partially assuming the parent/homemaker role (Haas, 1981; Hood, 1983).

Research on Mexican-American Families

In most social scientific research before the late 1970s, Mexican-American families were characterized as rigidly patriarchal. The father was seen as having full authority over mother and children, and wives were described as passive, submissive, and dependent (Zinn, 1980).

William Madsen (1973) emphasized the destructive aspects of Mexican-American *machismo* by comparing the men to roosters: "The better man is the one who can drink more, defend himself best, have more sex relations, and have more sons borne by his wife" (p. 22). According to such depictions, Chicano men were aloof and authoritarian, and rarely participated in the everyday business of running a household. In contrast, some contemporary scholars have rejected such stereotypes as misguided. For instance, Mirandé (1988) asserted that *machismo* implies respect, loyalty, responsibility, and generosity and noted that contemporary Chicano fathers are now participating more actively in child care than in the past.

Some recent research on marital interaction in Mexican-American families supports the notion that gender relations are more egalitarian than the traditional model assumes. Studies of marital decision making have found that Chicano couples tend to regard their decision making as relatively shared and equal (V. Cromwell & R. Cromwell, 1978; Hawkes & Taylor, 1975; Ybarra, 1982). Most researchers agree, however, that marital roles are not truly egalitarian in dual-earner Mexican-American households any more than they are in dual-earner Anglo-American households (Hartzler & Franco, 1985; Segura, 1984; Williams, 1988, 1990; Zavella, 1987). Because Mexican cultural ideals require the male to be honored and respected as the head of the family, Zinn (1982) contends that Chicano families maintain a facade of patriarchy even as mothers assume authority over day-to-day household activities. A key factor according to some researchers, is that Mexican-American women, like their Anglo-American counterparts, exercise more marital decision-making power if they are employed outside the home (Ybarra, 1982; Zinn, 1980).

Because research on Latino families is still exploratory, we cannot yet describe the most important social processes, nor make accurate predictions about the causes of the division of labor. For instance, Vega (1990) notes that researchers often aggregate divergent groups of Chicanos, Cubans, and Puerto Ricans, and typically fail to control for socioeconomic status (p. 1019). Although studies of Anglo couples tend to focus on the middle class, past studies of ethnic minority families have tended to include a preponderance of working-class people. We concur with Zinn (1990) that "marriage patterns, gender relations, kinship networks, and other family characteristics result from the social location of families, . . . where they are situated in relation to societal institutions allocating resources" (p. 74). To understand Chicano families' divisions of labor, we need to consider their social context and examine the simultaneous impacts of race, class, and gender. This chapter focuses on the allocation of tasks among a small group of relatively affluent Chicano couples with young children and is part of a larger study of Chicano family life (see Coltrane & Valdez, 1991; Valdez & Coltrane, 1993).

Research Design

We collected data from a sample of Chicano couples by interviewing husbands and wives separately using a semistructured format. We relied on snowball sampling techniques (Biernacki & Waldorf, 1981) to select 20 couples with one child at least 4 years old, but without children of high school age or beyond. Interviews were tape-recorded and portions transcribed for coding into emergent categories (Glaser & Strauss, 1967).

Sampling Strategy

We selected our sample on the basis of several conceptual concerns. Relying on large samples of mostly Anglo couples, other researchers had reported that couples in the "childless" or "empty nest" stages of the family life cycle share more housework than those living with young children in the home (Rexroat & Shehan, 1987). Past studies also documented the arrival of a first child typically occasioning a shift toward more conventional and gender-based allocations of household tasks (Cowan et al., 1985; R. LaRossa & M. LaRossa, 1981). Because we were primarily interested in exploring how and why Chicano couples might share both child care and housework over the long term, we avoided selecting childless couples and those in the initial transition to parenthood. Because researchers have also reported that teenage daughters often assume responsibility for significant amounts of housework and child care (Goodnow, 1988), we avoided sampling families with children of high school age. By restricting the age range of the oldest child to 4-14 years, we were able to reduce, somewhat, the impact of life cycle stage on the division of household labor.

To explore the potential impacts of sharing the provider role, we selected only couples in which both spouses were employed at least 20 hours per week. Because most previous studies of upper-middle-class dual-career couples included few ethnic minority families (R. Rapoport & R. Rapoport, 1971), and because many previous studies of Latino families focused on the working class (e.g., Lewis, 1960; Ruiz, 1987; Zavella, 1987), we felt that an exploratory look at role allocation in middle-class Chicano couples would be fruitful. Because the majority of Latino dual-earner families are composed of husbands and wives with service sector jobs (Segura, 1984), we began by interviewing Chicano white-collar workers. Because these clerk and secretary positions offer modest wages, limited autonomy, and few chances for upward mobility, they are more accurately classified as white-collar working class rather than middle class. Other white-collar positions held by our informants, such as teacher or administrator, entail both giving and taking orders and can be appropriately labeled middle-class occupations (Collins, 1988).

We began our interviews with staff employees of a university, but soon obtained referrals to couples far removed from this venue (over three quarters of the final sample were unconnected to the university). In the initial phase of the study, we were concerned that there might be too little variation in occupational status, so we explicitly included some families in which the men held professional jobs (i.e., lawyer, agency director) or blue-collar jobs (i.e., mechanic, laborer). The resulting sample varied from what might be termed lower middle class (or "comfortable" working class) to upper middle class. These terms, however, are too simple to capture the complexity of the class and status positions of the husbands and wives we interviewed (see Stacey, 1990).

Characteristics of the Sample

Table 8.1 shows that husbands in the sample ranged in age from 26 to 43 years old, with two thirds between the ages of 35 and 38. Wives tended to be slightly younger, with most between the ages of 33 and 36. Spouses' ages in 14 of 20 couples were within 2 years of each other, but four husbands were at least 3 years older than their wife, and one wife was 4 years older than her husband. At the time of the interviews, couples had been married an average of 13 years, with five couples married less than 10 years, and eight couples married for 15 years or more. Thus, the sample is composed of couples with long-standing marriages and tends to represent more stable, and perhaps more "successful," marriages than exist in the population at large.

Four couples had one child, nine couples had two children, five couples had three children, and two had four children. The ages of the children ranged from 1 to 14 years, with a median age of 7. Two thirds

Table 8.1 Demographic Characteristics of Sample Families

Couple No.	*Spouse*	*Age*	*Occupation*	*Hrs/Wk Employed*	*Annual Income*	*Yrs Education*	*Children's Sex and Age*	*Domestic Labor Index*
MAIN/SECONDARY PROVIDER COUPLES								
4	Husband	33	Public Admin.	45	$39,000	18	boy 8	1.6
4	Wife	30	Secretary	40	$15,000	12	girl 6	
11	Husband	26	Law Clerk	40	$19,000	19	boy 4	1.8
11	Wife	25	Bookkeeper	20	$ 7,000	16	boy 1	
12	Husband	36	Mechanic	55	$40,000	14	boy 11	1.9
12	Wife	38	Teacher's Aide	30	$ 8,000	13	boy 9	
17	Husband	37	Admin/Tech	45	$48,000	22	boy 5	1.8
17	Wife	28	Teacher's Aide	20	$ 6,000	16	girl 4	
19	Husband	36	Law Clerk	45	$29,000	19	girl 10	1.7
19	Wife	36	Teacher's Aide	20	$ 4,000	12	boys 6, 3	
MAIN/SECONDARY PROVIDER COUPLES WITH FAILED ASPIRATIONS								
8	Husband	31	House Painter	50	$30,000	18	girl 5	2.4
8	Wife	34	Secretary	40	$13,000	13		
15	Husband	37	Utility Lineman	40	$34,000	13	boys 13, 8, 4, 3	2.0
15	Wife	33	In-Home Day Care	45	$10,000	13		
20	Husband	42	Elem. Teacher	50	$31,000	17	girl 9	2.3
20	Wife	42	Public Admin.	20	$ 5,000	25		

AMBIVALENT CO-PROVIDER COUPLES								
1	Husband	35	City Planner	40	$38,000	17	girls 8, 11	2.0
1	Wife	39	Office Manager	40	$23,600	14	boy 4	
2	Husband	33	H. S. Teacher	35	$41,000	26	girl 4	1.9
2	Wife	35	Education Admin.	40	$38,000	17	boy 3	
16	Husband	38	H. S. Teacher	40	$45,000	17	boys 8, 4	1.3
16	Wife	35	Registered Nurse	26	$29,000	16	girl 8	
AMBIVALENT CO-PROVIDER COUPLES WITH PAID OUTSIDE HELP								
13	Husband	37	Attorney	45	$40,000	19	boys 8, 5	1.8
13	Wife	36	Social Worker	40	$36,000	18		
14	Husband	35	Const. Laborer	45	$30,000	12	boys 14, 9, 2	2.2
14	Wife	34	Social Worker	40	$24,000	18		
CO-PROVIDER COUPLES								
3	Husband	38	Contractor	40	$30,000	16	boy 12	2.6
3	Wife	37	Public. Admin.	50	$36,000	16	girl 9	
5	Husband	36	Mail Carrier	40	$29,000	12	boys 13,7	2.4
5	Wife	36	Exec. Secretary	40	$19,000			
6	Husband	36	Educ. Outreach	50	$29,000	16	girls 12, 10	2.5
6	Wife	34	Exec. Secretary	40	$22,000	12	boy 13	
7	Husband	36	Public. Admin.	50	$25,000	16	girls 7, 6, 1	2.7
7	Wife	35	Exec. Secretary	45	$19,000	15	boy 8	
9	Husband	34	Public Admin.	55	$40,000	16	boy 4	2.5
9	Wife	33	Clerk	40	$21,000	14	girl 2	
10	Husband	35	Engin. Technician	40	$27,000	14	boy 7	2.6
10	Wife	36	Engin. Technician	40	$27,000	15		
18	Husband	43	Public Admin.	40	$34,000	16	boy 6	2.3
18	Wife	40	Preschool Teacher	40	$22,000	17		

of the couples had at least one child in the family who was 5 years old or younger, but only four couples had youngest children under 3 years old. Thus, the sample consists of couples with multiple children of preschool and school age, with few infants or older teenagers.

Fifteen of the couples lived in suburban communities of southern California, and five in rural communities of the same region. Just one of the husbands and four of the wives spent some time growing up in Mexico; the rest were born and raised in the United States. Although most currently considered themselves to be middle class, the vast majority came from working-class backgrounds. Of the 40 husbands and wives interviewed, none had a parent with more than a high school education, and the average educational attainment of the parents was eighth grade. Most of the informants' fathers worked in menial jobs in agriculture or construction. Roughly half of informants' mothers were employed at least seasonally, most in low-paying agricultural jobs. Over 90% of informants identified their current religion as Catholic, and most reported that they went to church at least monthly.

All husbands and 14 wives were employed at least 35 hours per week, and 6 wives spent 20-30 hours per week on the job. Unlike their own parents and Latinos in general, the informants were relatively well educated: 15 husbands and 9 wives had at least a B.A. degree; 3 husbands and 7 wives had attended some college; and just 2 husbands and 4 wives had only a high school diploma. In contrast, 78% of all U.S. Hispanics in dual-earner couples had a high school education or less at about the time of the interviews (U.S. Bureau of the Census, 1989). Annual family incomes for the sample families ranged from $26,000 to $79,000, with a median of $53,400, well above the national median for Hispanic dual-earner families of $32,185 (U.S. Bureau of the Census, 1989). Individual incomes also varied widely: from $4,000 to $48,000. Ninety-five percent of the men, but only 25% of the women earned at least $25,000 per year. Five husbands were employed in blue-collar jobs such as painter, laborer, and mechanic; 11 in semiprofessional white-collar jobs such as teacher, administrator, or technician; and 4 in more prestigious professional jobs such as lawyer or agency director. Six wives were employed in low-status, low-paying jobs such as teacher's aide or day care provider; eight worked in skilled female-dominated jobs including secretary, bookkeeper, and clerk; and six wives had a professional or semiprofessional career as a social worker, teacher, administrator, nurse, or technician.

Comparison to Previous Research

Our sample and method of data collection differ somewhat from the few previous studies of household labor or conjugal decision making in Chicano couples. We interviewed both husbands and wives in mostly middle-class southern California dual-earner families with children. In contrast, Zavella (1987) interviewed only working-class women cannery workers in northern California. Zinn (1980) and Ybarra (1982) focused primarily on employed and nonemployed wives in both middle-class and working-class Chicano families in New Mexico and central California, respectively. Hartzler and Franco (1985) used structured scales and inventories to study 25 Anglo and 25 Chicano families (class not specified) in New Mexico, and Williams (1990) used interviews to collect information from both husbands and wives in a sample of 75 stable working- and middle-class Texas Chicano couples.

Like Hartzler and Franco (1985), we collected structured data about the performance of specific household chores, but our instrument included three times as many tasks (see below). Others focused on broad issues of "conjugal role patterns" (Ybarra, 1982) or "role making" (Williams, 1988) assessed with just a few global survey items or by coding depth interviews. Like Williams (1988), we collected information from both husbands and wives and focused on relatively privileged working-class and middle-class Chicano couples. We chose not to sample both Anglo and Chicano couples as Hartzler and Franco (1985) did, because we felt that an explicitly comparative research design with a small unrepresentative sample might be misleading. Our decision to focus only on Chicano couples with children, most of whom were broadly middle class, restricted the range of variation within our sample. This research strategy limited the number of potential exogenous variables we could consider and constrained our ability to make conclusions about relative levels of sharing in Chicano versus Anglo or in working-class versus middle-class families. Because making such comparisons based on snowball samples is risky at best, we were content with ensuring that our small sample had enough couples of various emergent "types" to describe some social processes and offer some theoretically informed generalizations. For grander theorizing, our results must be compared to other small studies with diverse samples or used for developing hypotheses to test on larger, more representative, populations.

Measuring Household Labor

We collected detailed data on housework and child care by asking each individual to sort stacks of cards listing various household and child care tasks. Husbands and wives separately indicated who had performed each of 64 tasks during the previous 2 weeks: (a) wife mostly or always, (b) wife more than husband, (c) husband and wife about equally, (d) husband more than wife, and (e) husband mostly or always. Following Smith and Reid's (1986) "strict criteria" for evaluating the extent of sharing in dual-earner couples (pp. 72-74), we computed a mean husband-wife score for each task and considered scores in the 2.5-3.5 range to be shared. The 64 tasks were grouped into six major areas: (a) housecleaning (vacuum, mop, sweep, dust, clean bathroom sinks, clean toilets, clean tub/showers, make beds, pick up toys, tidy living room, hang up clothes, take out trash, clean porch, wash windows, and spring cleaning), (b) meals (plan menus, shop for food, put food away, make breakfast, make lunch, cook dinner, prepare snacks, bake, wash dishes, put dishes away, and wipe kitchen counters), (c) clothes care (laundry, hand laundry, ironing, shoe care, sewing, and buy clothes), (d) home maintenance (inside repairs, interior painting, exterior painting, redecorate, wash car, maintain car, automotive repairs, maintain yard, water, mow lawns, garden, and external house maintenance), (e) finances and home management (bills, taxes, insurance, investments, major purchases, run errands, plan couple dates, and write/phone relatives and friends), and (f) child care (awaken, help dress, bathe, put to bed, supervise, discipline, drive, take to doctor, care for when sick, arrange baby-sitting, play with, and go on outings with).

For the following analysis, we combined the first three areas, housecleaning, meals, and clothes, into an additive 32-item index and refer to these activities as housework. When we discuss the sharing of child care, we refer to scores for the 12-item Child Care Index. In order to focus on the extent to which husbands share in the most time-consuming and repetitive household tasks, which are also conventionally performed by wives, we combined all housecleaning items except trash and porch, and all meals, clothes, and child care items to produce a 42-item Domestic Labor Index. Domestic Labor Index scores are listed for each couple in Table 8.1 and discussed below. Scores lower than 1.5 indicate that wives always perform the associated domestic tasks; scores between 1.5 and 2.5 indicate that wives perform the tasks more than husbands; and scores between 2.5 and 3.5 indicate that the tasks are relatively evenly shared.

Findings

The results of the interviews and card sorts showed that wives were primarily responsible for housecleaning, clothes, meals, and child care; husbands were primarily responsible for home maintenance; and finances/home management tended to be shared. These results are not surprising. Similar to findings on dual-earner Anglo couples, these dual-earner Chicano couples shared more child care tasks than housework tasks, but divisions of household labor still conformed to conventional expectations.

The families we interviewed did not conceive of themselves as having chosen to become two-job families. Like the dual-earner couples in some previous studies (Hood, 1983), our informants reported that they were simply responding to financial necessity. Although all husbands and almost three fourths of wives were employed full-time, the couples varied in the extent to which they accepted the wife as a permanent co-provider. By considering the employment and earnings of each spouse, along with each spouse's attitudes toward the provider and homemaker roles, we divided the 20 families into two general groups: main/secondary providers and co-providers (see Hood, 1986). In analyzing the couples' divisions of market and household labor, we further subdivided the two groups. Main/secondary provider couples were isolated for special analysis if the husband's career aspirations were unfulfilled. Co-provider households were divided into those who relied on paid household help, those who were ambivalent co-providers, and those who were full co-providers (Table 8.1 lists the sample families according to these five categories). We focus on the division of family labor in each of these groups below.

Main/Secondary Providers

In 8 of 20 families (40%), husbands made substantially more money than wives and assumed that men should be the primary breadwinner and women should be responsible for home and children. Such families were categorized as main/secondary providers because they generally considered the wife's job to be secondary and treated her income as "extra" money to be earmarked for special purposes (Hood, 1986). The eight main/secondary provider couples included all five wives who were employed part-time and three wives who worked in low-status full-time jobs. Wives in these families made substantially less than their husband, contributing an average of 20% to the total family income. In main/secondary provider households, wives typically took pride in the homemaker role and readily accepted responsibility for managing the household. This often meant limiting their employment to a part-time job so that the women could be home when their children were home.

Most wives in main/secondary provider households talked about their husband creating domestic work rather than lessening it. In general, secondary provider wives not only performed virtually all housework and child care, but both spouses accepted this as "natural" or "normal." The wife's commitment to outside employment was generally limited, and her income was considered supplementary rather than primary. Main provider husbands felt that financial support was their main responsibility and often made light of their wife's contribution to the family income. Similarly, secondary provider wives made light of their husband's child care or housework, and both spouses referred to his domestic contributions as "helping out." In their talk about who did what around the house, and in their sorting of the household task cards, main provider husbands took much more credit for their housework than their wife was willing to grant them (Valdez & Coltrane, 1993). Nevertheless, when we averaged husbands' and wives' ratings, we still arrived at scores indicating wives did most of the housework and child care. The first five main/secondary couples listed in Table 8.1 had Domestic Labor scores ranging from 1.6 to 1.9, with an average of 1.7. A score of 1.5 would mean that wives "mostly or always" performed all 42 chores that make up the Household Labor Index. Thus we find that main provider husbands with secondary provider wives in this sample contributed little to housework and child care.

The Impact of Failed Aspirations

Three main provider husbands with unfulfilled career goals tended to share more domestic labor than the others. One, a house painter with 6 years of college, wished he was doing something more "worthwhile" and was encouraged by his wife to change occupations. Another made good money working as a telephone line worker, but regretted dropping out of school and was told by his wife that he should go to college and make more of himself. The third husband in this category was a successful elementary school teacher, but his real love was art, and he and his wife openly lamented that he was not pursuing his true calling. Like the other main provider husbands, these three husbands earned substantially more money than their wife. Even though the three men earned over $30,000 per year, and their wife contributed an average of just 22% to family earnings, the fact that these men had failed career goals altered negotiations over household labor. Whereas other main provider husbands were able to minimize contributions to housework by claiming they were tired from long hours on the job, the three husbands with unfulfilled career goals were not able to use their outside job as an excuse to avoid family work. Whereas other main provider husbands were able to claim incompetence for tasks like laundry or cooking, the husbands with failed aspirations were pressed by their wife to learn the necessary domestic skills. Because they were not fulfilling their "true potential," the failed aspirations husbands were not able to translate their superior earnings into avoiding mundane household chores.

Whereas the first five main provider couples listed in Table 8.1 had an average Domestic Labor Index score of 1.7, the three main provider husbands with failed career aspirations had an average Domestic Labor score over 2.2 (see Table 8.1). Although wives in failed aspirations couples were more likely than husbands to perform stereotypical "feminine" household tasks, both husbands and wives rated the husbands' contributions as coming much closer to equal sharing.

Most secondary provider wives, regardless of their husband's perceived level of success at fulfilling career goals, reported that they received little help unless they "constantly" reminded their husband to contribute to housework or child care. When main provider husbands assumed some domestic chores in response to "necessity" or "nagging," they clung to the idea that it was not their responsibility. According to their accounts, this seemed to justify their resentment at having to do "her" chores. What generally kept a wife from resenting her husband's reluctance was her acceptance of the homemaker role and appreciation for his substantial financial contributions. When performance of the provider role was deemed to be lacking in some way—for example, failed aspirations or low occupational prestige—wives' resentment appeared closer to the surface and couples reported that she was more persistent in demanding his help.

Co-Provider Couples

Based on an evaluation of their employment, earnings, and ideology, we classified the remaining 12 families in our sample as co-providers. Compared to main/secondary provider couples, co-providers tended to have more equal earnings and to value the wife's employment more highly. Among the 12 co-provider couples, wives averaged 44% of the family income as compared to 20% for the 8 main/secondary provider couples. There was considerable variation among co-provider husbands, however, in terms of their willingness to accept their wife as an equal provider or to assume the role of equal homemaker. Accordingly, we divided these families into ambivalent co-providers (five couples) and co-providers (seven couples). The ambivalent co-provider husbands accepted their wife's job as important and permanent (Hood, 1986), but often used their own job commitments as justifications for doing little at home. We discuss each group in turn, considering variation between subgroups in terms of earnings, job status, ideology, role attachments, and divisions of household labor.

Ambivalent Co-Providers

Compared to their wife, ambivalent co-provider husbands usually held jobs that were roughly equivalent in terms of occupational prestige and worked about the same number of hours per week. All of these husbands earned more than their wife, however, with husbands' average annual earnings of $39,000, compared to the wives' average of $30,000. Although both husbands and wives thus had careers that provided "comfortable" incomes, the husbands, and sometimes the wives, were ambivalent about treating her career as equally important to his. For example, few ambivalent co-provider husbands let their family work intrude on their paid work, whereas wives' family work often interfered with their paid work. Such asymmetrically permeable work-family boundaries (Pleck, 1977) are common in single-earner and main/secondary provider families, but must be supported with subtle ideologies and elaborate justifications when husbands and wives hold similar occupational positions.

Ambivalent co-provider husbands remained in a helper role at home, perceiving their wife to be a more involved parent and assuming that housework was also their wife's responsibility. Husbands used their breadwinner responsibilities to justify their absence, but most lamented not being able to spend more time with their family. For instance, one husband who worked full-time as a city planner was married to a woman who worked an equal number of hours as an office manager. In talking about the time he puts in at his job, he commented, "I wish I had more time to spend with my children, and to spend with my wife too, of course, but it's a fact of life that I have to work." His wife, in contrast, indicated that her paid job, which she had held for 14 years, did not prohibit her from adequately caring for her three children, nor from taking care of "her" household chores. With an average Domestic Labor Index score of 1.8, ambivalent co-provider husbands did not perform significantly more housework and child care than main provider husbands, and generally did fewer household chores than main provider husbands with failed career aspirations (see Table 8.1).

Two of the five ambivalent co-provider couples attempted to alleviate stress on the woman by hiring outside help. For example, a self-employed male attorney making $40,000 per year finally agreed with his social worker wife that they should hire a housekeeper to help with "her" chores. Another couple paid a live-in baby-sitter/housekeeper to watch their three children during the day while he worked full-time in construction and she worked full-time as a psychiatric social worker. Although she labeled the outside help as "essential," she also noted that her husband contributed more mess than he cleaned up. He saw himself as an involved father because he played with his children, and although she acknowledged his role, she also complained that he competed with them in games as if he were a child himself. His participation in routine household labor was considered optional and he tended to select where and when he would contribute, usually focusing on the fun activities. Only one other family—Couple 3—talked about paying for household help. This co-provider couple, as described below, hired a gardener to do some of "his" chores, freeing him to do more child care and housework. This strategy reflects an assumption that the husband "should" share in family work, an assumption that main provider and ambivalent co-provider husbands did not willingly embrace.

Co-Provider Couples

Unlike the ambivalent co-providers discussed above, the seven true co-provider couples fully accepted the wife's employment and considered her career to be just as important as his. Like the ambivalent couples, co-provider spouses each worked about the same number of hours, but on the whole, these couples worked more total hours than their more ambivalent counterparts. The mean total amount of time per week that couples spent in paid labor for the ambivalent group was 78 hours and for the co-provider group, 87 hours. Co-providers also tended to have lower incomes. Men's average annual income for this group was

$30,000—$9,000 less than for the ambivalent group. Similarly, co-provider wives' incomes averaged $24,000, or $6,000 less than for wives in the more ambivalent co-provider families. Nevertheless, the average percentage income contribution from wives was similar in both groups: 43%-44%.

The sharing of housework and child care was substantially greater for co-providers (mean Domestic Labor Index score = 2.5) than for main/secondary providers (mean = 1.7), main providers with failed aspirations (mean = 2.2), or ambivalent co-providers (mean = 1.8) (see Table 8.1). No co-provider couple had a mean Domestic Labor Index score over 3.0—the true midpoint of the index—but five of the seven families had mean husband-wife scores of 2.5 or higher, indicating substantial sharing of these tasks. Because husbands often take more credit for family work than their wives grant them, we also analyzed husbands' contributions to domestic chores using only the wife's ratings (results not shown). Six of seven co-provider wives rated their husband over 2.5 for child care tasks, and two of these wives rated husbands over 2.5 for housework tasks as well. The co-provider families thus represent the most egalitarian families in this sample. On the following pages we investigate how similar or different these families are from the others and discuss some of the factors that the couples identified as reasons for their allocation of household labor.

Like the more ambivalent co-providers, husbands in these families discussed conflicts between work and family and sometimes alluded to their occupational advancement being limited by their commitments to their children. Nevertheless, co-provider husbands were less likely to use paid work as an excuse to avoid child care or housework. Comparable occupational status and earnings, coupled with relatively egalitarian ideals, led to substantial sharing of both child care and housework among the co-providers. Although some co-provider wives complained that husbands wouldn't do certain chores or didn't always notice when things were dirty, they were generally appreciative of their husband's contributions.

Although co-provider husbands, like the other husbands, tended to take more credit for their involvement than their wife granted them, we observed a difference between their talk and that of the husbands discussed above. When other husbands complained about their wife's high standards, they treated housework, and even parenting, as primarily the wife's duty. Main provider husbands and ambivalent co-providers talked about resenting being "nagged" to do more around the house, and even when they reluctantly complied with their wife's requests, they rarely moved out of a helper role to consider it *their* duty to anticipate, schedule, and take care of family and household needs. In many co-provider households, however, that asymmetric allocation of responsibility was taken less for granted. Because of this, negotiations over housework and parenting were sometimes more frequent than in the other families. Because both held expectations that each would fulfill both provider and caretaker roles, resentments came from both spouses—not just from the wife.

Our data suggest that it might be easier for couples to share both provider and homemaker roles when the wife's earnings and occupational prestige equal or exceed her husband's. For instance, in one of the co-provider couples reporting the most sharing of child care and housework, the wife earned $36,000 annually as a management consultant and director of a nonprofit organization, and her husband earned $30,000 as a self-employed contractor. According to both spouses, they shared most of the housework. What differentiates this couple from most others is that the wife made more money than the husband and had no qualms about demanding help from him. Not yet accepting the idea that interior chores were equally his, he reluctantly performed them. In the card sorts, she ranked his contributions to child care to be equal to hers and rated his contributions to housework only slightly below her own. Even though the husband did not eagerly rush to do the cooking, cleaning, or laundry, he nonetheless complied with her frequent reminders. The power dynamic in this family, coupled with their willingness to pay for outside help to reduce "his" yard work, and the flexibility of his self-employed work schedule, led to substantial sharing of domestic labor. Because she was making more money and working more hours than he was, he was unable to claim priority for his provider activities.

A similar dynamic was evident in other co-provider couples with comparable earnings and career commitments. Even when wives' earnings did not exceed husbands', some co-providers shared the homemaker role. A male college admissions recruiter and his executive secretary wife shared substantial housework according to mutual ratings and most child care according to her rating. He made $29,000 per year working an average of 50 hours per week; she made $22,000 working a 40-hour week (see Couple 6 in Table 8.1). Like some other co-providers, this wife was willing to give her husband more credit than he claimed for child care. Like all of the men in this study, however, he was reluctant to perform many housecleaning chores and took more credit for housework than she granted him. Like many of the co-provider husbands, however, he had redefined many routine housework chores as shared responsibilities. When asked what he liked least about housework, he laughingly replied, "Probably those damn toilets, man, and the showers, the bathrooms; gotta scrub 'em, argghh! I wish I didn't have to do any of that, you know, the vacuuming and all that, but it's just a fact of life."

Although secondary provider wives and ambivalent co-provider wives assumed that men were incapable of performing many domestic chores and allowed them to use their job as an excuse for doing less family work, co-provider wives did not accept such excuses. Like the wives of main providers with failed aspirations, co-provider wives rejected the assumption that all the housework was naturally "woman's work," and some refused to do certain chores. Hood (1983) describes this strategy as "going on strike," and suggests that it is most effective when husbands feel the specific task *must* be done (p. 131). As appearing neat and well dressed was a priority for one husband, when his wife stopped ironing his clothes, he started doing it himself. Because he felt it was important for his children to be "presentable" in public, he also began to remind them to iron their own clothes before going visiting or attending church. Ironing has *not* been identified as one of the tasks performed frequently by husbands in other studies. In our study, ironing was one of the only housekeeping tasks that a majority of both wives and husbands indicated was shared. High levels of church attendance among Chicanos and the symbolic importance of being well dressed in public probably makes Chicano men more likely than Anglo men to share the ironing.

Although some co-provider couples reported overt ongoing contentious struggles over housework, other co-providers claimed that their divisions of labor evolved "naturally." Such claims should not be taken to mean that these couples have not "negotiated" a division of household labor. Hood (1983) notes that because family processes involve chains of hundreds of little bargains over long periods of time, family patterns like household task divisions appear to "just happen" when in fact they have been subtly negotiated (p. 176).

Once co-provider spouses assume that household tasks are a shared responsibility, negotiation can become less necessary. For example, a co-provider husband who worked as a mail carrier commented, "I get home early and start dinner, make sure the kids do their homework, feed the dogs, stuff like that." He and his wife, an executive secretary, agreed that they rarely talk about housework. She said, "When I went back to work we agreed that we both needed to share, and so we just do it." Although she still reminded him to perform chores according to her standards or on her schedule, she summed up her appreciation by commenting, "At least he does it without complaining."

Although co-provider husbands were often reluctant contributors to housework, they were very involved with their children and bristled when friends or co-workers characterized their parenting efforts as "helping" the wife. Although most of the co-provider husbands were rated by their wife as performing almost half of the child care tasks, none of the main providers or ambivalent co-providers fell into this category. This is not to suggest that the other husbands did not love their children or interact with them on a regular basis. But there was something different about the way that co-providers characterized what they were doing as a decision to put their children's needs first. Main providers tended to use their job as excuse for spending little time with their children. Ambivalent co-providers lamented how children sometimes detracted from their careers. Co-provider husbands, on the other hand, even though they were employed at least as many hours as the others, talked about making a definite choice to spend time with and care for their children.

Discussion

Our interviews with dual-earner Chicano couples revealed considerable sharing in several areas. First, as in previous studies of ethnic minority families, wives were employed a substantial number of hours and made significant contributions to household income. Second, like Hawkes and Taylor (1975), V. Cromwell and R. Cromwell (1978), and Ybarra (1982), we found that couples described their decision making as relatively fair and equal. Third, fathers in these families were more involved in child rearing than their own fathers had been, and 7 of 20 husbands were rated as sharing most child care tasks. Finally, although no husband performed fully half of the housework, a few made substantial contributions in this area as well.

One of the power dynamics that appears to undergird the household division of labor in these families is the relative earning power of each spouse, though this is modified by occupational prestige, provider role status, and personal preference. In 40% of the families, the wife earned less than a third of the family income, and in all of these families the husband performed little of the routine housework or child care. In two families, wives earned more than their husband and shared much of the domestic labor with him. Among other couples sharing significant amounts of housework and child care, a preponderance had relatively balanced incomes. In two families with large financial contributions from wives but little household help from husbands, couples hired housekeepers to reduce the total household work load.

Although relative income makes a difference, we are not suggesting a simple or straightforward exchange of market resources for domestic services. Other factors like failed career aspirations or occupational status differentials influenced resource/power dynamics and helped us understand why some wives were willing to push a little harder for change in the division of household labor. In most cases, husbands responded reluctantly to requests for help. Only when wives actively demanded help did some of the day-to-day burden of housework begin to shift toward husbands. Even when they shared housework and child care, men tended to do more pleasant tasks like playing with the children or putting clean dishes away. Comparing these men to their fathers and their wives' fathers, we can see that they are sharing more domestic chores than the generation of parents that preceded them.

Even when wives made much less money than their husband, if they expected husbands to "make more" of themselves, pursue "more important" careers, or follow "dream" occupational goals, then they were able to get them to do more around the house. This perception of failed aspirations, if held by both spouses, served as a reminder that husbands had no excuse for not helping out at home. In these families, wives were not at all reluctant to demand assistance with domestic chores, and husbands were rarely able to use their job as excuse for getting out of housework. When husbands accepted wives as co-providers, either because of her earnings and job status, or because of his own failings, the division of household labor was more symmetrical. Similarly, when wives relinquished a portion of the homemaker role by delegating duties to husbands, household labor allocation became more balanced. If wives made lists for their husbands or offered them frequent reminders, they were more successful than if they waited for husbands to take the initiative. Even when they received help, however, remaining responsible for managing home and children was cause for resentment on the part of many wives.

Over a third of the families we interviewed exhibited divisions of household labor that contradicted cultural stereotypes of male-dominated Chicano families. Particularly salient in these families was the lack of fit between their own class position and their parents'. Most of the parents were immigrants with little education and low occupational mobility. The couples we interviewed, in contrast, were well educated and relatively secure in middle-class occupations. Although the couples could have compared themselves to their parents, evaluating themselves to be egalitarian and financially successful, most compared themselves to their Anglo and Chicano friends and co-workers. These social comparisons occasionally motivated both husbands and wives to negotiate further changes in the household division of labor, in part because their referents were perceived as more egalitarian than themselves. Still, there was no absolute or fixed standard against which the couples were making judgments. Rather, implicitly comparing their earnings, occupational commitments, and perceived aptitudes to those of their spouse, these individuals negotiated new patterns of work-family boundaries and developed new justifications for their emerging arrangements. These were not created anew, but emerged out of the popular culture in which they found themselves. Judith Stacey (1990) labels such developments the making of the "postmodern family," because they signal "the contested, ambivalent, and undecided character of contemporary gender and kinship arrangements" (p. 17). Our findings confirm that families are an important site of new struggles over the meaning of gender and the rights and obligations of men and women to each other and over each other's labor (Hartmann, 1981). Overt and covert negotiations over who should do what in the home also suggest that some subtle shifts may be under way.

Because we sampled only parents with school-aged children and used more detailed measures of housework and child care than previous researchers studying Chicano families, it is difficult to compare our results directly to previous findings. The extent of sharing we uncovered, particularly for child care, contradicts monocausal analyses that depict Latino households as patriarchal (e.g., Lewis, 1960; Madsen, 1973) and supports Mirandé's (1988) suggestion that Chicano fathers are relatively involved in their families. Nevertheless, with fathers doing so much less than mothers, our findings also contradict the notion that Chicano families are essentially egalitarian (V. Cromwell & R. Cromwell, 1978; Hawkes & Taylor, 1975; Ybarra, 1982). Like Zinn

(1980), Williams (1988), and Zavella (1987), we found that gender is the primary axis of labor allocation in Chicano families, but that Chicanas actively struggle against oppressive assumptions about their duty to perform all domestic labor. Like these researchers, we found that when Chicanas are employed, their bargaining power can increase, but that the simple fact of employment is not sufficient to bring about changes in the domestic division of labor. We did find that Chicana wives who had more income, were employed more hours, and whose occupation was comparable in status to that of their husband, were the most likely to be considered co-providers and demand help with domestic chores.

One of our most interesting findings has to do with the class position of Chicano husbands and wives who shared domestic labor. The white-collar working-class families shared more than the upper-middle-class professionals. Contrary to findings from nationwide surveys predicting that higher levels of education for either husbands or wives will be associated with more sharing (Ross, 1987), the most highly educated of our well-educated sample of Chicano couples shared only moderate amounts of child care and little housework. Contrary to predictions from Zavella (1987), Stacey (1990), and others, neither was it the working-class women in this study who achieved the most sharing. It was in the middle group, the executive secretaries, clerks, technicians, teachers, and midlevel administrators who extracted the most help from husbands. Their husbands were similarly in the middle in terms of occupational status for this sample—administrative assistants, a builder, a mail carrier, a technician—and in the middle in income. What this means is that the highest status wives—the program coordinators, nurses, social workers, and office managers—were not able, or chose not to transform salaries or occupational status into more participation from husbands. This was probably because their husbands had even higher incomes and more prestigious occupations. The lawyers, program directors, ranking bureaucrats, and "community leaders" parlayed their status into extra leisure at home, either by paying for housekeepers or ignoring the work. Finally, Chicana wives at the lowest end fared least well. The teacher's aides, entry-level secretaries, day care providers, and part-time employees did the bulk of the work at home whether they were married to mechanics or lawyers. When wives earned considerably less than their husbands, they were only able to enlist husbands' assistance if the men held jobs considered "below" them—a telephone line worker, a painter, an elementary school teacher.

In general, then, our analysis suggests that researchers must consider the education and occupational achievement of both husbands and wives simultaneously. Only by comparing incomes, occupational prestige, and ideology of both spouses can we understand how men and women assume provider role status and justify domestic divisions of labor. Focusing on wives alone, or husbands alone, gives us only half of the picture.

Although we studied only Chicano couples, our results are similar to most in-depth interview studies of Anglo couples (Hochschild, 1989; Hood, 1983). Our interpretation is that the major processes shaping divisions of labor in middle-class Chicano couples are similar to those shaping divisions of labor in other middle-class couples as well. That is not to say that ethnicity did not make a difference to the people we interviewed. They grew up in recently immigrating working-class families, watched their parents work long hours for minimal wages, and understood firsthand the toll that various forms of racial discrimination can take. Probably because of some of these experiences, and their own more recent ones, our informants looked at job security, fertility decisions, and the division of household labor somewhat differently than their Anglo counterparts. In some cases, this may give Chicano husbands in working-class or professional jobs license to ignore more of the housework and might temper the anger of some working-class or professional Chicanas who are still called on to do most of the domestic chores. If our findings are generalizable, however, it is couples in between the blue-collar working class and the upper-middle-class professionals that might be more likely to share housework and child care.

Assessing whether our findings apply to other dual-earner Chicano couples will require the use of larger, more representative samples. If the limited sharing we observed represents a trend—however slow or reluctant—it could have far-reaching consequences. More and more Chicana mothers are remaining full-time members of the paid labor force. With the "postindustrial" expansion of the service and information sectors of the economy, more and more Chicanos and Chicanas will enter white-collar working-class occupations. As more Chicano families fit the occupational profile of those we studied, we may see more assumption of housework and child care by Chicano husbands.

References

Becker, G. (1981). *A treatise on the family.* Cambridge, MA: Harvard University Press.

Berk, S. (1985). *The gender factory.* New York: Plenum.

Biernacki, P., & Waldorf, D. (1981). Snowball sampling. *Sociological Methods and Research, 10,* 141-163.
Collins, R. (1988). Women and men in the class structure. *Journal of Family Issues, 9,* 27-50.
Coltrane, S. (1988). Father-child relationships and the status of women. *American Journal of Sociology, 93,* 1060-1095.
Coltrane, S. (1989). Household labor and the routine production of gender. *Social Problems, 36,* 473-490.
Coltrane, S., & Valdez, E. (1991, April). *Not seeing is believing.* Paper presented at the Pacific Sociological Association Annual Meetings, Irvine, CA.
Cowan, C., Cowan, P., Heming, G., Garrett, E., Coysh, W., Curtis-Boles, H., & Boles, A. (1985). Transitions to parenthood: His, hers, and theirs. *Journal of Family Issues, 6,* 451-482.
Cromwell, V., & Cromwell, R. (1978). Perceived dominance in decision-making and conflict resolution among Anglo, Black, and Chicano couples. *Journal of Marriage and the Family, 40,* 749-760.
Glaser, B., & Strauss, A. (1967). *The discovery of grounded theory.* New York: Aldine.
Goodnow, J. (1988). Children's household work. *Psychological Bulletin, 103,* 5-26.
Haas, L. (1981). Domestic role-sharing in Sweden. *Journal of Marriage and the Family, 43,* 957-965.
Hartmann, H. (1981). The family as the locus of gender, class, and political struggle. *Signs, 6,* 366-394.
Hartzler, K., & Franco, J. (1985). Ethnicity, division of household tasks and equity in marital roles. *Hispanic Journal of Behavioral Sciences, 7,* 333-344.
Hawkes, G., & Taylor, M. (1975). Power structure in Mexican and Mexican-American farm labor families. *Journal of Marriage and the Family, 37,* 807-811.
Hochschild, A. (1989). *The second shift.* New York: Viking.
Hood, J. (1983). *Becoming a two-job family.* New York: Praeger.
Hood, J. (1986). The provider role: Its meaning and measurement. *Journal of Marriage and the Family, 48,* 349-359.
LaRossa, R., & LaRossa, M. (1981). *Transition to parenthood.* Beverly Hills, CA: Sage.
Lewis, O. (1960). *Tepoztlan.* New York: Holt, Rinehart & Winston.
Madsen, W. (1973). *Mexican-Americans of South Texas* (2nd ed.). New York: Holt, Rinehart & Winston. (Originally published 1964)
Mirandé, A. (1988). Chicano fathers: Traditional perceptions and current realities. In P. Bronstein & C. Cowan (Eds.), *Fatherhood today* (pp. 93-106). New York: John Wiley.
Pleck, J. (1977). The work-family role system. *Social Problems, 24,* 417-427.
Rapoport, R., & Rapoport, R. (1971). *Dual career families.* Baltimore: Penguin.
Rexroat, C., & Shehan, C. (1987). The family cycle and spouses' time in housework. *Journal of Marriage and the Family, 49,* 737-750.
Ross, C. (1987). The division of labor at home. *Social Forces, 65,* 816-833.
Ruiz, V. (1987). *Cannery women/cannery lives.* Albuquerque: University of New Mexico Press.
Segura, D. (1984). Labor market stratification: The Chicana experience. *Berkeley Journal of Sociology, 29,* 57-91.
Smith, A., & Reid, W. (1986). *Role-sharing marriage.* New York: Columbia University Press.
Stacey, J. (1990). *Brave new families.* New York: Basic Books.

U.S. Bureau of the Census. (1989). *Current Population Reports* (Series P-20, No. 431). Washington, DC: U.S. Government Printing Office.

Valdez, E., & Coltrane, S. (1993). Work, family, and the Chicana. In J. Frankel (Ed.), *Employed mothers and the family context* (pp. 153-179). New York: Springer.

Vega, W. (1990). Hispanic families in the 1980s. *Journal of Marriage and the Family, 52,* 1015-1024.

Williams, N. (1988). Role making among married Mexican-American women. *Journal of Applied Behavioral Science, 24,* 203-217.

Williams, N. (1990). *The Mexican American family.* New York: General Hall.

Ybarra, L. (1982). When wives work: The impact on the Chicano family. *Journal of Marriage and the Family, 44,* 169-178.

Zavella, P. (1987). *Women's work and Chicano families.* Ithaca, NY: Cornell University Press.

Zinn, M. B. (1980). Employment and education of Mexican-American women. *Harvard Educational Review, 50,* 47-62.

Zinn M. B. (1982, Summer). Qualitative methods in family research. *California Sociologist,* 58-79.

Zinn, M. B. (1990). Family, feminism, and race in America. *Gender and Society, 4,* 68-82.

9

Balancing Work and Single Fatherhood

GEOFFREY L. GREIF
ALFRED DEMARIS
JANE C. HOOD

Increasingly fathers have found themselves trying to balance the demands of raising children alone while working outside of the home. The number of single custodial fathers in the United States (defined here as fathers who have primary responsibility for the children a majority of the time) raising at least one child under 18 has grown from 393,000 in 1970 to 1,351,000 in 1990. During the same period, the proportion of fathers grew from 10% to 14% of all single parents (U.S. Bureau of the Census, 1990).

In spite of these changes, researchers have paid little attention to how single fathers manage the competing demands of work and family (Hansen, 1991). Further, there are hardly any systematic comparisons of the kinds of work-family problems faced by single fathers as opposed to single mothers. The few studies that do compare male and female single parents' problems in combining work and family find that women generally have a harder time than men due to lower incomes and less flexible lower status jobs (Burden, 1986). However, because single-parent men are less likely than women to have been primary caretakers before the separation, men may have to make more changes in their work patterns and may be more likely to find these changes problematic than will women who combined full-time work and child care while married. Bosses and co-workers unsympathetic to men's parenting needs (Keshet & Rosenthal, 1976; Pleck, this volume) will make the transition to single fatherhood even more difficult. If work problems affect the amount and quality of attention a father gives his children, we could expect work-family conflicts to decrease the quality of men's relationships with their children. This chapter follows a causal chain from custody through work-family conflicts and work changes to parenting relationships.

Literature Review

Research on families headed by single fathers has focused almost exclusively on the employed middle- and upper-middle-income father. Early studies documented the difficulties fathers have in managing the competing demands of work and child care. Keshet and Rosenthal (1976) found that nearly two thirds of their sample of 49 fathers reported being hampered in the number of hours they could give to their work, the type of work assignments they could accept, and the priority they could give to work over other aspects of life. Earnings suffered for slightly over half of the fathers, as did their ability to accept job transfers. In addition, one out of five fathers reported that relationships with co-workers and bosses suffered.

From interviews with 32 fathers, Mendes (1976) learned of a number who, in order to facilitate child care, had changed their job or had children change schools to be closer to the father's place of work. Fathers who hired day care providers to come to their home were less satisfied than those who used out-of-home supervision. Both high turnover and the belief that in-home caretakers were not as competent contributed to this dissatisfaction. One father reportedly quit his job and became a welfare recipient so that he could provide day care for his young children.

Chang and Deinard's (1982) survey of 80 single fathers asked respondents to compare the difficulties of handling a variety of family-related tasks. Finding time for work was ranked as one of the most difficult. Lack of employment flexibility and interference with job performance was a problem for nearly one third of the fathers. In spite of difficulties reported by many fathers, other research using small samples has found the fathers to be well adjusted in a variety of areas related to single parenting (Nieto, 1990; Orthner, Brown, & Ferguson, 1976). In addition, researchers have found that fathers with college educations have a special advantage because they are more able than other workers to reduce their work hours so that they can arrange their parenting responsibilities (Facchino & Aron, 1990).

National sample research is limited to two surveys (N = 1136 and 1135) of single-parent fathers (Greif, 1985, 1990; Greif & DeMaris, 1990). The data for this chapter come from the second of these two surveys. Both samples were drawn primarily from the membership of Parents Without Partners, the largest self-help organization for single parents in the United States. The second sample also included respondents drawn from court records in three East Coast locations.

In previous analyses of the 1987 survey data, Greif (1990) found that over three quarters of his respondents had experienced at least one job change as a result of gaining sole custody. Arriving late or leaving work early because of child care related demands was the most frequently reported change (by 39% of the fathers). Missing work altogether because of these demands was also common. Other kinds of adjustments included reducing work-related travel, assuming a flextime schedule, bringing work home, and taking on an additional job to make ends meet. One out of 14 fathers reported quitting, and 1 in 20 reported being fired as a result of his sole-parenting responsibilities. A longitudinal examination of 28 fathers who had participated in earlier research revealed no significant changes in the difficulty of work over a 3-year period spanning, on average, 4 to 7 years after the father gained custody (Greif, 1987).

In-depth interviews provided qualitative illustrations of Greif's survey findings. For instance, some fathers benefited from their ex-wife's continued involvement in their life by receiving assistance with child care that then gave the fathers more job flexibility. Other fathers experienced the mother's involvement as interference, when, for example, they received harassing phone calls at work from their ex-wife (Greif, 1990). In addition, fathers had to make psychological adjustments related to their job. Some suffered because child care demands impeded their progress at work. Yet others flourished after being removed from the pressures of competition in the workplace. For this second group, having an attractive alternative to focusing on work, that is, taking care of their children, helped them make what they considered a healthy transition to a more child-centered life-style (Greif, 1990).

This chapter uses the same 1987 survey data to answer the following three questions:

1. What contributes to the ease or difficulty single-parent men encounter when attempting to combine work and family?

2. How does social status condition single fathers' work-family relationships?
3. Do difficulties with work scheduling, day care, overtime work demands, and so on adversely affect the quality of single fathers' relationships with their children?

Because the data were not intended for a detailed analysis of work and family, they lack the specificity that would allow us to look at effects of given occupations, work settings, or workplace policies on different types of work-family role strain. For example, working afternoon or night shifts can be particularly difficult for parents of school-aged children (Hood & Milazzo, 1984; Staines & Pleck, 1983). However, because these data include no information on work schedules, we must infer work schedules from what we know about given occupational categories. Nonetheless, findings from one of the largest data sets of custodial fathers should provide fruitful suggestions for studies that do focus more specifically on work-family links. Because the data come from a diverse sample of fathers, relationships unearthed in this analysis may serve as better guidelines for further research than those based on smaller, more specialized samples.

Methodology

The data presented in this chapter come from a 4-page, 104-item questionnaire published October 1987 in *The Single Parent,* the membership magazine of Parents Without Partners (PWP). PWP had more than 160,000 members at the time the survey was published. Fathers raising children 18 and younger a majority of the time were asked to complete the instrument and fold it into a postage-guaranteed envelope for mailing. Although exact return rates are difficult to calculate, we estimate that the rate was approximately 20%. Questionnaires were also mailed to fathers whose names we obtained from court records in the Baltimore; Washington, D.C.; and Philadelphia areas. Because we believed that those with less custody had an arrangement that more closely resembled joint custody, the survey included only fathers with sole custody at least 5 nights a week. The final sample from these procedures totalled 1,132, 18% of whom came from the court systems.

One weakness of this approach was that it only surveyed members of a self-help group or those who chose to respond to a questionnaire mailed to them because their name appeared in court records. Further, we have no independent measures and must rely solely on the father's report of his situation. In contrast to past research on this population though, the sample's size and heterogeneity have produced a data set large enough to justify the use of multivariate statistical analysis. (For further details on methodology, see Greif, 1990.)

The Sample

The average age of this sample of fathers was 40.8. Their marriage had lasted an average of 12 years, and they had had sole custody for about 4 years. At the time of the survey, almost all of the fathers were divorced rather than separated. They were raising an average of 1.7 children 18 or younger with the oldest child aged 13.1. They were more likely to be raising only sons (42%), as opposed to only daughters (27%), with the remainder raising both boys and girls.

Occupations ranged from professional to unskilled laborer, with nearly half of the sample describing themselves as professional or business people. The fathers had completed an average of 2 years of college and had a mean income of $33,400, with half the sample earning less than $30,000. By comparison, the mean income for white male householders (96% of these fathers were white) with no wife present was $26,247 in 1986 (U.S. Bureau of the Census, 1987).

Measures

In the first stage of this analysis we look at how parenting demands, resources, and workplace flexibility affect the ease with which the men combined work and family after obtaining custody. Independent variables include father's education, income, and occupation (10 categories) as SES measures; parenting demands measured by number and age of custodial children; parenting resources measured by age of father, preseparation experience as primary caretaker, social support, cooperation with ex-wife, and motivation to parent (as indicated by obtaining custody though court contest).

With the exception of social support, these variables are either continuous variables measured in exact numbers (age and income), ordinal categories (census occupational code), or nominal categories coded as 1/0 (primary caretaker was ex-wife; present conflict with ex-wife;

father obtained custody from court contest). We measured social support with a series of items asking the father, "Rate how supportive the following have been of your having custody." This question was followed by "your parents," "your in-laws," "your friends," "your co-workers," "your boss," "your neighbors," "the children's teachers," "your clergyman," "your ex-wife," and "your dates." Response choices were "very supportive," "somewhat supportive," and "not at all supportive." Additionally, we constructed an additive social support scale using the 10 items (with higher values indicating higher perceived levels of support from significant others). For some analyses, we separated "support at work" (support from bosses, co-workers, and friends) from familial support (parents, ex-wife, in-laws).[1]

Dependent variables include two work-family measures (number of job changes, difficulty in combining work and family) and an index measuring parental attitudes. These were measured as follows:

Job Changes. We measured adjustments in the work routine by asking fathers to identify which of the following job changes they had experienced as a result of being single parents: bringing work home, reducing travel, working flexible hours, having to miss work, arriving late or leaving early, taking on additional jobs, being fired, or quitting. To assess the cumulative effect of multiple changes on the difficulty of fulfilling both work and child care obligations, we created a variable representing the total number of such changes experienced.[2]

Difficulty in Combining Work and Child Care. To measure perceived difficulty in simultaneously fulfilling both work and child-rearing obligations, we asked: "How difficult has the combination of working and raising your children alone been for you?" Of the 1,102 fathers who responded to this item, 21.4% perceived this combination to be "very difficult," 61.8% said it was "somewhat difficult," and 16.8% considered it "not at all difficult."

Problematic Relationships. We measured the quality of the father's relationship with his children with the Index of Parental Attitudes (IPA), one of nine short-form scales that taken together make up the Clinical Measurement Package (Hudson, 1982). The scales in this package were designed to measure the severity of problems that people have in different areas. The IPA measures the severity of problems in parent-child relationships as perceived by the parent. The instrument consists of 25 statements such as "My child gets on my nerves," "I get along well with my child," and "I feel that I can really trust my child." Respondents indicate how frequently they experience these feelings toward a referent child or children, with responses ranging from "rarely or none of the time" to "most or all of the time." In this study, fathers were asked to complete this scale in reference to "the children living with you."

Scores on the IPA range from a low of 0 to a high of 100, with higher scores signifying more problematic relationships with children. Thirty is the clinical cutting point.[3]

Results

Easily Combining Work and Family

To find out what kinds of fathers composed the minority that found combining work and family relatively easy, we dichotomized the ease/difficulty measure and then used logistic regression to separate the effects of SES, parental demands, and parental resources on the ease of combining work and family. For this analysis, explanatory variables included father's age, annual income, the ages of his children (coded as all under 13, all over 13, or mixed), the number of children living with him, whether he had obtained custody through a court contest, which parent was most involved in child care in the year before the breakup (coded mother vs. father or both parents equally), the total number of job changes experienced, the present degree of conflict existing between the father and his ex-wife (on a scale from l—none to 4—a great deal), and his degree of social support for having custody. The results are shown in Table 9.1.

The coefficients listed under "Regression Coefficients" represent the impact of each predictor on the natural logarithm of the odds of giving the "not difficult" response. The second column of the table shows the impact of each predictor on the odds of giving the "not difficult" response, whereas the last column of the table indicates which predictors are significant. The last two rows of the table present the Model Chi-square, which tells whether the set of predictors makes a significant contribution to the prediction of the dependent variable, and a coefficient of the predictive ability of the model, called "PRE_{CV}." The figure of .38 suggests that we would improve our prediction by about 38% if we use the model to predict which fathers give the "not difficult" response (DeMaris, 1992).

We see that of the 10 predictors examined, only 5 are significant after all other effects are accounted for. Thus, after controlling for the impact

Table 9.1 Logistic Regression Results for Predicting Lack of Difficulty in Combining Work and Child Care Based on Salient Explanatory Variables

Variable	*Regression Coefficient*	*Impact on Odds*	*Wald Chi-Square*
Intercept	−5.81		
Primary caretaker was father or both parents[a]	0.65	1.92	7.91**
Father obtained custody through a court contest[b]	0.49	1.63	5.70*
All children over 13	−0.12	0.89	0.28
Children are mixed ages[c]	−0.49	0.61	2.31
Present conflict with ex-wife	0.04	1.04	0.19
Father's age	0.04	1.04	9.38**
Father's annual income	0.01	1.01	2.60
Number of custodial children	−0.11	0.90	0.78
Number of job changes	−0.54	0.58	50.64**
Social support	0.70	2.01	8.87**
Model chi-square	128.24**		
PRE_{cv}	0.38		

NOTES: $N = 1{,}102$. Mean (interval variables) or mode (qualitative variables) substituted for missing values.
a. "Primary caretaker was ex-wife" is reference category.
b. "Father obtained custody without a court contest" is reference category.
c. "All children under 13" is reference category.
$*p < .05$; $**p < .01$.

of the other variables, we find that fathers were more likely to consider combining work and child care "not difficult" if they were older, had helped with child care before the marital breakup, had obtained custody through a court contest, and had high levels of social support. Those who have experienced more changes in their work life as the result of being single parents are also less likely to find combining work and child care "not difficult."

Job Changes

In the second stage of our analysis, we explored the effects of occupation, education, income, and life cycle stage on the number of work changes fathers had to make to accommodate to parenting demands. Using analyses of variance (not shown) we found that professional and managerial workers made more changes than blue-collar workers, but that this difference disappeared after controlling for education. Income level was not significantly associated with job changes, and there were no significant interactions between occupational category and either income or education. Men with the highest levels of education report making the most changes in work routines.

To what extent are changes in work routine associated with life cycle stage among single fathers? Insofar as younger children need more supervision than others, one would expect the greatest number of changes to be associated with fathers' having either preschoolers or preteens in the home. In fact, this is precisely what we found. Figure 9.1 shows the mean number of job changes plotted against stage in the family life cycle for all 1,104 fathers in the sample. Having teenagers in the home is associated with markedly fewer work changes. Both those with preschoolers and those with preteens have had to make significantly more job changes than those with teenagers. The most obvious explanation for this finding is that fathers can either leave teenagers alone to fend for themselves or enlist their aid in caring for younger siblings.

In sum, we find that the key factors associated with changes in a father's work routine are a high level of education and having custody of younger children. Because the number of job changes a man makes could be an indicator of either a flexible work environment that allowed these changes or an inflexible one that forced the worker to demand changes, it is hard to interpret these results. However, in general, workers with high levels of education enjoy more control over the timing and conditions of their work (Simpson, 1985, p. 422; Staines & Pleck, 1983, p. 61). Wage workers generally have less control over their work schedules and may simply not be able to make needed changes in their work, short of quitting their job.

Although Table 9.1 shows that men who made the fewest job changes had the easiest time combining work and family, making many work changes in order to parent (and therefore reporting problems in combining work and family) need not necessarily lead to problematic relationships with children. In fact, we might just as easily expect the reverse. Men who give their children priority over their work, and therefore take time from work to be with them, may have better relationships with their children than those who do not.

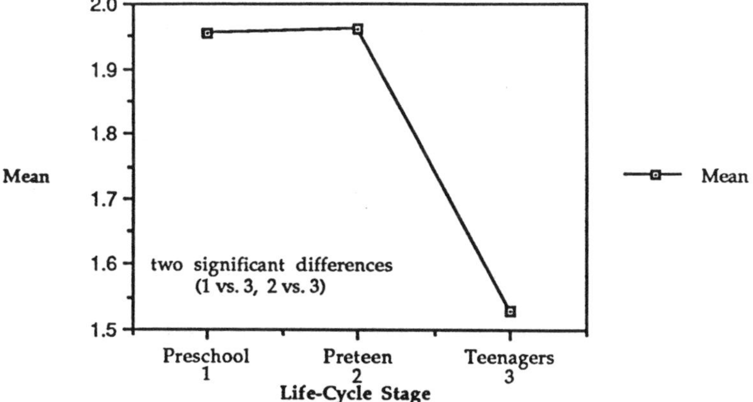

Figure 9.1. Mean Number of Job Changes by Life Cycle State

Work-Family Conflict and IPA

As it turns out, job changes may be related to parent-child problems in both ways. The zero-order correlation between job changes and IPA is only .04, suggesting that having to change one's work routine to accommodate children may be associated with better parent-child relationships for some men and worse relationships for others. We might, however, expect that men who are still reporting difficulty in combining work and child care may also be having problems with their children. Figure 9.2 presents mean IPA scores plotted against responses to the question about the difficulty experienced in combining work and child care. As fathers report greater difficulty, mean IPA increases. Moreover, all differences are significant. Hence, fathers reporting that combining work and child care was "somewhat difficult" experienced significantly more problems in their relationships with their children than those who said that this task was "not difficult." Similarly, those who said that this task was "very difficult" experienced significantly more problems than those giving either of the other two responses.

We could stop here and assume that, indeed, problems in combining work and family do translate into poorer parent-child relationships for single-parent fathers. However, the same men who are having problems combining work and family may be the ones who did the least child care before separation, are having conflicts with their ex-wife, or are getting the least social support from their friends and co-workers. All of these

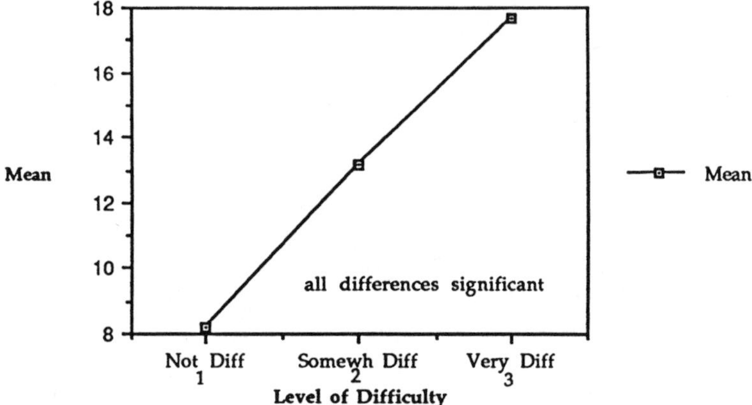

Figure 9.2. Mean IPA Score by Level of Difficulty in Combining Work and Child Rearing

factors could produce bad parent-child relationships whether or not a man was having trouble juggling his work and parent roles.

Further, the predictor variables used in Table 9.1 are interrelated in a number of complex ways. Although the multivariate analysis identified the best predictors for "ease in combining work and family," such an analysis obscures the complex interrelationships among patterns of predictor and outcome variables.

For example, men who fight for custody in court may fight for children with whom they already have a good relationship (Greif & DeMaris, 1989). However, if they do have a court battle, they are unlikely to get along well with their ex-wife or get much help from their ex-wife's family. Men who were primary caretakers before custody may get along with their children better and also have to make fewer job changes because, like their wife, they had to make job changes before the separation in order to be primary caretakers. Further, although having young children is associated with more schedule changes due to day care needs, most parents have more relationship problems with teenagers (Morawetz & Walker, 1984).

To get at this web of relationships, we drew from the results of the first two stages of our analysis to construct a causal model using LISREL.

LISREL Model and Data Analysis

Figure 9.3 presents a structural model (Joreskog & Sorbom, 1989) relating father's social characteristics to social support for custody,

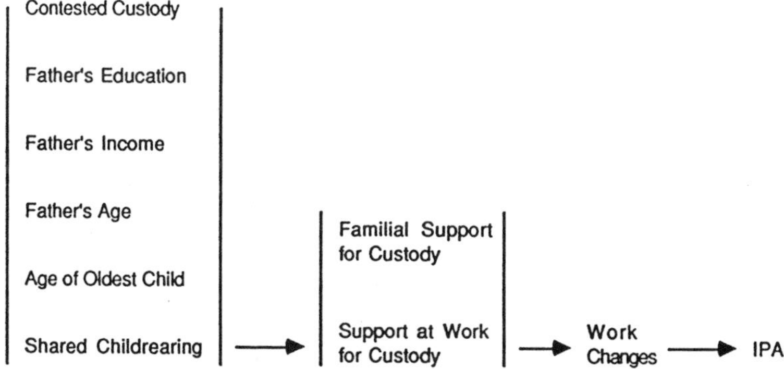

Figure 9.3. Structural Model Relating Father's Social Characteristics to Social Support for Custody, Changes in the Father's Work Routine, and the Index of Parental Attitudes (IPA)

changes in the father's work routine, and the Index of Parental Attitudes (IPA). The model shown is a chain in which each block of variables is considered to directly affect only those variables to its immediate right. Hence, father's social characteristics are assumed to affect only support for custody directly, and support for custody is assumed to affect only work changes directly. Any effects of these blocks of variables on variables that are "one link" removed from them in the chain are assumed to be indirect, through the intervening block of variables. This is, in a sense, a "perfect" intervening-variable model, in which intervening variables account completely for the effects of prior variables on variables of interest.

The resulting trimmed structural model for the entire sample is presented in Figure 9.4 and Table 9.2. The model has a good fit to the data, with a chi-square of 24.08 ($df = 20$, $p = .239$). The goodness-of-fit index at the bottom of the table also suggests that the model fits the data well, as index values above .9 are indicative of a good fit (Bollen, 1989; Wheaton, 1988). The coefficient of determination of .104 indicates that the model accounts for about 10% of the generalized variance in the set of endogenous variables.[4]

According to Table 9.2, fathers who contested their custody are estimated to be about .21 points lower in familial support, on average, than those who did not achieve custody through a court contest. Because both ex-wives and in-laws are counted as part of the family in this analysis, it is easy to understand why men who contest custody might have less family support. Those who contested custody are also estimated to have

Table 9.2 Unstandardized Direct, Indirect, and Total Effects of Predictor Variables on Outcome Variables in Trimmed Structural Model: Sample Is All Single Custodial Fathers

Predictor	*Outcome*	*Total Effect*	*Direct Effect*	*Indirect Effect*
Contested custody	Familial support	−.212**	−.212**	—
Work Changes		.076**	.000[a]	.076**
	IPA	−1.943**	−1.943**	.000
Father's education	Work changes	.066**	.066**	
.000				
Father's income	Work support	.002*	.002*	—
Work changes		−.001	.000	−.001
-	IPA	−.008*	.000	−.008*
Father's age	Work changes	−.025**	−.025[b]**	.000
Age of oldest child	Work changes	−.025**	−.025[b]**	.000
	IPA	.213**	.213**	.000
Shared child rearing	IPA			
		−3.089**	−3.089**	.000
Familial support	Work changes	−3.58**	−.358[c]**	—
Work support	Work changes	−.358**	−.358[c]	—
	IPA	−3.667**	−3.667**	.000
Chi-square ($df = 20$)		24.080		
Probability		.239		
Goodness-of-fit index		.996		
Coefficient of determination		.104		

NOTES: $N = 1{,}104$.
a. .000 indicates a parameter constrained to equal zero.
b. Parameters constrained to be equal to each other.
c. Parameters constrained to be equal to each other.
$^{*}p < .05$; $^{**}p < .01$.

made very slightly (but significantly) more changes (.08) at work than those who did not contest custody. Interestingly, this effect is all indirect, through familial support. That is, those who contested custody, compared to those who did not, have relatively less familial support (direct effect = −.212), but those who have relatively less familial support have, in turn, made relatively more changes at work (because the direct effect of familial support on work changes is −.358). Therefore, the overall indirect effect on job changes is positive ($-.212 \times -.358 = .076$).

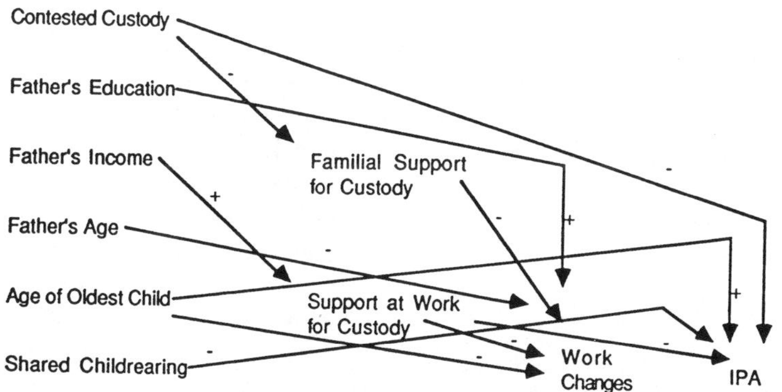

Figure 9.4. Structural Model Relating Father's Social Characteristics to Social Support for Custody, Changes in the Father's Work Routine, and the Index of Parental Attitudes (IPA) Based on Trimmed Structural Model in Table 9.2

Contested custody is also a predictor of having less problematic relationships with one's children. Perhaps contesting custody indicates a determination to be a responsible parent to one's children. In addition, fathers may work harder to get along with children they have had to fight for and may also be more likely to fight for the children they get along with best (Greif & DeMaris, 1989).

In sum, it appears that those who must struggle to obtain custody of their children by engaging their ex-wife in court battles report lower familial support for custody and therefore end up making more adjustments at work to accommodate parenting demands. Men who contest custody are also more likely than those who don't to report nonproblematic relationships with their children. Although our model predicted a direct relationship between job changes and IPA (after controlling for relationships among predictors), we did not find evidence for this link. Instead, this multivariate model suggests that work changes and problems with children are separate end points on two different causal chains. Although contesting custody is related to both work changes and fathers' attitudes toward the children, the number of changes a father must make appears to have no direct effect on the quality of his relationship with his children.

We expected fathers to be more likely to both contest custody for and get along best with children they have cared for prior to the separation.

The LISREL model shows us that each of these variables independently predicts fathers' positive attitudes toward children. In other words, men who contest custody report more positive attitudes toward their children whether or not they shared child care responsibility while married.

Fathers with more education make, on average, more work changes than those with less education (holding constant other factors in the first two columns of Figure 9.3). Salary level appears to affect both work support and the IPA score. Fathers with higher incomes tend to report more support at work for being a single parent and tend also to report fewer problems in relationships with their children. However, the latter effect is all indirect via work support, because the more his co-workers, boss, and friends are supportive of his single parenting, the fewer problems the father reports having with his children. Again, we see that making changes at work is not itself directly related to the number of problems the father has with his children. Instead, social support at work is related simultaneously to having to make fewer changes and to having more positive relationships with one's children.

As we would expect, older fathers tend to make fewer adjustments in their work routines as a result of single parenting (as do fathers with older children). However, having to make fewer work adjustments does not, in turn, lead to having fewer problems with one's children. In fact, the older the children, the more problems the father reports in his relationships with them. As Greif points out in *The Daddy Track and the Single Father* (1990), teens pose particular problems for single fathers because they are harder to control than younger children, more often leave fathers alone while they spend time with peers, and may attempt to reestablish contact with their mother against the father's wishes.

Although the LISREL model explains a modest amount of variance in the two outcome variables, the analysis clarifies the complex relationships among fathers' backgrounds, social support, work changes, and the quality of relationships with children.

Occupational Differences

Although one is tempted to generalize these results to single fathers regardless of occupational category, it would be unwise to do so. The demands of different occupations as well as the different social characteristics associated with people in these positions led us to hypothesize that the model in Figure 9.4 might not hold equally across occupations. Our next step, therefore, was to reexamine the fit of this model in each of four occupational groupings: (a) craftworkers, (b) managers and salespersons, (c) military and police, and (d) professionals.[5] Although we did find some differences among occupational groups, limitations of the data (and existing literature) did not permit full explanation of the findings. We therefore summarize the findings below and suggest directions for future research.

Comparing models across four broadly defined occupational groups, we found that contested custody had no direct effect on work changes for craftworkers, managers and salespersons, and professionals, but had a large positive direct effect for men in the military and police. As both the military and police officers are more likely than the other categories of workers to have rigid work schedules, they may be forced to make more changes at work.

We also found that among craftworkers only, father's age had a direct positive (although not quite significant) effect on work support, whereas the age of the oldest child had a significant direct negative effect on work support. Unfortunately, we have no good interpretation of this finding.

Lastly, we found that for professional men only, the more money earned, the fewer problems reported with children. In addition, among professionals shared child rearing had a positive (although not quite significant) direct effect on work support. It is difficult to understand why income should affect the quality of parent-child relationships for professionals only. However, shared child rearing may have a greater impact on work support because professional and managerial workers may have had the freedom to make adjustments in their work schedules even before the separation, whereas other workers in less responsive work settings may have asked for concessions only after they became single parents. All other effects are the same across all groups.

Because this analysis grouped fathers into four very general occupational categories, we were somewhat surprised to find any differences among occupational types. Although neither our data nor the existing literature allow us to explain our results, our findings do demonstrate the need for a new category of work-family research focusing on the interaction between occupational cultures, workplace policy, and men's work-family conflicts.

Because women are usually primary caretakers, whether in single- or dual-parent homes, studies of employer responsiveness to parenting needs have generally been limited to organizations employing large numbers of women. Due to occupational sex segregation, these kinds of work organizations are unlikely to employ large proportions of men. As

Haas found (this volume), Swedish men working in the primarily male private sector were less willing than those in the public sector to take time off for child rearing. And as both Pleck (this volume) and Haas point out, male workers often experience considerable informal pressures against fulfilling parenting responsibilities. Our study finds that the more support single fathers get from co-workers and bosses, the fewer changes they have to make in their work routines and the more positive their attitudes toward their children. As the proportions of both single-parent and co-parenting fathers continue to grow, fathers will need the same kinds of concessions from their workplaces that working mothers have been demanding for years. Because workplace support and ease of combining work and family are crucial for single-parent fathers, researchers need to focus more attention on men's workplaces. As Haas's and Pleck's chapters in this volume suggest, for all kinds of fathers the gendered organization of work may pose as many as or more problems than does the gendered nature of parenting.

Implications and Conclusions

The popular stereotype is that men, when compared with women, are able to handle workplace pressures easily. Although research may indicate that they do not have the same trials that women have, it is still clear that most of the men who participated in this research experienced significant problems balancing the demands of work and single parenting. The fathers who are successfully coping found more cooperative work situations and support networks than those who are not. The first step in building more supportive work environments for fathers is to recognize that men as well as women are parents and that, as working parents, they must make adjustments in their work to respond to family needs. If work organizations do not begin to take men's parenting needs more seriously, our research suggests that both fathers and their children will continue to suffer the consequences.

Notes

1. Friends were included in the measure because of the possible overlap between friends and co-workers.

2. Because some of these changes indicate employer flexibility (i.e., working flexible hours) and others suggest a nonresponsive workplace (being fired or quitting), the

combined measure is admittedly an ambiguous indicator of workplace characteristics. We hope it is a better indicator of the need for making changes at work.

3. The IPA has good convergent, discriminant, and construct validity (Hudson, 1982). For the current sample, Cronbach's alpha for the IPA was .91, suggesting strong internal consistency. The scale mean for the entire sample was 13.3 with a standard deviation of 9.9.

4. Because they are unstandardized coefficients, the parameter estimates in the body of the table are interpreted as the change in units of a given endogenous variable for a unit increase in the relevant predictor variable, controlling for all other variables preceding that endogenous variable in the model. For dummy variables, the coefficients represent the estimated mean difference in the endogenous variable between those in the category of interest and those in the contrast category.

5. Because occupations were originally coded using the census 10-category code, we had to collapse those codes and could not create new ones that might better reflect work settings and conditions. We dropped farm workers and service workers from this analysis because they included a total of only 2.5% of the sample and we could not justify adding them to another category.

References

Bollen, K. A. (1989). *Structural equations with latent variables.* New York: John Wiley.

Burden, D. S. (1986). Single parents and the work setting: The impact of multiple job and homelife responsibilities. *Family Relations, 35,* 37-43.

Chang, P., & Deinard, A. S. (1982). Single-father caretakers: Demographic characteristics and adjustment processes. *American Journal of Orthopsychiatry, 52,* 236-243.

DeMaris, A. (1992). *Logit modeling: Practical applications.* Newbury Park, CA: Sage.

Facchino, D., & Aron, A. (1990). Divorced fathers with custody: Method of obtaining custody and divorce adjustment. *Journal of Divorce, 13,* 45-56.

Greif, G. L. (1985). *Single fathers.* Lexington, MA: Lexington.

Greif, G. L. (1987). A longitudinal examination of single custodial fathers: Implications for treatment. *American Journal of Family Therapy, 15,* 253-260.

Greif, G. L. (1990). *The daddy track and the single father.* Lexington, MA: Lexington/Macmillan.

Greif, G. L., & DeMaris, A. (1989). Single fathers in contested custody suits. *Journal of Psychiatry and Law, 17,* 223-238.

Greif, G. L., & DeMaris, A. (1990). Single fathers with custody. *Families in Society, 71,* 259-266.

Hansen, G. L. (1991). Balancing work and family: A literature and resource review. *Family Relations, 40,* 348-353.

Hood, J. C., & Milazzo, N. (1984, December). Shiftwork, stress and wellbeing: How workers and their families cope with shiftwork. *Personnel Administrator,* pp. 95-108.

Hudson, W. (1982). *Clinical measurement package: A field manual.* Chicago: Dorsey.

Joreskog, K. G., & Sorbom, D. (1989). *LISREL 7: A guide to the program and applications.* Chicago: SPSS.

Keshet, H. F., & Rosenthal, K. N. (1976). Single parent families: A new study. *Children Today, 7*(3), 13-17.

Mendes, H. (1976). Single fathers. *Family Coordinator, 25,* 439-444.

Morawetz, A., & Walker, G. (1984). *Brief therapy with single-parent families.* New York: Brunner/Mazel.

Nieto, D. S. (1990). The custodial single father: Who does *he* think he is? *Journal of Divorce, 13,* 27-43.

Orthner, D. K., Brown, T., & Ferguson, D. (1976). Single parent fatherhood: An emerging lifestyle. *Family Coordinator, 25,* 429-437.

Simpson, R. (1985). The social control of occupations and work. *Annual Review of Sociology, 11,* 415-436.

Staines, G. L., & Pleck, J. H. (1983). *The impact of work schedules on the family.* Ann Arbor: University of Michigan Press.

U.S. Bureau of the Census. (1987, July). *Money income and poverty status of families and person in the United States: 1986* (Series P-60, No. 157). Washington, DC: U.S. Government Printing Office.

U.S. Bureau of the Census. (1990). *Household and family characteristics: March 1990 and 1989* (Series P-20, No. 447). Washington, DC: U.S. Government Printing Office.

Wheaton, B. (1988) Assessment of fit in overidentified models with latent variables. In J. S. Long (Ed.), *Common problems/proper solutions: Avoiding error in quantitative research* (pp. 193-225). Newbury Park, CA: Sage.

10

Meanings of Housework for Single Fathers and Mothers

Insights Into Gender Inequality

POLLY A. FASSINGER

Who does the housework in your home? Since the 1970s, this has been a popular question for researchers interested in changing gender roles (e.g., R. A. Berk & S. F. Berk, 1979; Coverman & Sheley, 1986; Walker & Woods, 1976). With an almost exclusive emphasis on married couples, these quantitative portraits have provided useful records of shifts in men's and women's involvement in housework; yet they have not enabled us to investigate the meaning of housework for women and men. In our struggle to understand why most married men contribute relatively little to housework, we should examine men's and women's interpretations of this activity (Thompson & Walker, 1989).

This chapter explores gender inequality in housework through interviews with divorced fathers and mothers. By focusing on single parents, we compare men and women who have similar structural pressures to do housework. Children are single parents' primary source of housework help; few rely on nonhousehold members to do their weekly housekeeping (Gasser & Taylor, 1976; Greif, 1985; Orthner, Brown, & Ferguson, 1976; Risman, 1986). Given similar structural pressures, how

AUTHOR'S NOTE: The author thanks Barrie Thorne, Jane Hood, Nancy Gilliland, Linda Johnson, and Mary Jo Neitz for their helpful comments.

do men's and women's interpretations of family roles and the nature of housework shape their involvement in household activities?

This question is informed by both microstructural and interactionist theoretical perspectives. Microstructuralists (see Risman & Schwartz, 1989) argue that structural forces are often responsible for creating gender differences. They believe that men and women would be more similar (and presumably equal) if their daily lives were more structurally alike. One interactionist inquiry that helps motivate my central question is Hochschild's (1989) study of gender strategies. A gender strategy, according to Hochschild, is a "plan of action through which a person tries to solve problems at hand, given the cultural notions of gender at play" (p. 15). Hochschild studied the ways in which two-paycheck families manage family care, the "second shift" of daily work. Overall, Hochschild discovered that married women's gender strategies for the second shift included: (a) indirect and direct attempts to get their husband to participate, (b) doing everything alone, (c) reducing their involvement in paid work, (d) spending less time on housework, their marriage, themselves, and/or their children, and (e) getting help from children or paid workers.

Married men, according to Hochschild, either cooperated with their wife's desires and got involved in family work, or they resisted it. Although Hochschild outlined no specific strategies of cooperation, strategies of resistance included: (a) asserting that many things need not be done because they were unnecessary (e.g., "We don't need new clothes, so we don't need to shop"), (b) getting minimally involved in tasks, which often caused wives to step in and complete the work, and (c) offering praise and encouragement to wives for family care and other activities, a tactic that made husbands' noninvolvement seem less onerous to wives.

Hochschild's enlightening findings come from research on married, two-paycheck couples. Of course, single fathers and single mothers with custody also have second shifts. They also must combine paid work with family care. Their gender strategies will inherently differ from those of married parents, as they usually cannot rely on another adult for help around the house. To expand Hochschild's insights about gender strategies and further develop our understanding of the forces that perpetuate gender inequality in housework,[1] this chapter discusses how single parents' gender strategies differ from those of Hochschild's married parents.

Following S. F. Berk's (1985) and West and Zimmerman's (1987) interactionist interpretation, I view gender not as a role or a trait, but rather as something humans "manufacture" during daily interactions. These authors believe men and women engage in producing gender when they do housework. As a result, husbands and wives reproduce relations of submission and dominance as they negotiate their domestic labor. In my study, the example of a single mother who called her ex-spouse "Susie Spotless" illustrates the "production of gender":

> And it seemed like the only time he would ever have a smile on his face when he walked in the door was if I was scrubbing or pushing the vacuum cleaner around. It was just that the house had to be just so all the time. And it got to the point where I hated it.

Although husbands and wives are constantly involved in gender production work, they typically recognize only the household tasks themselves. The following analysis uncovers the gender production process embedded in the ways single-parent fathers and mothers manage household work.

Study Background

I contacted divorced single parents living with their children in 1985 through notices in newsletters from: (a) 27 public and parochial schools, (b) a local social service agency, (c) two day care centers, (d) Parents Without Partners, and (e) a support group for the widowed and divorced. Additional names were obtained from the single parents I interviewed. I saw four parents on two occasions and interviewed the rest once. By their choice, I met most at their homes; six asked to be seen at their offices.

All 34 interviewees were residents of a Midwestern city of about 130,000. The city is predominantly white (97%), and all interviewees were white. The 20 mothers, whose ages ranged from 26 to 40, averaged 34 years of age; the fathers averaged 39 years old, with ages spanning from 33 to 46. These parents had one to three children at home. Whereas the mothers had been single parents for 4 months to 13 years, fathers' tenure as single parents spanned from 1 to 7 years. Therefore, compared to an average of almost 5 years for the mothers, the fathers had been single parents for about 3 years. All parents had high school educations, and eight mothers and six fathers had college degrees. The nine mothers who were professionals were mostly nurses, teachers, and counselors. Six mothers did clerical work. The fathers' 1984 median income was \$22,000, whereas the mothers' incomes ranged from \$5,700 to \$24,000 and averaged \$16,000, which was a bit higher than the mean for female householders with school-aged children (\$14,773) (U.S. Bureau of the

Census, 1986). The sample's higher income may be related to the lack of minorities and high percentage of college graduates. The study community contains four higher educational institutions, which attracted some of the women to the town and may help account for the sample's high number of college graduates. In addition, newsletters may have provided more middle-class contacts. The taped and transcribed semistructured interviews initially focused on how single parents organized their daily family and work activities. Grounded theory research (Glaser & Strauss, 1967) allows investigations to change direction and focus on topics of concern to the persons being studied. As a result, my later interviews touched on numerous dimensions of single parents' lives that were overlooked in earlier conversations.[2]

Analysis with the constant comparative method (Glaser & Strauss, 1967) began after the first five interviews. At this time, it became apparent that parents were not interested in describing their daily behaviors; they wanted to discuss their attitudes and feelings about their changed responsibilities. The Charmaz (1983) strategy of line-by-line coding helped me recognize that parents' comments reflected their reactions to changes in responsibilities, including changes in decision making, parenting, financial management, paid work, and housework. This report focuses on housework, which includes the sundry chores of cleaning, cooking, shopping, and household maintenance and repair.[3]

To understand variations in parents' responses, I analyzed factors associated in the literature with single parents' reactions to life changes, including their reasons for becoming single parents (e.g., desertion, own choice), tenure at single parenting, current income, age, education, number of children, gender of children, and reason for custody (e.g., see Gasser & Taylor, 1976; Greif, 1985; Hetherington, M. Cox, & R. Cox, 1976; Rosenfeld & Rosenstein, 1973; Schorr & Moen, 1979; Weiss, 1979). However, when I sorted data along these dimensions, I did not find consistent themes in single parents' responses to housework.

I then compared single parents' feelings about their changed responsibilities by using inductively derived factors not discussed in the literature, such as tenure as a married parent, beliefs about why the marriage ended, and previous personal investment in the marriage. None of these factors explained patterns in the parents' reactions. Instead, fathers' reactions to housework seemed shaped by the degree to which they had been involved in housework as married parents. Two fathers described themselves as "uninvolved" in housework while married. They had seen homemaking as their wife's domain and helped with cooking, cleaning, shopping, or household maintenance only on rare occasions. Seven men talked of being "helpers" around the house. They described their contributions as having been regular and specific (e.g., doing the weekly shopping with their wife). A third group of five fathers said they "shared" the housekeeping with their wife while married. They perceived themselves as having been very actively involved in daily household tasks. In contrast, mothers' feelings about their changed housework responsibilities were rarely influenced by their spouse's past contributions to housework. In the following section, I compare the diverse perceptions of fathers who were previously uninvolved, helpers, or sharers to the mothers' descriptions of becoming a single householder.[4]

Findings

Learning About Housework

When they became single parents, single fathers in this study set out to learn new tasks. One father remembered the day his 7-year-old daughter begged him to make cookies:

> I baked cookies once. That was an experience. My daughter told me I was doing it wrong. As it turned out, she was right. I didn't know that they expanded when you put them in the oven. I made them the size I wanted them to be when they were finished. She said, "They are going to get big when you put them in there." I said, "No, they aren't." Often she knows what she is talking about.

Only fathers spoke of learning new housework tasks. This is a coping strategy because it reflects the men's decision to "solve the problem at hand" by becoming involved in housework, rather than ignoring tasks, hiring someone to do them, or having only their children do them. It is also a gender strategy because single fathers' behaviors were clearly colored by cultural notions about men's and women's work and the gendered nature of domestic chores, as will be shown below. I believe Hochschild discovered this gender strategy among married fathers also, yet because these men did not fully embrace their new tasks or do them to their wife's satisfaction, Hochschild chose to interpret these actions as "resistance" rather than as "cooperation." Men's need to learn new daily tasks varied according to the fathers' past involvement in housework.

Uninvolved Men

When the "uninvolved" men became single parents, they were faced with new responsibilities for indoor household care. They had minimal experiences with the cooking, cleaning, shopping, and planning duties of housework. These fathers described both the obstacles they faced while learning these tasks and the skills they cultivated in the early months and years of single parenting. Eric commented on why his experience was so difficult:

> Well, I didn't really do the laundry. You know, I didn't do the house [when I was married]. . . . All the other little things, like cleaning the house, doing the dishes after you had cooked . . . making sure that when you went shopping you had exactly what you needed. That was all new. It was . . . there were times when it was disgusting, my ignorance. . . . It wasn't as natural as a woman, a woman's instincts with the children, with the family, with the house. It's a naturalistic thing for a mother, for a woman, where it wasn't for a man. [Q: What instincts didn't you have that a woman would have?] Washing clothes. If you could have seen some of my whites! After my first couple of loads. When to add bleach . . . that was the instinct there . . . I didn't know that. I had to learn that. And I ruined a lot of clothes.

The large disjuncture between their old cluster of household responsibilities and their newer, vastly enlarged sphere of duties set these fathers apart from the fathers who had "shared" or "helped" with housework while married.

Helpers

The seven fathers who had been "helpers" had some experience with household care before they became single parents. Some had helped with cleaning, others had done occasional cooking, a few had shopped frequently or done the laundry. These fathers had to learn a number of new tasks and skills. However, the change from having some involvement in household care to having total responsibility was less substantial than the change experienced by uninvolved fathers. Helpers commented that being in charge of household care meant that one had to expand one's elementary skills, rather than master a group of foreign ones. Dave explained:

> I had to diversify my cooking. I always thought of myself as a fairly good cook, but it was fairly one-dimensional. I would make a main course and it

> would be something like spaghetti or I couldn't do it. So I had to broaden my horizons. . . . I think ironing was something I didn't know how to do. I had to iron a shirt and I had to do that, pants and stuff. But I knew how to run a dishwasher and a dryer. At least I knew how to use one setting. I don't know what all those settings are.

Even those helpers who thought of themselves as poor housekeepers did not feel lost in alien territory, as had the uninvolved fathers. The basic skills of homemaking were familiar to them. Most helpers had a few new tasks to learn as single parents. These chores were the hardest for them to feel comfortable about and incorporate into daily life.

Steve felt that scheduling had been a difficult task to master. He mentioned it on numerous occasions during our talk:

> Well, you are gonna have a real goofed-up night if you don't pick the kids up till 6:30. By the time you get done eating, it's about 7:30-8:00. It doesn't give them much time to do their homework or spend time with them before they go to bed. Whereas if you somewhat keep on a schedule and get those types of things done as far as housekeeping duties early in the morning before they get up, it takes a lot of pressure off the evening.

As single fathers, helpers grew increasingly sensitive to the organization of household routines and the need to create daily schedules.

Sharers

When they were married, the five fathers who had "shared" housework were involved with household care more than either the helpers or the uninvolved men. Most said they had shared or done housework jointly with their spouse. These fathers felt quite able to do housework and reported the fewest adjustments in their daily household activities. Each took on only one or two additional household tasks after becoming a single parent. For Roger, the new task was shopping:

> Shopping is one [new] thing. . . . I didn't do groceries and making meals wasn't, making meals wasn't too bad, but getting the groceries from the grocery store to here was, I guess would be a big step for me. Cause to go out and sit down and make a grocery list out. And what the kids are gonna eat, and what's good for them. And what I can prepare without really screwing it up [laughs], involves a lot.

Overall, these fathers found their new housework tasks easy to master. Sometimes, however, they saw the new tasks as trivial or mildly annoying. For example, Martin explained:

> There were some things I had to learn to do over. Little silly things that women learn to do. Part of the household tasks that I never had before, now I had to do. You don't know the proper tools, equipment, or soap. Dumb little things. If you never wash floors, for example. I can make an extraordinarily inefficient job of washing the floor. Or if you don't know that foam cleans chrome. Or what you use to take grease off the walls.

Learning new tasks was enjoyable for some fathers (e.g., when they felt they had completed a difficult job), whereas others learned new tasks grudgingly. Nonetheless, it is clear that single fathers recognized components of family care to which they had previously been oblivious. Fathers were gradually being oriented to the "invisible nature" of housework (Daniels, 1987; DeVault, 1987). As DeVault (1987) notes, people often overlook the complex and varied tasks entailed in housework. For example, feeding a family involves recognizing the likes and dislikes of household members, organizing schedules, planning menus, maintaining variety, and keeping in line with cultural standards. Ignorance of these "invisible" elements may help explain some men's resistance to household tasks. Although some men may consciously avoid housework, others may merely lack awareness of the full nature of the project at hand. When left alone to complete household tasks and unable to rely on someone who may "instinctively" know how to do a particular job, these single fathers seem better able to recognize and appreciate the labor and training required to do housework well.

Enjoying Greater Control

Two fathers enjoyed the greater control they had over housekeeping when they became single parents. When married, these men had been helpers around the house; housework was one component of family life their wife seemed to control. In contrast, when they became single parents these men exercised new discretion and power. This autonomy was appreciated most by men who previously had little input into household care and who did not approve of their wife's standards. For example, Vince enjoyed being in charge of housekeeping:

> One of the great pleasures of being divorced is that I can live neatly, and my ex-wife was in practice a slob. Rotting food in the refrigerator, papers and clothes lying all over the house. Dirty dishes in the sink. The place was always a mess. . . . Essentially she was responsible for leaving the place a mess and I was not able to affect that in any way. . . . It's wonderful to be single in terms of housekeeping, cause I can keep it neat.

This response parallels some single mothers' greater enjoyment of control over decision making (see Fassinger, 1989b). Mothers who saw themselves as decision-making "helpers" were the most pleased with the greater control they gained over decision making. Although fathers from traditional marriages controlled housework more as single parents, they did not seem to enjoy this change, perhaps because they felt rather overwhelmed by tasks. Fathers from egalitarian homes thought the changes in control were minimal. It seems that parents who considered themselves helpers (vs. those from either very traditional or egalitarian marriages) were in the best position to enjoy new authority over their daily life.

Getting Children's Help

Another way single parents dealt with housework was to get children's help. This finding complements one of Hochschild's discoveries: Mothers used paid helpers and children to do housework in two-paycheck families. (Hochschild did not identify using children's help as a strategy of fathers, although she offers evidence that at least one father did this.)[5]

There were two major differences between single mothers' and single fathers' use of children's help. First, single fathers relied on their offspring much more heavily than did single mothers. For fathers who had been in very traditional marriages, children seemed to become substitute spouses or housekeepers. This finding raises interesting questions about fathers' and mothers' strategies in married couple homes (e.g., Do married fathers rely on their children's help around the house more than do married mothers? Do they rely on children to help keep down their own involvement?).[6]

Of all the sons and daughters, children of uninvolved fathers did the most housework. These children also were parenting supports: They baby-sat and assisted with the care of their younger siblings. Carl not only had his sons do all the daily cooking, cleaning, and dishes, but also had his older son teach the younger one how to do all the necessary chores. Eric, a previously uninvolved father with daughters aged 7, 8, and 10, described his children's daily after-school activities:

> The oldest one will make the beds. Joyce will check the garbage and if there is any, she will take it out. Start the dishwasher. The youngest will pick up the clothes and run them downstairs. . . . Now Joyce [the 8-year-old], she does the dishes and vacuuming, and when I go to wash clothes, she is learning to wash clothes. She knows how to sort. If I fold, they will put them away. It's working and I believe it's working 'cause of the cooperation between all of us.

Fathers who had helped with housework often agreed that after their marriage ended, their children's household chores increased a bit. For example, Gene said that his two children "probably do a little more of the general housekeeping like vacuuming and things for the general population and not just their own rooms."

Interestingly, fathers who had shared housework seemed to expect less household help from children than the other men. These fathers observed that their children's chores changed minimally after divorce.[7] Roger described his son's chores as "Pretty much [the same]":

> He does the vacuuming and dusting, and I do the rest: scrubbing the floors and the bathroom, the good stuff. And he's been doing that for a long time.

Rather than relying heavily on their children, fathers who had shared housework tended to be more self-reliant. Perhaps these men expected less help from their children because they had done housework as a married parent and were accustomed to it. This was the only group of single fathers to openly admit their dismay and fatigue with housework. For example, Martin noted:

> I mean it's just a hell of a lot of work. I wish I didn't have to do it. I must admit that when a date washes dishes it makes me feel pretty good. And I don't want to overreact and go out, I don't want to have a partner that is subservient. But the relief is nice. To have someone wait on you after you have waited on the children and everything is a very nice break.

The mothers also differed in their beliefs about what their children's roles should be at home. The rather pronounced differences among the mothers varied according to whether or not the women regarded their husband as having been uninvolved or a helper. (None of the mothers with whom I spoke felt that their husband had shared the housework with them.)

Most of the women whose former husband was uninvolved had been full-time homemakers when they were married. Of all single mothers, these women expected the least help around the house from their children. They generally felt that after they became single parents there had been little change in the amount of aid they asked of their sons and daughters. They consistently explained that there was not much need for their children's help or that they wanted their children to be free to do other things with their time.

Mothers who had been married to helpers demanded more help around the house than did mothers who had uninvolved husbands. Some of them believed they asked for more help at home after they became single parents than they had previously. For example, Jo, who enrolled in college after she became a single parent, said that her daughters were her "saving grace." They would start meals and help with washing clothes and cleaning. Mothers like Jo said they felt comfortable asking for a bit more help from their children, but not for an amount that differed greatly from the children's previous work loads. These mothers were sensitive to how their children's lives had changed due to divorce and did not take their children's help lightly. However, none of the mothers relied on their children as heavily as did the uninvolved fathers.

Overall, it seems parents who were most involved in housework as married parents expected the least amount of housework help from their children. Too, men expected more help than did women. This gender difference may reflect women's perception of housework as part of their mother role; in contrast, fathers seemed to think of housework as a family task, as discussed below.

Perceiving Responsibility for Housework

Parents' use of children's help also was related to whether or not they thought of housekeeping as a basic parental obligation. Fathers were much more likely than mothers to feel that housekeeping was not a parental responsibility. When describing their housekeeping arrangements, fathers often asserted that responsibility for housework should not have to rest on their shoulders. Only fathers who had shared housework did not hold this view. Not uncommonly, fathers gained help from their children by insisting that housework was a family chore. When his daughters were preschoolers, Eric talked with them about housework:

> I guess I came out and said, "Dad doesn't want to do this anymore, and you are going to have to start doing this yourself." They decorate and I let them do little things and I leave it. I let them do things cause I am an easy person when it comes to cleaning up this house. I'll do anything to get out of it. That's the way it is.

Irv also felt that his children should participate around the house. He explained:

> I have been very consistent with them, and it is expectant [*sic*] of them and they know they have to do it. 'Cause everybody has got to do something. I refuse to go through this place every day after work and clean it. I have done it and can do it. But I don't want to do it and shouldn't have to do it. . . . Beds made in the morning. Put clothes away. You don't even think of all those responsibilities but they make a world of difference. 'Cause I'll be damned if I'm going to go around and put them all away.

Single mothers, on the other hand, seemed to feel that housework was their responsibility. They explained to me (and to their children) that they could not (rather than should not have to) do all the housework alone. When they asked their children for help around the house, mothers suggested they needed help because there were limits to what they could do. (This plea is reminiscent of married mothers in Hochschild's study.) Fathers said they deserved help because they did not enjoy housework or felt that it was unreasonable for them to do all of it. Fathers also asked for help because they wanted their sons and daughters to feel part of a team or a family unit.

Although some mothers also admitted that they did not like doing housework, fathers were more likely to admit not being interested in housework and to dismiss themselves from these tasks. For example, Vince described his feelings about cooking:

> If I were into that, I could do it. I could cook meals, get a simple cookbook and just do it and stuff. But it just feels like an effort and a burden. And who's gonna care if a kid will eat a meal? I suppose I could make greater effort to find out exactly what he likes and cook it just the way he likes it. But I am not interested in that. I don't want to spend a lot of my time and energy trying to make him happy with food.

Fathers' tendency to demand more help from their children has implications for differences in the amount of freedom and leisure time single parents experience. If a parent asks for help and still assumes ultimate responsibility for a task, it is likely that this person will not be able to experience much "down time" in their domestic activities. Down time is when one feels fully relieved of a task and can direct one's attention elsewhere (R. LaRossa & M. M. LaRossa, 1989). Instead, these parents probably are obtaining "secondary time" (R. LaRossa & M. M. LaRossa, 1989). In other words, they are able to do other things while being responsible for and attentive to the domestic labor of their helpers. Fathers who seem to view housework as a family duty can more easily relinquish their responsibility for various tasks and move away from monitoring others. In contrast, mothers will likely maintain secondary involvement in housework and ultimately invest greater emotional and mental energy in this work.

Feeling Less Frustration

When they were married, all of the mothers in this sample had done most of the housekeeping and felt responsible for the vast majority of housework. One might expect very little change in their reactions to housework because most mothers felt they had received little or no help around the house from their spouse while married.

In fact, in contrast to single fathers, many women felt that housework became easier to manage as single mothers. Some mothers felt less stressed about the upkeep of their home because they no longer were frustrated by their spouse's participation (or lack thereof) in this task. Their husband's delinquent or irresponsible behavior with regard to household chores had caused considerable tension. Judy felt this way. When asked if it was different to keep up a home as a single parent, she reflected:

> It was easier. 'Cause I don't expect him to. There isn't that anger that he should be home to do this for the kids once in a while. He should be home to take out the garbage. . . . I just got mad that he wasn't. I would hire someone to mow the lawn, whatever. And after I was here alone with the kids that was one thing I noticed. That I wasn't angry about taking out the garbage and all that cause there was no one to expect to do it. It was a question of expectations.

The strategy these single mothers followed is what I call "reduced emotion work" associated with family care. I see "emotion work" as the component of family care that involves motivating or nurturing those who work with you (see Hochschild, 1983). As other researchers have noted, women often see their work as a blend of task involvement and "person involvement" or relationship building and caretaking (Statham, Miller, & Mauksch, 1988). Single mothers said they put less time and energy into trying to encourage the help of others around them than they did when they were married. As a result, they felt less frustrated about housework as single parents; it seemed easier to manage. In comparison with when they were married, some single women felt relief over not having to cajole or coax another adult to help with family care. Of course, they could have transferred these demands to their children or to other adults (such as close family members), but these women did not. In reality, these mothers may have had more family care tasks to do alone as single parents, yet they defined them as less strenuous because the emotional energy once directed at encouraging their spouse to help (and monitoring him, supporting him, or getting angry at him) was no longer draining them. Family care work clearly is not just the accomplishment of discrete physical tasks; it is recognized by these mothers as a combination of instrumental tasks, socioemotional treatment of one's co-workers, and one's own emotional response to this labor.

Mothers Doing Less; Fathers Doing More

Mothers also said they lowered their standards for housework following the end of their marriage by putting less effort into these tasks. This pattern parallels findings that suggest single women tend to devote less time to housework than do married women with similarly sized families (Burden, 1986; Morgan, 1978; Sanik & Mauldin, 1986).

Mothers provided four explanations for their lowered housework standards. To begin with, their values changed; they often spoke of a deeper commitment to devoting time to their children in comparison with when they were married. This response parallels some fathers' reactions to paid work following divorce (see Fassinger, 1987). Second, after divorce mothers spent less time doing housework due to longer work schedules or the demands of schooling. Women felt they had to reevaluate what they could accomplish in a day after they took on these additional burdens. As a result, mothers became more tolerant of less rigorous or continuous household care. Third, mothers put less effort into housework because they felt fewer social pressures about household care. Their friends' and neighbors' opinions of housework seemed to be less important to these single mothers than when they were married. As a consequence, their self-esteem was less intimately linked with their household work. Jo explained:

> It used to be that if somebody came to visit me my house used to have to be just so or they would think I was really a bad person. Now I think they have to accept me for who I am and not how my house looks. And if they come to see me, they shouldn't worry about my house. Not that I would let it be a filthy mess.

In contrast with mothers, fathers devoted more time to housework as single parents. Yet, men's greater involvement in housework was not fueled by their desire to live up to others' expectations; nor did these tasks have a new or enlarged impact on the men's sense of self. Fathers did not refer to others' standards as a way to measure their housekeeping performance, even when advice or support from others indicated that their housework might be judged as lacking. One 42-year-old father noted:

> Mom has tried to help more. She wants to come over here and clean the house all the time. She thinks it's dirty, and I don't think it's so dirty. She wants to come over right now and wash that window; that's her. I say don't worry about it, the rain will come and wash it off.

This example reinforces the conclusion that fathers did not see housework as integral to their parent role. Instead, housework was merely a set of tasks to do.

Finally, some women lowered their standards for homemaking because they no longer felt constrained by their spouse. Through their requests and demands, husbands had put restrictions and pressures on women's behavior around the house. For example, Marilyn thought her husband was tyrannical about housework:

> He was just so picky. It was so bad that he would go around and inspect the house. He was always looking for something to put me down for. And it was so bad that after I left [him] I was used to keeping such a clean house that it made people uncomfortable. I had a friend come to my apartment one day and she said, "This is awful," and she picked up a burner [and it was spotless] and I moved out my stove and cleaned underneath, the whole thing, every Saturday. And she said, "There is not a speck on this stove. You've got to sit down and relax a little bit. You make me uncomfortable."

S. F. Berk's (1985) and West and Zimmerman's (1987) understanding of gender and housework helps to explain why some mothers found household labor less cumbersome after becoming single. Single mothers like Marilyn may have found housework less frustrating because while they were married they were burdened by household activities that shaped gender and reinforced their secondary status. These mothers seemed to recognize how their housework served to reinforce their husband's dominance; they commented on their husband's high standards for housekeeping and their own need to do housework in ways that would please their spouse. As single parents these mothers no longer needed to use others' standards for housework and were free from interactions about housework that reinforced their spouse's dominance.

Single mothers' major plan of action was to lower standards for housework. This gender strategy corresponds directly with some married mothers' attempts to cut back on time devoted to housework and children (Hochschild, 1989). For example, some single mothers reduced their standards for housework because they gave priority to other parts of their lives (e.g., paid work or school). However, some feelings and thoughts that informed this gender strategy were expressed only by single mothers. For example, while married, some single mothers felt constrained by their husband's family care standards. In other words, it seems that husbands may have created family care work for their wife by demanding certain standards of cleanliness and care (Hartmann, 1981). Who sets standards for family care? Hochschild implies that standards are set by the main caretaker of a household. She suggests this when she calls men's redefinition of women's standards one of men's "strategies of resistance." When men redefine family needs by curtailing them, they may be resisting personal involvement in family care. However, when they assert tougher requirements for family care, they are employing a strategy that attempts to expand their control over their spouse's labor.

These single parents' comments add the following observations to Hochschild's (1989) discussion of gender strategies: (a) some married men make more work for their spouse by "raising standards" for household care, (b) some women actively reject their spouse's family care standards,[8] and (c) some women reduce their work load by redefining the relationship between housework and their self-worth.

Discussion

This study expands Hochschild's (1989) insights about "gender strategies." Through interviews with single parents, I discovered gender strategies not outlined by Hochschild. I learned that when single fathers are responsible for housework, they are likely to learn new household tasks, ignore some tasks, and get children's help with housework more than do mothers. While married, some men also set standards for their family's care. These are gendered strategies; men's experiences and their notions of masculinity and femininity influence their responses. For example, although necessity may require single fathers to learn new household tasks, their interpretations of male and female roles affect their impressions of these tasks. Eric's comments about women's "instinctive" ability to do laundry unmask his assumption that washing clothes is more challenging for men than for women. Martin's depiction of some housework as "silly," "dumb," and "little" links housework and gender by the use of adjectives most often associated with women in our culture.

These gendered images have important ramifications. In Eric's and Martin's cases, one can see effects on both self-esteem and use of help. For example, Eric's assessment of these tasks enables him to gain esteem and feel a sense of accomplishment (when he learns how to add bleach), whereas Martin's image of housework devalues the work and makes the use of children to do "silly" and "little" chores seem more reasonable.

Some housework went undone in these single fathers' homes, but not necessarily because of men's resistance as Hochschild (1989) implies. Instead, because they lacked exposure to housework, some fathers failed to understand the nature of tasks that had been "invisible" to them. For example, when married, these fathers took for granted the structure their wife had built into their daily life; it was only when they became single fathers that the logistics and routines of family care became obvious to them. The need to develop schedules became a common concern, especially for fathers who had been helpers or uninvolved. Housework's hidden dimensions contribute to gender inequality in the distribution of household labor. If men cannot see the tasks, they are unable to take part in them.

Although both fathers and mothers secured children's help with housework, I discovered that fathers use this strategy more than do mothers. Fathers and mothers also offer different rationales for requesting their children's aid. Whereas mothers ask for help because they "need it," fathers tell their children that housework is "not my job." This observation highlights an important insight from my research: Men may do more housework as single fathers, but they do not necessarily feel responsible for these activities. Single parenting may produce greater equality in men's and women's behavior (e.g., more housework for men, less for women) while preserving gendered differences in the interpretations of this behavior. Parents' sense of responsibility for housework has important implications for the degree to which fathers and mothers can expect relief from this duty. It is likely that when children do housework, fathers and mothers may experience very different amounts of down time (because mothers remain responsible). Particularly if fathers use children's help more than do mothers, the difference in down time could be quite dramatic.

Mothers in this sample utilized two gender strategies that Hochschild did not uncover. First, mothers did less emotion work in conjunction with housework. Previously mothers' emotion work involved encouraging spouses to help around the house. Second, some mothers weakened the connection between housework and their self-esteem. This strategy, if more widely adopted, could promote gender equality. The more detached from housework women become, the more willing they will be to share responsibility for housework with family members.

These discoveries offer three important insights for future research. First, it is important to distinguish between doing and being responsible for a job. Many researchers seem to imply that gender equality in family care will exist when women and men do equal amounts of work, finish equal numbers of tasks, or spend equivalent time at this labor. Surveys rarely ask respondents to distinguish between who does and who is responsible for housework.[9] However, these single parents demonstrate that fathers can do household work and not feel responsible for it. Thus, in married couple homes men may do housework but still see it as their wife's responsibility.

Second, if men and women define their responsibility for housework differently, we should not expect microstructural forces alone to create gender equality. Microstructuralists argue that greater structural similarity in men's and women's situations will help bring about gender equality. For example, Risman's (1986) microstructural survey indicated that when men are single parents, their behavior is quite similar to mothers' behavior. However, Risman's quantitative portrait was largely unable to uncover the meaning that fathers attached to their acts. My findings indicate that behavioral equality may accompany distinctly different perceptions and motivations of men and women. As a result, quantitative microstructural analyses might best be combined with an interactionist perspective to unmask qualitative distinctions that shape men's and women's lives.

Third, fathers who shared housework are an important exception to men's tendency to see housework as a family task. These men did not refer to housework as a family chore and did not utilize children's labor extensively. They also felt involved in housework when married and seemed to see housework as part of their role as parent and spouse, as did women. My interviews did not investigate what might cause some married men to share housework. Future research might examine how men form their early perceptions of their responsibility for housework.

Conclusion

A key factor that helps perpetuate gender inequality in housework is the different perception men and women have of responsibility for these tasks. This pattern was well developed during these men's and women's marriages. When single mothers reflected on the standards their former spouse imposed on their housework, they did not challenge the men's right to do this; mothers did not question women's greater obligation to do housework. Likewise, when some fathers remarked that housework was not their job, they showed that they thought of their housework involvement as an aberration, as for example a 42-year-old father who said:

> I don't feel like I should have to do that, but I will if I have to. . . . See, when I got married I figured, well, there it is. I got rid of that whole job. I don't have to do [housework] anymore.

Housework clearly is an arena in which gender and gendered relations are produced. As long as housework helps to reproduce gender, we should not be surprised when men see their involvement in housework as temporary or exceptional. By physically participating in housework, men take initial steps toward gender equality. A more difficult but essential step involves men's and women's willingness to critically examine their gendered interpretations of housework.

Notes

1. Hochschild (1989) studied "family care," which incorporates housework and child care activities. I discussed child care with single parents, but our conversations centered on the parents' relationships with their children and infrequently drew us into conversation about the physical care of children. In this sense, Hochschild's focus on child care is

broader than is mine. I use the term "family care" when attempting to draw the discussion beyond my immediate findings.

2. In addition, some interviewees are not included in this sample of 34 parents. My first 10 interviews were with divorced single parents. When I began to interview never-married parents, I realized that their experiences could not be incorporated in the categories of analysis that were developed for divorced single parents.

3. For an analysis of single parents' reactions to decision making, see Fassinger (1989b); single mothers' feelings about their paid work is discussed by Fassinger (1989a).

4. Clearly, this sample is skewed toward the middle class. During data analysis I concluded that this bias did not need to be corrected, inasmuch as the parents' marital histories seemed to be the strongest predictors of their reactions to their changed lives (see Fassinger, 1987). Working-class and middle-class parents were found within each marital history type.

5. All parents in Hochschild's sample had preschoolers at home. Most of the single parents I interviewed had school-aged children. This may help account for some of the differences in our findings.

6. Hood (1983) found that when mothers became employed, teenage daughters (not fathers) did more housework (Hoffman, 1958). Fathers did do more housework when the children were "too young to be depended upon" (Hood, 1983, p. 108). However, the children relied on by uninvolved fathers in this study were no older than 11 years.

7. Although women were a bit more likely to divorce when their children were preschoolers, the majority of these children were elementary school age at the time of this study. Thus, it would seem that age played less of a role in the parents' decisions about how much the children would help around the house than did the parents' own history of involvement in housework.

8. This is consistent with studies that show women workers long for and often devise ways to increase autonomy (Statham et al., 1988). Some single mothers in this study seem to see single parenting as an opportunity for just such autonomy; their new standards for housework contradict or subvert their ex-husband's old patterns.

9. Important exceptions include Haas (1981), Lein (1984), and Slocum and Nye (1976).

References

Berk, R. A., & Berk, S. F. (1979). *Labor and leisure at home: Content and organization of the household day.* Beverly Hills, CA: Sage.

Berk, S. F. (1985). *The gender factory: The apportionment of work in American households.* New York: Plenum.

Burden, D. S. (1986). Single parents and the work setting: The impact of multiple job and homelife responsibilities. *Family Relations, 35,* 37-43.

Charmaz, K. (1983). The grounded-theory methods: An explication and interpretation. In R. Emerson (Ed.), *Contemporary field research* (pp. 109-126). Boston: Little, Brown.

Coverman, S., & Sheley, J. (1986). Change in men's housework and child-care time, 1965-1975. *Journal of Marriage and the Family, 48*(2), 413-422.

Daniels, A. K. (1987). Invisible work. *Social Problems, 134*(5), 403-415.

DeVault, M. (1987). Doing housework: Feeding and family life. In N. Gerstel & H. E. Gross (Eds.), *Families and work* (pp. 178-191). Philadelphia: Temple University Press.

Fassinger, P. A. (1987). *Transitions in the lives of single parents: Heading a household and parenting alone.* Unpublished doctoral dissertation, Michigan State University, East Lansing.

Fassinger, P. A. (1989a). Becoming the breadwinner: Single mothers' reactions to changes in their paid work lives. *Family Relations, 38*(4), 404-411.

Fassinger, P. A. (1989b). The impact of gender and past marital experiences on heading a household alone. In B. Risman & P. Schwartz (Eds.), *Gender in intimate relationships* (pp. 165-180). Belmont, CA: Wadsworth.

Gasser, R., & Taylor, C. (1976). Role adjustment of single parent fathers with dependent children. *Family Coordinator, 25*(4), 397-401.

Glaser, B., & Strauss, A. (1967). *The discovery of grounded theory.* Chicago: Aldine.

Greif, G. L. (1985). *Single fathers.* Lexington, MA: Lexington.

Haas, L. (1981). Domestic role-sharing in Sweden. *Journal of Marriage and the Family, 43*(4), 957-965.

Hartmann, H. (1981). The family as the locus of gender, class, and political struggle: The example of housework. *Signs, 6*(3), 366-394.

Hetherington, E., Cox, M., & Cox, R. (1976). Divorced fathers. *Family Coordinator, 25*(4), 417-428.

Hochschild, A. (1983). *The managed heart: Commercialization of human feeling.* Berkeley: University of California Press.

Hochschild, A. (1989). *The second shift.* New York: Viking.

Hoffman, L. (1958). *Some effects of the employment of mothers on family structure.* Unpublished doctoral dissertation, University of Michigan, Ann Arbor.

Hood, J. (1983). *Becoming a two-job family.* New York: Praeger.

LaRossa, R., & LaRossa, M. M. (1989). Baby care: Fathers vs. mothers. In B. Risman & P. Schwartz (Eds.), *Gender in intimate relationships* (pp. 138-154). Belmont, CA: Wadsworth.

Lein, L. (1984). *Families without villains.* Lexington, MA: Lexington.

Morgan, J. (1978). A potpourri of new data gathered from interviews with husbands and wives. In G. Duncan & J. Morgan (Eds.), *Five thousand American families* (Vol. 6). Ann Arbor: University of Michigan, Institute for Social Research.

Orthner, D., Brown, T., & Ferguson, D. (1976). Single-parent fatherhood. *Family Coordinator, 25*(4), 429-437.

Risman, B. (1986). Can men mother? *Family Relations, 35*(1), 95-102.

Risman, B., & Schwartz, P. (Eds.). (1989). *Gender in intimate relationships: A microstructural approach.* Belmont, CA: Wadsworth.

Rosenfeld, J., & Rosenstein, E. (1973). Towards a conceptual framework for the study of parent-absent families. *Journal of Marriage and the Family, 35*(1), 131-135.

Sanik, M. M., & Mauldin, T. (1986). Single versus two parent families: A comparison of mothers' time. *Family Relations, 35*(1), 53-56.

Schorr, A., & Moen, P. (1979). The single parent and public policy. *Social Policy, 19,* 15-21.

Slocum, W. L., & Nye, F. I. (1976). Provider and housekeeper roles. In F. I. Nye with H. M. Bahr, S. J. Bahr, J. E. Carlson, V. Gecas, S. McLaughlin, & W. L. Slocum (Eds.), *Role structure and analysis of the family* (pp. 81-99). Beverly Hills, CA: Sage.

Statham, A., Miller, E., & Mauksch, H. (1988). The integration of work: A second-order analysis of qualitative research. In A. Statham, E. Miller, & H. Mauksch (Eds.), *The worth of women's work* (pp. 11-35). Albany: State University of New York.

Thompson, L., & Walker, A. (1989). Gender in families: Women and men in marriage, work, and parenthood. *Journal of Marriage and the Family, 51*(4), 845-871.

U. S. Bureau of the Census. (1986). *Money income of households, families, and persons in the United States: 1984* (Current Population Report, Series P-60, #151). Washington, DC: U.S. Government Printing Office.

Walker, K. E., & Woods, M. (1976). *Time use: A measure of household production of goods and services.* Washington, DC: American Home Economics Association.

Weiss, R. (1979). *Going it alone.* New York: Basic Books.

West, C., & Zimmerman, D. (1987). Doing gender. *Gender and Society, 1*(2), 125-151.

PART THREE

WORKPLACE ORGANIZATION AND POLICY

11

Are "Family-Supportive" Employer Policies Relevant to Men?

JOSEPH H. PLECK

As the rate of labor force participation among married women with children steadily increased in the last two decades in the United States, policy analysts argued that U.S. workplaces should change their policies to make it easier for employed mothers to combine their work and family roles (e.g., Kamerman & Kahn, 1981; Kamerman, Kahn, & Kingston, 1983). Rather quickly, however, the language used to describe what had originally been labeled "working mothers'" issues became gender neutral. By the late 1980s, "work and family" had clearly become the dominant term for these concerns. As recent illustrations, the *Wall Street Journal* began a biweekly "Work and Family" column in 1990, and the National Research Council's (1991) recommendations for family-supportive employer policies were published under the title *Work and Family: Policies for a Changing Work Force.*

Several related factors motivated this transformation in perspective. To some feminists, labeling this domain as working mothers' or women's issues reinforces the traditional notion that women alone are responsible for homemaking and child care. Thus, gender-neutral language conveys the expectation that men *should* share responsibility for the family. Other feminists, who perceive women to be the main beneficiaries of family-supportive workplace policies, believe that labeling them gender neutrally reduces opposition to them: corporate decision makers and male co-workers are more likely to go along with the new practices if it is not made explicit that they will predominantly be used by women. To many employers, the new terminology is also preferable because they fear that providing policies specifically designed to help employed mothers might make them vulnerable to charges of sex discrimination.

However, at conferences and workshops, I have observed negative responses to the inclusion of men that the "work and family" language implies. Many react to the term cynically or view it as a wistful fantasy. One leading policy analyst told me, for example, "Of course, no one seriously thinks these issues impact on fathers the way they do on mothers." Some women have told me they feel affronted by "work and family" and other gender-neutral terms that make women invisible. "They're not work and family issues, they are *working mothers'* issues!" On numerous occasions, I have also witnessed male managers becoming extremely uncomfortable when they realize that some others in a workshop or discussion group are using gender-inclusive language not as a polite fiction, but because they actually believe that a significant subgroup of men currently experience work-family conflicts and ought to be able to make use of family-supportive policies.

Thus, among most people there is considerable skepticism that family-supportive policies are relevant to men. Among those favoring the idea, it is more a matter of faith about what should be than belief about what is true now. Few, however, have considered the question seriously enough to examine it systematically. Based on the evidence presented in this chapter, I conclude that men make use of various employer policies to accommodate their work role to their family obligations to a far greater degree than is generally realized.

Much of the information bearing on the question of men's use of family-supportive policies is fairly technical, concerning specific details of the implementation and utilization of workplace policies that are often not widely known. At the same time, this analysis touches on other issues that are far more general. Again based on my observations in conferences and workshops, discussion of these issues quickly brings to the surface differing, deeply rooted beliefs about how substantial men's family involvement is and how much it has increased in recent decades. To view family-supportive policies as relevant to men, one must believe that a significant proportion of men has a substantial level of family responsibility. Recent publications arguing that men accept little family responsibility and are not doing more in the family than they used to (Hochschild, 1989; LaRossa, 1988) have reinforced doubts that men will use family-supportive policies to any significant degree.

In addition, data on men's use of parental leave ("paternity leave") often trigger a variety of strong positive and negative responses. To some, the availability of paternity leave is central to future change in gender roles. To others, data on paternity leave show how truly uninterested most fathers are in greater paternal responsibility. Depending on underlying assumptions one makes about the structural constraints faced by men and what kinds of behaviors represent real accommodations, these data indicate that men are making accommodations in their work life to meet their family needs either a lot or hardly at all.

In the remainder of this chapter, I first present a perspective on men's average level of family involvement and the extent to which it has increased in recent decades, issues that have recently become a matter of debate and set the stage for the potential impact of family-supportive employer policies on men. I then review evidence in several areas: levels and consequences of work-family stress in men, child care supports, flextime and other alternative work schedules, and parental leave. I conclude by analyzing some broader issues about the implementation and impact of these policies on men.

The Context: Levels and Trends in Men's Family Participation

In earlier publications (Pleck, 1985, 1987), I reported that U.S. men's average level of housework and child care combined was about 1.85 hours per day in 1975. I also recounted research findings showing that men's time in these activities increased between the mid-1960s and the early 1980s, with men's share of the total performed by both sexes rising from 20% in 1965 to 30% in 1981. In some studies the increase is evident among males or husbands overall (see also Shelton, 1989), whereas in others it is evident only among those with young children (see also Coverman & Sheley, 1986). Later investigations, employing time use data collected through 1986, have provided further documentation that time spent in family roles has continued to increase among men as a whole (Robinson, Andreyenkov, & Patrushev, 1988; Gershuny & Robinson, 1988), as well as among married and unmarried men, and among fathers and nonfathers (Robinson, 1988). Women's average time in family roles has correspondingly decreased, both among women as a whole, and among married, single, employed, nonemployed, mother, and nonmother subgroups. In the most recent available national data

(1985), married men do 34% of the housework performed by couples (Robinson, 1988). Although married men's 34% share of housework in 1985 is still far from the 50% that would denote equality, the increase from men's 20% share of housework and child care in 1965 is substantial.

Two other recent and widely cited analyses have offered different conclusions about men's levels of housework and child care, and trends in these levels. First, Hochschild (1989, p. 4), citing Szalai (1972), stated that in U.S. national data in 1965, husbands' average time in housework averaged 17 minutes per day and child care 12 minutes. These figures are the only quantitative estimates for men's average time in family roles provided in Hochschild's book, and they have been widely repeated in the media (e.g., Skow, 1989). Hochschild also asserted that husbands' time in housework and child care did not increase between 1965 and 1975.

However, the two figures Hochschild cites are actually the time spent by employed fathers only on *workdays*, when both employed men and women spend less time in family roles. The housework estimate is the smaller of the two categories of household work reported by Szalai. The larger housework category omitted in this figure includes such activities as shopping, administrative services, repairs, and waiting in line. When nonworkdays are factored in, and time spent in all housework and child care is included, these 1965 data show that employed fathers actually spent an average of 91 minutes per day in housework and child care combined. This figure is close to other published calculations based on these data, for example, Juster's (1985) estimate of 1.6 hours per day for men as a whole. It is also noteworthy that although more current data were easily available, the data Hochschild selected to report were over two decades old.[1]

Hochschild's (1989) further assertion that "between 1965 and 1975 . . . men weren't doing more housework" (p. 272) is incorrect. The study she cites on this point (Robinson, 1977), which used a narrower definition of family tasks than most other studies, actually reported that men's time in housework and child care rose from 9.0 to 9.7 hours per week between 1965 and 1975.[2] In this respect as well as by highlighting the 17- and 12-minute figures as summary estimates of men's housework and child care, Hochschild does not accurately convey what time use research has found about men's family involvement.

In a critical overview of men's family role performance focusing on fatherhood, LaRossa (1988) asserts that since the turn of the century "fatherhood has not changed (at least significantly), if one looks at the conduct of fatherhood—how fathers behave vis-a-vis their children" (p.

451). However, the two specific sources of data LaRossa discusses to support this point contradict this conclusion. The first is Lamb's (1987) report of Juster's (1985) time use data from a national sample of couples aged 25-55 interviewed in 1975 and again in 1981, which found that husbands' time in child care increased about a half hour per week, from 2.29 to 2.88 hours. LaRossa's critique is that wives' time with children also increased by this amount, and that the time use measure assessed only one of several theoretical components of father involvement.[3] Second, in the Middletown studies, Caplow, Bahr, Chadwick, Hill, and Williamson (1982) reported that the average amount of time fathers spent with children increased between 1924 and 1977 (see Pleck, 1985, 1987, for more detail). LaRossa comments that the time use measure did not distinguish between one-on-one interaction and less intense interaction. Although LaRossa's points about these two studies are valid, they in no way contradict that these studies clearly demonstrate increases in fathers' time with children.

Other data since 1981 further corroborate that fathers' average level of child care involvement is rising. Robinson et al. (1988) provides the most recent data on men's time in child care that makes a comparison to earlier decades. In making comparisons across years, it is critical to use child care figures derived from the same report, because different reports—even by the same investigator—can vary in how narrowly or broadly they define the specific activities to be considered in child care. Robinson et al. compare levels of child care (defined more narrowly than in Juster's analysis discussed above) among employed men nationally and in Jackson, Michigan, in 1966 and 1988. Employed men's time averaged 0.6 hours per week in both periods nationally, and 0.8 hours in both periods in Jackson. Making use of information that Robinson et al. provide about the proportion of the Jackson sample that had children in the two time periods (66% and 52%), employed fathers' time with children in Jackson rose from 1.21 to 1.53 hours per week between 1966 and 1986. If data were available to adjust the national figures in the same way, they would show a similar increase.

Another more recent indicator of levels and trends in men's child care responsibility derives from large-scale surveys of child care arrangements in families with employed mothers. According to the fall 1987 Current Population Survey (U.S. Bureau of the Census, 1990), in two-earner families with a child under 5 years, 18% of mothers reported that the father was the primary child care arrangement during the mother's working hours. Fathers are the primary care arrangement almost as often as are family day care homes (22%), and far more often than group care centers (14%) or grandparents (9%). Presser (1989) also reports evidence that father care for children during mothers' working hours increased between 1965 and 1985.

Father care is so frequent not because many fathers are unemployed, but because mothers and fathers often have nonoverlapping work schedules. Such "two-shift" families sometimes select these schedules as a conscious strategy to reduce child care costs, although they also occur involuntarily. The fact that fathers are the primary arrangement during mothers' work hours in almost one out of five dual-earner families with preschool children suggests that a much higher proportion of fathers have significant child care responsibility than is usually thought.

No one questions that men perform less housework and child care than women, and that the rate of change in males' share of these family responsibilities has been relatively slow. However, the level and rate of increase in men's family involvement are greater than Hochschild and LaRossa suggest. Recent evidence that husbands on average perform one third of the housework and one of five fathers with an employed wife is the primary child care arrangement for his preschool child suggests that family-supportive policies may be more relevant to men than is generally realized.

The Evidence

If men are spending more time in family roles, is there corresponding evidence that men experience conflict between their work and family responsibilities? If they do, what do we know about the extent to which men make use of the three most important family-supportive workplace policies: child care supports, flexible schedules, and parental leave? And what do we know about the impact of these policies on men's family behavior?

Levels and Consequences of Work-Family Stress

Many surveys of workers have documented that substantial proportions of working fathers report stress in combining work and family roles, or say they are interested in using specific policies to reduce this stress. In some surveys, men's stress levels or desire to use policies equals or exceeds women's. For example, in a 1987 study of 1600 employees at a public utility and a high-technology company in the Northeast, 36% of fathers (compared to 37% of mothers) reported "a lot of stress" in balancing their work and family lives. In another 1987 survey of 1200 employees in a Minneapolis company, higher percentages of fathers than mothers reported difficulties with child care (72% vs. 65%) and general "dual-career problems" (70% vs. 63%) (Trost, 1988; see also Pleck, Staines, & Lang, 1980).

Other studies find that fathers report lower rates of work-family problems. Nonetheless, the proportion of fathers reporting difficulties in these studies is substantial, for example, 23% in a 1987 survey of employees in Portland, Oregon (Regional Research Institute for Human Services, 1987). Some research also finds that although fathers report work-family problems less frequently than mothers, when stress occurs it has more negative consequences for men than for women (Bolger, DeLongis, Kessler, & Wethington, 1989). Another study found that although men were less likely to miss work when child care arrangements broke down, missing work for this reason is more strongly associated with stress, poor health, and diminished well-being among men than among women (Shinn, Ortiz-Torres, Morris, & Simko, 1987). It has also been documented that fathers miss work and are late for work more frequently than nonfathers (Emlen, 1987; Regional Research Institute for Human Services, 1987).

Men's interest in using specific policies to reduce work-family stress is also increasing. In surveys of large samples of Dupont employees, the proportion who said they wanted the option of part-time work to allow them to spend more time with their children rose from 18% in 1985 to 33% in 1988 (Thomas, 1988). The percentage expressing personal interest in leave to care for newborn children increased from 15% in 1986 to 35% in 1991; the proportion interested in leave to care for sick children rose from 40% to 64% in the same period ("Labor Letter," 1991).

Child Care Supports

Affordable, high-quality child care is perhaps working parents' greatest need. It is becoming widely recognized that employers can help workers meet their needs for child care. Companies can do this not only or primarily by providing on-site centers, but by purchasing slots or otherwise subsidizing local child care centers, fostering family day care networks, providing information and referral services, and by making it possible for workers to pay for child care with pretax income (dependent care reimbursement programs).

No systematic data concerning the availability or utilization of these child care policies by men are available. Anecdotal information occasionally appears, such as the reports that 8% of the clients of the child care information and referral service at Hallmark Cards are fathers ("Labor Letter," 1988) and that 40% of the parents dropping off children at a Massachusetts on-site center are fathers ("Fathers make more use of on-site day care," 1991). The reports and the findings noted earlier that fathers miss and are late for work more often than nonfathers and that child care problems have a negative effect on fathers' health suggest that fathers will use employer-provided child care supports when present.

Flextime and Other Alternative Work Schedules

The second main workplace policy supporting families is flexible work schedules. A particularly important example is "flextime," in which workers have some latitude to set their starting and ending times, but continue to work a full day. Several studies have investigated the impact of flextime on men's family involvement and on the marital division of labor. Winett and Neale (1980) interviewed parents of children under age 13 working in the Washington, D.C., headquarters of two federal agencies before and after the introduction of flextime. The study found that 16 of 34 fathers (47%), compared with 18 of 37 mothers (49%), changed their schedule. In all cases workers chose to start work earlier so that they could leave work earlier.

Those who changed their schedules when flextime was introduced spent more time with their spouse and children. Although Winett and Neale do not report data on this point for fathers and mothers separately, they suggest that the two sexes showed the same patterns. In the first agency, parents who changed their schedule increased their family time by over an hour a day (most of the increase was in time with children), whereas those who kept the same schedule reported no change. In the second agency, averaging over the 28 weeks for which data were collected following the introduction of flextime, schedule changers increased their family time by 37 minutes a day, compared with a 5-minute increase in the nonchangers. The increment in the schedule changers' overall family time was slightly less by the end of the period studied, but it was still substantial (31 minutes per day greater than it was before flextime). The increase in child care showed no diminution. In both agencies, parents who altered their schedules also reported that it was easier for them to spend time with their children.

Another study, using a sample of British male scientific workers, confirmed that the introduction of flextime was associated with an increase in child care and child socialization activities among men with employed wives (Lee, 1983). A third study found no difference in child care time between fathers working in an agency on flextime and those working in an agency on standard schedules (Bohen & Viveros-Long, 1981). However, because this study did not compare fathers before and after flextime began, or focus on the subgroup who used flextime to change their schedules, its results are less meaningful.

Many analysts have been skeptical of the potential positive effects of flextime, particularly in promoting a more equitable marital division of labor (Bohen, 1984; Presser, 1989). Actually, because flextime promotes family time among both men and women, and is equally available to both sexes, it is likely to have no overall average impact on couples' division of family responsibility. Nonetheless, the two available experimental studies clearly show that flextime increases fathers' involvement with their children. Maklan (1977) earlier found that another alternative schedule, the 4-day (or "compressed") work week, also fostered fathers' spending more time with their children.

In my experience, when fathers use flextime and other alternative work schedules to increase their time with their children, it is generally not recognized as such. This use of flextime as a male work-family "accommodation" strategy (Bailyn, 1978) tends to be invisible because of gender role stereotypes. If a father with flextime changes his schedule, it may simply not occur to co-workers and supervisors that a child care need or a desire to spend more time with his child is the reason for the change. Many fathers may likewise find it simplest to let others think that something else motivated their change in schedule. The resulting invisibility of flextime as a male work-family accommodation then further reinforces the stereotype that fathers do not adjust or limit their work role to meet family obligations.

Formal Paternity Leave

Parental leave differs from the policies previously discussed in two important respects. When employers began to provide child care supports and flexible work schedules over the last two decades, many probably assumed that all or most users would be women. Even so, companies adopting these policies routinely made them available to both sexes. Doing so did not require any basic shift in employers' perception of men's family role. In addition, as noted above, fathers and employers collude to keep invisible men's use of these policies as work-family accommodations. By contrast, employers providing parental leave benefits to women have had great difficulty extending them to men. Men who take parental leave invariably generate considerable interest. Unlike child care supports and flexible schedules, employers offering, and fathers using, parental leave requires a fundamental shift in how employers view men.

Formal paternity leave is available to a substantial minority of male workers (Pleck, 1986). In the most recent (1989) Federal Employee Benefits Survey covering workers in medium-sized and large private establishments (those with 100 or more workers), 18% of full-time male workers had unpaid paternity leave and 1% had paid leave, compared to 37% of women covered by paid maternity leave and 3% with unpaid leave (Hyland, 1990). In 1990, 8% of such workers in firms with fewer than 100 workers were eligible for paternity leave (U.S. Bureau of Labor Statistics, 1991). Thirty-three percent of full-time male workers in state and local governments had paternity leave in 1990 ("Employee benefits in state and local governments address family concerns," 1991). Surveys of large companies likewise show that a large minority offer paternity leave, for example, 44% in Christensen's (1989) analysis of 502 large manufacturing and service firms in 1988.

Only two U.S. studies have collected systematic data on fathers' utilization of parental leave. Of the 119 companies offering unpaid leave to fathers in a 1984 investigation, only 9 reported that a father had taken leave under this policy, and in most of these, only 1 father had done so (Catalyst, 1986). A survey conducted by a national recruiting firm in 1990 concluded that slightly more than 1% of eligible fathers use leave (Vrazo, 1990). Recent reports about specific companies indicate that the number of fathers taking leave is zero or extremely low in many companies (e.g., Cray Research, Campbell Soup, Dow Jones; Alexander, 1990).

However, these recent accounts also suggest that in some other large firms, fathers' use of parental leave is becoming more common. At Commonwealth Edison (Chicago), 25 fathers applied for child care leave between 1985 and 1988 (Trost, 1988). The number of fathers taking leave is increasing at Aetna, Eastman Kodak, American Telephone and Telegraph (AT&T), 3M, and Lotus Development (Hammonds, 1991). For example, 23 fathers took leaves at Lotus in 1990, compared with 29 in the previous 2 years combined. At Eastman Kodak, 61 men took paternity leave in the last 3 years. At AT&T, men account for 1 of every 50 employees taking family leave, compared to 1 in 400 a decade ago; 82% do so for 3 months or longer, a higher rate than for women. About 10% of the employees taking family leave at IBM are men (Vrazo, 1990).

It is noteworthy that enough fathers have wanted paternity leave strongly enough that a body of case and administrative law has established fathers' entitlement to child care leave when employers provide it to mothers. In the most recently settled case, the U.S. Court of Appeals for the Third Circuit ruled in May 1990 that the Pittsburgh Board of Education's policy providing 1-year unpaid child care leave only to female teachers was discriminatory and ordered reinstatement and back pay to Gerald Schafer, a teacher who had been denied leave (*Schafer vs. Board of Public Education,* 1990). In August 1990, the Equal Employment Opportunity Commission subsequently adopted the position that child care leave must be afforded to women and men on an equal basis (Bureau of National Affairs, 1991). Pleck (1988) recounts details of five earlier paternity leave cases during the 1980s.

Data from Sweden are also relevant to understanding the father's utilization of paternity leave. Although Sweden is not the only European country providing paternity leave (Norway, Denmark, Finland, Iceland, West Germany, France, and Portugal do also; Pleck, 1988), the Swedish policy is of particular interest because it is the most generous, the oldest, and the most consciously intended to promote paternal involvement. As noted by Haas (this volume), in the most recent available data, for 1989, 44% of fathers in married couple families used some of the couple's parental leave entitlement. Among fathers who took leave, the average number of days taken was 43. The typical pattern is for fathers and mothers to take leaves sequentially rather than simultaneously, that is, the father takes leave only after the mother completes whatever period of leave she takes.

Swedish fathers' rate of leave taking rose in several stages since the policy was introduced in 1974. The percentage of eligible fathers taking leave during the child's first year rose from 3% to 10% in the first 4 years of the policy, and then jumped to 21% in 1978 when the period of leave available was markedly lengthened. Fathers' utilization stabilized at around this figure through 1986 (Haas, 1992). The rate has increased since 1986 through a combination of public education to promote fathers taking leave and increasing the period paid at a high rate (90%-100% of salary), as opposed to a subsistence rate, from 9 to 12 months. In addition, Swedish fathers use two other categories of leave at high rates. Parents can take paid leave to care for a sick child; 30% of married fathers drew some of this benefit in 1984, for an average of 5.3 days, compared to 40% of mothers, for 6.5 days. About 85% take a special 10-day leave at the birth of a child (Pleck, 1988; Sandqvist, 1987; see also Haas, this volume).

"Informal" Paternity Leave

Before considering the factors influencing fathers' use of parental leave, it is important to call attention to a form of leave-taking behavior that has only recently been recognized: "informal" paternity leave. The data considered so far concern the extent to which fathers take parental leave made available through formal policies. Almost all the U.S. data derive from surveys of companies, in which personnel offices report how many fathers have used these policies. Because I was concerned that such information might not fully reflect what fathers actually do, I collected relevant data directly from fathers themselves. In surveys conducted in 1988, 1990, and 1991, I interviewed 142 fathers with preschool children to find out whether and how much time they took off from work when their child was born. These fathers came from a college-sponsored nursery school, the hometown networks of college students, and the birth records of a working-class town.

Of the sample of 142 fathers, 124 (87%) reported they had taken at least some days off work. The average number of days taken was 5.3. On the average, about half this time consisted of vacation and sick days, but the other half appeared to be discretionary days off. That is, following a birth, supervisors and co-workers appeared to allow a father to take a few extra days off without loss of pay as long as he does not abuse this flexibility. It is also noteworthy that fathers generally did not label this time as "paternity leave"; 82% of the fathers who took days off work in my 1988 survey reported that they did *not* think of their days off in this way.

Two studies conducted since I first collected these data confirm fathers' high rates of leave taking when it is assessed by measures asking whether fathers take time off from work rather than whether they used a formal leave policy. The Four State Parental Leave Study found that 75% of a sample of 1,395 fathers of newborns in Minnesota, Oregon, Rhode Island, and Wisconsin took at least some leave from work (Bond, Galinsky, Lord, Staines, & Brown, 1991). Essex and Klein (1991) also found that 75% of a sample of 55 Wisconsin fathers took some leave.

Some may question the meaningfulness of taking vacation and sick days off after a birth and be skeptical of the value of leaves averaging 5 to 6 days. Use of vacation and sick days may seem trivial, until one realizes that many workers' vacations are scheduled by the employer, not the worker, and that many employers require medical certification, often from a company doctor, to take paid sick days. Another indicator that use of vacation or sick days for parental leave is not to be taken for granted is that several company surveys show that substantial proportions of employers have explicit policies either permitting or prohibiting such use (Bureau of National Affairs, 1986).

Although longer leaves would no doubt have greater value, one should not minimize the benefits to mother and family of even these few days. Perhaps those who think 5 workdays off makes no difference should ask the new mother whose husband took *no* days off. In addition, I analyzed the relationship between the amount of time fathers took off and their later involvement in child care. In two of the three samples (1988 and 1991), the more days the father took off from work, the higher his reported current involvement in child care, even after controlling for the child's age and sex, mother's employment status, and father's work hours. Two of three available Swedish studies also suggest modest positive associations between paternity leave time and later involvement with the child (Hwang, 1987; Lamb et al., 1988). Although these associations do not necessarily show that taking time off from work at birth *causes* higher levels of later paternal involvement, they do indicate that leave taking is consistent with a broader pattern of greater paternal involvement.

Thus, although few fathers use formal parental leave policies, the large majority *do* take informal parental leave by arranging to take a small number of days off work, without loss of pay, in other ways. What makes this possible is that informal paternity leave involves no loss of pay, and usually no formal application procedure. By contrast, taking a formal parental leave almost always leads to loss of pay (a particularly important factor if the mother is also taking unpaid job leave or leaving her job), besides requiring formal application and approval.

What Influences Whether Fathers Take Paternity Leave?

The way the question is often put is "Why do so few fathers take paternity leave?" The data presented above, however, suggest that the question should really be why so few fathers take formal, long-term, unpaid leaves. The most important reason is that the majority of fathers simply do not feel a desire to take this kind of leave. For most men, taking such a leave is not part of their conception of their role as father. Unlike mothers, fathers have not grown up believing there is a special bond between themselves and their child that requires their being home full-time during the first months of their child's life.

Several other factors reinforce fathers' low motivation to take formal long-term leaves. These additional influences also act as disincentives to formal leave taking among the minority of fathers who *do* want to take such leaves. Formal paternity leave for men is almost always unpaid. Even among fathers motivated to take time off, most will be reluctant to lose pay, especially at a time when the birth of a child has increased the family's economic responsibilities. In addition, fathers' choice about leave occurs in the context of the choices mothers make. Because most employed new mothers either take leave (usually unpaid) or stop working, most couples will perceive the father taking an unpaid leave at this time to be a luxury they cannot afford. There is also a disincentive for the alternative option of the father, but not mother taking leave, in that fathers usually earn more than mothers, and paternity leave thus "costs" more.

Because paternity leave in Sweden is paid, its utilization rates give some additional insight into how income loss may interact with mothers' leave taking in influencing fathers' behavior. It is often uncritically assumed that whether a father takes leave under the Swedish policy reflects only and directly whether he wants to. However, because the policy limits the total amount of leave time taken by the couple, the father's taking leave in effect reduces the amount available to the mother. Whether the father uses some of the leave allotment probably more often represents a couple's decision than the father's alone. In addition, an often-overlooked contextual factor is that Swedish pediatricians strongly emphasize full-time breastfeeding during the first 6 months (Haas, this volume). As noted earlier, Swedish fathers' utilization of birth leave increased markedly at two points, in 1978 and in the late 1980s, each corresponding to substantial expansion in the total amount of leave paid at full salary. In effect, each increase in the leave entitlement made it possible for a higher proportion of mothers to take the full length of leave they wanted, without entirely using up all the leave months available at full pay. Thus, the proportion of fathers using some of the leave allotment jumped sharply. At the same time, the fact that even with the most recent increase in the entitlement, the majority of fathers take no birth leave suggests that among this large group, loss of income is not the barrier to paternal leave taking.

A second general disincentive to paternity leave is that employers and co-workers have negative attitudes about it. As an extreme example, the late business leader Malcolm Forbes (1986) editorialized that "New daddies need paternity leave like they need a hole in the head" (p. 19). A human resource manager observed that "There's something in the corporate culture that says to men, 'Don't do it'" (Lawson, 1991, p. C1). As one father described it, "There was nothing in the policy that said that men could not take the leave, but there was an unwritten rule that men do not do it" (Lawson, 1991, p. C8). Another observer who interviewed fathers in a variety of businesses reported, "At a number of companies, there's a joke—'Sure, we have parental leave, and the first guy who uses it will have an arrow in his back'" (Levine, quoted in Vrazo, 1990, p. 17). In addition to being viewed as uncommitted to the job, men who take leaves are perceived as unmasculine. One researcher noted, "We haven't escaped the notion that house-husbands are, to a certain degree, wimpier than persons who are not" (Alexander, 1990, p. B1). The relatively high numbers of fathers noted earlier to take leave in a few companies indirectly corroborates the role of corporate cultures: Certain firms seem to have climates in which a father taking a formal paternity leave is more acceptable.

An employer survey provides some quantitative documentation of the general negative workplace attitude. Companies who currently provided paternity leave were asked how long a leave they thought would be reasonable for a father to take; 41% indicated that *no* amount of time was reasonable (Catalyst, 1986). This study also observed that many companies do not notify men that they have a parental leave entitlement and had extended parental leave to both parents only to avoid the appearance of sex discrimination, not because they intended or expected fathers to use it. In addition, even in Sweden, where there are explicit legal prohibitions against penalizing fathers who take leave, many fathers and employers report that employers do in fact view leave-taking fathers negatively and punish them in various ways (Hwang, 1987).

Finally, an additional reason that most U.S. fathers do not take long-term formal leave may be that it is relatively easy to take short-term informal leave. That is, most fathers have available an alternative that meets, at least to a limited degree, their need to be at home. Although this alternative is limited, it has the advantage that it does not lead to loss of pay or to being labeled as uncommitted to their jobs, odd, or unmasculine.

Conclusions

The inclusion of men has not been a central issue in the evolution of family-supportive workplace policies. Policies concerning alternative work schedules and child care benefits were initially developed on a gender-neutral basis, and there has been surprisingly little interest in monitoring the degree of male as compared to female utilization. It seems unlikely that anyone would interpret data showing lower male usage as a rationale for limiting them only to women. The extension of formal parental leave benefits to men has required more of an explicit cognitive shift by employers, and there has been somewhat more interest in the extent to which men use these benefits when they are available. But even here, few data have been collected, and the unions and employers who currently have formal policies providing gender-neutral leave generally show little interest in monitoring or reporting male usage.

In the areas for which direct evidence exists to make a comparison, men appear to use family-supportive policies in ways both similar to and different from women's. Men use flextime to about the same degree as women, and with the same consequences for their family participation, although these effects tend to be less visible. Most men do take time off from work when children are born. However, they typically do so on an informal, short-term basis in contrast to women's taking long-term, formal leave. There is also evidence that men experience work-family stress, and that this stress has negative consequences for them—in several studies actually greater than for women. Thus, to a far greater extent than is usually realized, men *do* engage in work-family accommodations or adaptations, that is, they negotiate the demands of their jobs to meet family needs. In spite of the assumption that only women accommodate their jobs to their family, many men do so as well.

Men's work-family accommodations tend to be less visible than women's. Some male adaptations, such as use of flextime, are usually perceived as motivated by other purposes. Other accommodations, such as informal paternity leave, are often not noticed at all, and when they are noticed, their significance is minimized or interpreted in other ways. On several occasions when managers have told me they have never seen any father take paternity leave, I have asked them to describe what happened the last time a male in their immediate work group had a child. Invariably managers describe a pattern of the man using vacation days, sick days, compensatory time off, and other informal time off totaling a week or more. When I respond that in some ways this sounds like paternity leave, they become extremely uncomfortable. To others, the data on informal paternity leave just show that men don't want to take *real* parental leave. In effect, many observers do not acknowledge men's parental leave patterns because they are comparing men's behavior to a standard derived from women, and because men do not fit this standard, conclude that men are not taking parental leave. This judgment parallels the way women's employment behavior has traditionally been discounted because it departs from the male model (e.g., women are not really attached to the labor force if they work part-time or interrupt employment for early child rearing).

Two principles appear to influence the extent to which men use particular family-supportive policies. Men use policies to the extent that their use (a) does not reduce their earnings, weakening their role and identity as breadwinners, and (b) does not cause them to be perceived as uncommitted to their jobs or unmasculine. Particular policies will be used most if their "cost" on these two dimensions are low and will be used far less if their cost is higher on either. These two rules are adequate to account for why men use flextime and informal paternity leave at relatively high rates, but formal paternity leave to a much lesser degree.

The second principle illustrates the important role of workplace culture in regulating how men use family-supportive policies. Attitudes held by others in the workplace culture determine whether a man's use of a particular formal policy is perceived as impugning his commitment to work and his masculinity. Workplace culture can create expectations for male performance that exceed "official" demands of the job. In some companies, if a father leaves work at 5:00 or 5:30, male co-workers will joke, "Are you working part time now?" (Levine, 1991, p. 3). Workplace norms also define some informal work-family accommodations, as in informal paternity leave, as well as stimulate the development of others. As illustrations of the latter, Levine (1991) identifies a number of strategies fathers use to leave work on time without appearing uncommitted: the "avoid the supervisor ploy" (not leaving until just after the supervisor leaves or parking in the back lot to avoid being seen leaving by others) and the "another meeting ploy" (saying you have to break away from work for a "meeting").

To reduce employed fathers' work-family conflicts and to promote greater family involvement, further attention to how men actually use formal family-supportive policies as well as the adaptations men develop informally are needed. Future research should focus particularly on the role of workplace culture in the men's use of formal policies and men's initiation of informal ones. As one consultant who works with large companies observed,

> When we first started doing this the groups of men and of women sounded very different. If the men complained at all about long hours, they complained about their wives' complaints. Now if the timbre of the voice was disguised, I couldn't tell which is which. The men are saying: "I don't want to live this way. I want to be with my kids." I think the corporate culture will have to begin to respond to that. (Galinsky, quoted in Quindlen, 1990, p. IV-19)

Notes

1. Hochschild (1989, p. 279, note 2) cites Szalai (1972, p. 668) as the source for the 17- and 12-minute estimates, but these numbers are actually taken from p. 642 and concern the subgroup of men who are employed and have children. My calculation is based on data reported on pp. 642, 644, and 646 for employed married men with children. Also, although Hochschild (pp. 3, 271-273) does discuss data from other and more recent studies concerning men's *total* time spent in work and family roles compared to women's (the "leisure gap"), she does not report their estimates of men's time in family roles by themselves, all of which are dramatically higher than the 17- and 12-minute figures she highlights.

2. Some other analyses of changes in men's family time comparing these two surveys find a decrease. Pleck (1985, pp. 143-146) discusses the inconsistencies among these analyses.

3. These figures are averages for a sample including husbands both with and without children, although LaRossa's summary does not make this clear. Also, LaRossa does not note that this is the only time use study finding that women's time in child care increased over time.

References

Alexander, S. (1990, August 24). Fears for careers curb paternity leaves. *Wall Street Journal,* pp. B1, B4.

Bailyn, L. (1978). Accommodation of work to family. In R. Rapoport & R. Rapoport (Eds.), *Working couples* (pp. 17-30). New York: Harper & Row.

Bohen, H. (1984). Gender equality in work and family: An elusive goal. *Journal of Family Issues, 5,* 254-272.

Bohen, H., & Viveros-Long, A. (1981). *Balancing jobs and family life: Do flexible schedules help?* Philadelphia: Temple University Press.

Bolger, N., DeLongis, A., Kessler, R. C., & Wethington, E. (1989). The contagion of stress across multiple roles. *Journal of Marriage and the Family, 51,* 175-183.

Bond, J. T., Galinsky, E., Lord, M., Staines, G. L., & Brown, K. R. (1991). *Beyond the parental leave debate: The impact of laws in four states.* New York: Families and Work Institute.

Bureau of National Affairs. (1986). *Work and family: A changing dynamic.* Washington, DC: Author.

Bureau of National Affairs. (1991). *Equal benefits for men: Avoiding corporate liability in parental leave programs* (BNA Special Report Series on Work and Family, #39). Washington, DC: Author.

Caplow, T., Bahr, S., Chadwick, B. A., Hill, R. E., & Williamson, M. (1982). *Middletown families.* Minneapolis: University of Minnesota Press.

Catalyst. (1986). *Report on a national study of parental leaves.* New York: Author.

Christensen, K. (1989). *Flexible staffing and scheduling in U.S. corporations.* New York: Conference Board.

Coverman, S., & Sheley, J. F. (1986). Change in men's housework and child-care time, 1965-1975. *Journal of Marriage and the Family, 48,* 413-422.

Emlen, A. C. (1987, August). *Panel on child care, work and family.* Paper presented at the American Psychological Association, New York.

Employee benefits in state and local governments address family concerns. (1991, October 31). *News,* Bureau of Labor Statistics, U.S. Department of Labor.

Essex, M. J., & Klein, M. H. (1991). The Wisconsin parental leave study: The roles of fathers. In J. S. Hyde & M. J. Essex (Eds.), *Parental leave and child care: Setting a research and policy agenda* (pp. 280-293). Philadelphia: Temple University Press.

Fathers make more use of on-site day care. (1991, September 4). *Wall Street Journal,* p. B1.

Forbes, M. S. (1986, July 14). Fact and comment. *Forbes,* p. 19.

Gershuny, J., & Robinson, J. P. (1988). Historical changes in the household division of labor. *Demography, 25,* 537-552.

Haas, L. (1992). *Equal parenthood and social policy: A study of parental leave in Sweden.* Albany: State University of New York Press.

Hammonds, K. (1991, April 15). Taking steps toward a daddy track. *Business Week,* pp. 90-92.

Hochschild, A. (1989). *The second shift: Working parents and the revolution at home.* New York: Viking.

Hwang, C. P. (1987). The changing role of Swedish fathers. In M. E. Lamb (Ed.), *The father's role: Cross cultural perspectives* (pp. 115-138). Hillsdale, NJ: Lawrence Erlbaum.

Hyland, S. L. (1990). Helping employees with family care. *Monthly Labor Review, 113,* 22-26.

Juster, F. T. (1985). A note on recent changes in time use. In F. T. Juster & F. Stafford, (Eds.), *Time, goods, and well-being* (pp. 313-332). Ann Arbor: University of Michigan, Institute for Social Research.

Kamerman, S. B., & Kahn, A. J. (1981). *Child care, family benefits, and working parents.* New York: Columbia University Press.

Kamerman, S. B., Kahn, A. J., & Kingston, P. W. (1983). *Maternity policies and working women.* New York: Columbia University Press.

Labor letter. (1988, July 19). *Wall Street Journal,* p.1.

Labor letter. (1991, April 30). *Wall Street Journal,* p. 1.

Lamb, M. E. (1987). Introduction: The emergent American father. In M. E. Lamb (Ed.), *The father's role: Cross-cultural perspectives* (pp. 3-25). Hillsdale, NJ: Lawrence Erlbaum.

Lamb, M. E., Hwang, P., Broberg, A., Bookstein, F., Hult, G., & Frodi, M. (1988). The determinants of paternal involvement in a representative sample of primiparous Swedish families. *International Journal of Behavior and Development, 11,* 433-449.

LaRossa, R. (1988). Fatherhood and social change. *Family Relations, 37,* 451-457.

Lawson, C. (1991, May 26). Baby beckons: Why is daddy at work? *New York Times,* pp. C1, C8.

Lee, R. A. (1983). Flexitime and conjugal roles. *Journal of Occupational Behaviour, 4,* 297-315.

Levine, J. A. (1991, June 11). *The invisible dilemma: Working fathers in corporate America* (Testimony at the hearing "Babies and briefcases: Creating a family-friendly workplace for fathers"). Washington, DC: U.S. House of Representatives, Select Committee on Children, Youth, and Families.

Maklan, D. (1977). *The four-day workweek.* New York: Praeger.

National Research Council. (1991). *Work and family: Policies for a changing work force.* Washington, DC: National Academy Press.

Pleck, J. H. (1985). *Working wives, working husbands.* Newbury Park, CA: Sage.

Pleck, J. H. (1986). Employment and fatherhood: Issues and innovative policies. In M. E. Lamb (Ed.), *The father's role: Applied perspectives* (pp. 385-412). New York: John Wiley.

Pleck, J. H. (1987). The contemporary man. In M. Scher, G. Eichenfield, M. Stevens, & G. Good (Eds.), *Handbook on counseling and psychotherapy with men* (pp. 16-27). Beverly Hills, CA: Sage.

Pleck, J. H. (1988). Fathers and infant care leave. In E. Zigler & M. Franks (Eds.), *The parental leave crisis: Toward a national policy* (pp. 177-191). New Haven, CT: Yale University Press.

Pleck, J. H., Staines, G. L., & Lang, L. (1980). Conflicts between work and family life. *Monthly Labor Review, 102*(3), 29-32.

Presser, H. B. (1989). Can we make time for children? The economy, work schedules, and child care. *Demography, 26,* 523-543.

Quindlen, A. (1990, February 18). Men at work. *New York Times,* p. IV-19.

Regional Research Institute for Human Services. (1987). *Employee Profiles: 1987 Dependent Care Survey.* Unpublished report, Portland State University.

Robinson, J. P. (1977). *Changes in Americans' use of time, 1965-75: A progress report.* Cleveland, OH: Cleveland State University, Communications Research Center.

Robinson, J. P. (1988). Who's doing the housework. *American Demographics, 10* (12), 24ff.

Robinson, J. P., Andreyenkov, V. G., & Patrushev, V. D. (1988). *The rhythm of everyday life: How Soviet and American citizens use time.* Boulder, CO: Westview.

Sandqvist, K. (1987). Swedish family policy and the attempt to change paternal roles. In C. Lewis & M. O'Brien (Eds.), *Reassessing fatherhood: New observations on fathers and the modern family* (pp. 144-160). Stockholm: Almqvist & Wiksell.

Schafer v. Board of Public Education, Bureau of National Affairs, Special Report No. 39, 26 (3rd Cir. 1990).

Shelton, B. A. (1989). *"Real" change or pseudo change? Sources of change in men's and women's domestic labor time, 1975-1981.* Unpublished manuscript, State University of New York at Buffalo.

Shinn, M., Ortiz-Torres, B., Morris, A., & Simko, P. (1987, August). *Child care patterns, stress, and job behaviors among working parents.* Paper presented to the American Psychological Association, New York.

Skow, J. (1989, August 7). The myth of male housework. *Time,* p. 62.

Szalai, A. (Ed.) (1972). *The use of time: Daily activities of urban and suburban populations in twelve countries.* The Hague: Mouton.

Thomas, E. (1988, December 18). The reluctant father. *Newsweek,* pp. 64-66.

Trost, C. (1988, November 1). Men, too, wrestle with career-family stress. *Wall Street Journal,* p. 33.

U.S. Bureau of the Census. (1990). *Who's minding the kids? Child care arrangements: Winter 1986-7* (Current Population Reports, Series P-70, No. 20). Washington, DC: U.S. Government Printing Office.

U.S. Bureau of Labor Statistics. (1991). *Employee benefits in small private establishments, 1990* (Bulletin 2388). Washington, DC: U.S. Department of Labor.

Vrazo, D. (1990, October 15). Paternity leaves offered more often. *Providence Journal,* p. 17.

Winett, R. A., & Neale, M. S. (1980, November). Results of experimental study on flexitime and family life. *Monthly Labor Review, 113,* 29-32.

12

Nurturing Fathers and Working Mothers

Changing Gender Roles in Sweden

LINDA HAAS

Increasing attention is being paid in the U.S. media and in the social scientific literature to the changing roles of women and men in U.S. families. As wives' and mothers' labor force participation rates have increased, more people have suggested that men take on greater responsibility in the home for housework and child care. Surveys have found that Americans believe women and men should be equally responsible for housework and child care when both work for pay outside the home (Haas, 1986; Hiller & Philliber, 1986; Huber & Spitze, 1983). However, this interest in changing roles in the family has not led to an appreciable increase in the extent to which women and men share domestic work (Hochschild, 1989; Hood, 1986; LaRossa, 1988; Pleck, 1985).

What might bring an end to the gender-based division of labor? One way to approach this question is to study a society that has been striving deliberately to abolish gender roles. For over 25 years, Sweden has had an official policy of gender equality (*jämställdhet*) that calls for the sexes' equal involvement in employment and parenting. The purpose of this chapter is to (a) discuss this policy and explain how it came about, (b) report how well Swedish men in fact live up to the egalitarian model, and (c) examine the barriers to complete realization of the goal of gender equality in Sweden.

Methods

Findings in this chapter are based on seven study trips to Sweden in 1975-1990. These trips involved library research; interviews with researchers, officials, feminists, and parents; and a mail survey of parents of young children.

The survey was conducted in 1986 in Gothenburg, a city of half a million inhabitants. A sample was obtained from two local social insurance offices' lists of parents receiving parental leave benefits for a child born in 1984, or 15-27 months old at the time of the study. In order to be eligible for benefits, both parents had to be in the labor force before the baby was born. All couples who received benefits and still lived in the area were sent two questionnaires to complete. I was unable to improve upon the initial 44% response rate because insurance officials prohibited follow-ups ($N = 319$ couples). Despite the danger of bias from the low response rate and the small number of offices allowed for study, the responding group was similar to the general population of parents in Gothenburg with regard to social class, family structure, family size, and fathers' degree of participation in parental leave (Haas, 1992).

Jämställdhet—*The Ideal*

In 1968, the Swedish government submitted a report on the status of women to the United Nations. It presented a radical view on gender roles, advocating the abolition of separate spheres for men and women (Sandlund, 1971). No other government goes so far as to stipulate that men and women are equally responsible for children's economic support as well as their care and supervision (Kamerman, Kahn, & Kingston, 1983; Lamb & Levine, 1983; Qvarfort, McCrae, & Kolenda, 1988). Recently, other Nordic countries (notably Norway) have shown more interest in changing men's roles, but progress lags behind Sweden's (Nordic Council of Ministers, 1988).

This radical view on gender roles is reflected in governmental, political party, and trade union policy. For example, national curriculum guidelines set in 1969 require schools to:

> promote equality between the sexes—in the family, in the labor market, and in the community at large. . . . The schools should assume that men and women

> will play the same role in the future, that preparation for the parental role is just as important for boys as for girls and that girls have reason to be just as interested in their careers as boys. (Baude, 1979, p. 153)

In 1976, the most conservative political party expressed its commitment to "increase responsibility on the part of men for housework and child care" (Eduards, 1988, p. 7). The National Labor Market Board stated in 1977: "The right for men to take responsibility for their children on the same basis as women must be accepted and encouraged" (Arbetsmarknadsstyrelsen, 1977).

Programs Designed to Bring About Equality

Many programs and laws have been developed in line with the official policy for gender equality. These policies are designed to improve women's opportunities in the labor market, promote fathers' participation in child care, and help both parents combine work and family roles.

The most important initiatives to increase women's qualifications for and interest in employment include lifting of protective legislation that limits women's access to certain jobs, a tax reform making individuals rather than couples pay income taxes (thereby decreasing the tax burden on two-earner families), and a 1980 law banning employment discrimination. Efforts made to increase women's opportunities for nontraditional jobs include directives to school and employment office counselors, pilot training programs, financial subsidies for employers, well-financed campaigns to recruit girls and women into nontraditional jobs, and a 5-year plan to increase women's representation in several specific jobs. Although not specifically designed to improve women's economic situation, labor union efforts to boost the salaries of low-paid workers raised women's wages significantly and thereby encouraged them to enter the labor force (Baude, 1979; Ericsson & Jacobsson, 1985; Gustafsson, 1983; Gustafsson & Lantz, 1985; Ruggie, 1984).

Several programs encourage men to take on child care responsibilities. Prenatal, delivery, and parent education programs have been changed to include (or almost require) men's participation (Sellström & Swedin, 1987). At childbirth, men are granted 10 days off from work with full pay—so-called daddy days—to take care of family responsibilities and become acquainted with their new offspring. To help fathers maintain ties with their children, in 1983, joint custody of children became the rule at divorce (Forsberg, 1984). An official commission to study men's changing roles established in 1983 recommended that the government provide stronger encouragement for men to share child care (Arbetsgruppen om Mansrollen, 1985). Men's crisis centers opened, offering counseling to men undergoing gender role change (Arbetsgruppen om Mansrollen, 1985). Traveling exhibitions and idea fairs promoted new roles for men as did camps sponsored by the National Institute for Sex Education (Scott, 1982; Wistrand, 1981).

In addition to the daddy days at childbirth, Swedish men have access to a wide array of programs designed to help working parents care for children. Men's inclusion in these programs was not added as an afterthought or merely to avoid charges of reverse discrimination. The programs were deliberately designed to help fathers as well as mothers combine work and family roles.

The most noteworthy of these programs is parental leave. Since 1974, employers have been obligated to grant parents of both sexes paid leave with job security at childbirth or adoption. Parents receive at least 90% of their former salary. As of 1991, fathers and mothers could share up to 12 months of this generously paid leave, 3 additional months of low-paid leave (approximately $10 a day), and 3 months of unpaid leave.

Fathers as well as mothers are allowed to take up to 120 days off work per year, with pay, to care for sick children or to step in for sick caretakers. Parents are granted 2 days per year to attend children's programs or visit children at day care or school and may reduce their workday to 6 hours (with a corresponding loss of pay) until their children reach age 7.

A government-subsidized network of high-quality child care facilities helps working parents retain an attachment to the labor force. Parents pay only 8% of the cost of a place in a day care center or licensed day care home. After-school centers are similarly subsidized. As of 1990, 55% of all Swedish children under school age were in subsidized child care, and 29% used the after-school centers (Statistiska Centralbyrån, 1990).

Reasons for the Development of Equality Policy

This litany of innovative programs designed to improve women's breadwinner status and men's child-rearing capacities raises the question: Why has Sweden adopted such a radical approach to men's work and parenting roles? Economic, political, and ideological conditions have combined to make *jämställdhet* a popular social policy in Sweden.

In 1961, the feminist Eva Moberg wrote an essay that started the debate about men's roles in Sweden. Moberg argued that women would never enjoy equal employment as long as they held primary responsibility for child care and housework. She stated, "Both men and women have one major role, that of human beings" (Moberg, 1962, p. 108, author's translation). The "human being role" included responsibility for income provision, domestic work, and child care, as well as rights in the area of leisure time and opportunity for political involvement. Moberg specifically recommended that men become less absorbed in occupational achievement and more involved in child rearing. Her views caught on quickly, not only among feminists and academics, but also among political leaders, trade unionists, and government officials. This major ideological shift in how gender roles should be defined caught on so quickly because economic conditions made this new idea seem a compelling and timely one.

One circumstance was the desperate need for women's labor power. During the 1960s, the Swedish economy boomed, and there was a shortage of male workers to fill positions created by expanding private and public sectors, especially in service areas. Women's attachment to the labor force during their childbearing years thus was no longer discouraged. To free women to work, men were encouraged to share more in child care and the government developed work-family programs to keep women employed.

Another major economic reason for Sweden's interest in changing men's roles was a low birthrate, which reached an all-time low in 1978 of 1.59 children per woman. Economists warned that such a low birthrate would eventually make it difficult to financially support the growing number of older Swedes. Gender equality was seen as part of the solution to this problem. Working women might be more likely to have children if their partners were committed to sharing the care of them and if society supported motherhood via parental leave, sick leave, day care, and other programs. The solution seems to be a sound one. By 1991 the birth rate had risen to 2.1, one of the highest rates in Europe (Gustafsson, 1991).

Although there were important economic pressures pushing Sweden to adopt the "human being model" advocated by Moberg, the unique nature of politics in Sweden made it possible for this radical change to come about. One important characteristic of Swedish politics is the high level of female participation. Since the early 1970s, women have held at least a third of parliamentary and cabinet seats, which is one of the highest rates of female political representation in the world (Rhoadie,

1989). These women have taken advantage of their unusual political access to advocate equal participation of men and women in employment and child care.

In addition, the system of proportional representation leads to considerable competition between parties for voters, which in turn affects gender policies. To attract new adherents, most parties have taken the stance that women and men should be equal partners in the labor market and in the home and have supported programs that would create gender equality (Eduards, 1988).

It would still have been difficult to promote a policy as radical as the human being model if the ideological climate of the society had been hostile. This, however, was not the case in Sweden. Two aspects of the ideological climate deserve special mention. Swedes generally hold the well-being of children in the highest regard. This priority is reflected in the number of social programs designed to prevent children from living in poverty or suffering ill health as well as the number of rights enjoyed by Swedish children (e.g., court-appointed attorneys at divorce, outlawing of corporal punishment such as spanking). Since the 1970s, one of children's basic rights has been the opportunity to have close relations with fathers as well as mothers. In recent years, one argument used for extending parental leave benefits to men and for expanding the program is that children need intense contact with both parents early in life in order to develop good parent-child relations and to reach their full potential (Allen, 1988; Falkenberg, 1990).

An additional ideological reason for Sweden's gender policy is the relative lack of support for organizations that promote traditional roles for men and women. In some societies, the religious climate and religious-based organizations serve as upholders of tradition and impediments to gender equality. In Sweden, however, religious sentiment is not strong. Swedes do not report religion to be a significant factor influencing their values or conduct, and only about 5% attend church weekly (Swedish Institute, 1989b).

Gender policy in Sweden has thus developed as a result of a combination of immediate economic concerns, the nature of political institutions, and the ideological climate. Although it appears unlikely that many other societies will experience this exact combination, this outline of conditions in Sweden can inform us of the potential determinants of gender role change in other societies as well.

Jämställdhet—*The Reality*

Sweden has set a course for gender equality that is unparalleled in the world. To what extent has this goal been realized? Using the Swedish definition, we would expect to find women and men equally involved in the labor market as well as in child care; however, findings from the 1986 survey of working parents, as well as other studies of Swedish men and women, reveal how far Sweden still has to go to reach the goal of *jämställdhet* it set for itself.

Work Roles

Swedish women are almost as likely to be in the labor force as men, particularly if we look at those in younger generations. National statistics for 1988 showed 95% of men aged 25-54 in the labor market, compared to 91% of women. Having preschool-aged children had little effect on women's labor force participation, with 86% of women with children under 7 (the age of starting school in Sweden) being employed. Economists predict that by the year 2000, men and women will participate in the labor force to an equal extent (Persson, 1990).

Such a high rate of women's labor force participation suggests that the Swedish goal of equally involving women and men in paid work has been realized. This, however, is not the case, as we can tell from other statistics on work patterns and attitudes toward work. National data show that Swedish men tend to put in more hours of paid employment than women. In 1987, 43% of Swedish women worked part-time (less than 35 hours per week), compared to only 7% of men (Natti, 1990). Swedish women with preschoolers were even more likely to work part-time, with 60% doing so (Persson, 1990). The average mother in a dual-earner family with preschool-aged children works 29.2 hours per week for pay compared to a father's average of 42.5 hours (Statistiska Centralbyrån, 1990). The gap between men's and women's hours has lessened by a third over the past 15 years, but it will still take many years for the gap to be eliminated (Persson, 1990).

The 1986 survey of beneficiaries of parental leave in Gothenburg shows that there is also a significant gender gap in attitudes toward work. Only 6% of mothers preferred to work full-time, in contrast to three fourths (75%) of fathers. Most mothers preferred part-time work.

The pattern of different attitudes toward employment was also found with another question: "How important to you is it to be employed right now, in comparison with your other interests and activities?" Answers ranged on a 5-point scale from "Work is the main interest in my life" to "Work is not at all important compared with my other interests." Forty-two percent of the fathers, in contrast to only 19% of the mothers, reported work to be the main interest in their lives (see Table 12.1).

The survey respondents' attitudes about men's roles were also measured by their reactions to the statements: "Men should be the primary breadwinners in the family" and "Success on the job ought to be a man's main goal in life." Less than 10% of either sex agreed absolutely with either statement. This was substantially less than the 52%-68% support shown for men's traditional responsibility for breadwinning that was found in a study of U.S. couples (Vannoy-Hiller & Philliber, 1989). On the other hand, responses also indicated that most Swedes do not yet wholeheartedly agree with the goals of the human being model. Less than one fourth of fathers said the first statement was not at all true, and only one third felt that way about the second statement. Although women expressed significantly more egalitarian attitudes, less than half indicated complete agreement with the equality model (see Table 12.1).

At the time of the survey over three quarters (76%) of the sample were dual-earner couples. Significant gender differences in employment preference, work commitment, and breadwinning attitudes persisted among the subsample of couples where both partners were still in the labor force ($n = 242$).

In sum, the evidence suggests that Swedish fathers and mothers are not equally involved in paid employment. Substantial gender differences in work hours, work preferences, and work commitment were found. Although the majority of Swedish parents (especially mothers) rejected the notion that breadwinning and occupational achievement are the man's responsibility, it is clear that in practice they do not yet live up to their egalitarian ideals.

Child Care Roles

The second major component of the model for gender equality espoused by Swedish policymakers is equal participation in child care by mothers and fathers. (Sharing of housework has received little attention.) Past studies have indicated that Swedish fathers, although active in child care, are not yet as involved in child care as Swedish mothers (Haas, 1982; Sandqvist, 1987). The Gothenburg survey allows a close examination of parental sharing of child care in families with very young children.

Table 12.1 Work Attitudes of Swedish Parents ($N = 319$)

	Fathers		*Mothers*
Work Preference			
Full-time (1)	75%		6%
Part-time	24%		67%
Stay home (3)	1%		27%
Totals	100%		100%
Means	1.26	*	2.21
Importance of Work			
The main interest (1)	4%		0%
A main interest	38%		19%
One interest	46%		56%
Less important interest	8%		16%
Not important interest (5)	4%		9%
Totals	100%		100%
Means	2.71	*	3.13
"Men should be the primary breadwinners"			
Absolutely (1)	9%		5%
In certain cases	29%		24%
Don't know	26%		3%
Hardly ever	13%		25%
Not at all (5)	23%		43%
Totals	100%		100%
Means	3.14	*	3.76
"Success on the job should be men's main goal in life"			
Absolutely (1)	2%		1%
In certain cases	18%		13%
Don't know	33%		4%
Hardly ever	13%		36%
Not at all (5)	34%		46%
Totals	100%		100%
Means	3.60	*	4.12

*signifies that the difference between means was statistically significant at the .05 level, according to one-tailed t-tests.

Several dimensions of child care were examined: general responsibility for child care, participation in specific tasks, time spent with children, and usage of parental leave programs. Respondents were asked to answer the questions with the child born in 1984 in mind. There were some gender differences in reports of fathers' participation in child care, with men claiming more sharing of child care tasks and time than women acknowledged. Consequently, mothers' and fathers' answers were averaged to form a composite measure of fathers' participation in child care.

Respondents were asked: "Who has the main responsibility for the care and upbringing of the child born in 1984—the mother mostly, the mother more, both equally, the father more, or the father mostly?" Although the mother was said to be the one primarily responsible for child care in only 13% of the couples, both parents reported equal responsibility in only one fourth of the cases. Single-earner and dual-earner couples did not differ significantly.

A similar pattern was evident for the second measure of child care, sharing of 14 specific tasks. Fathers were more likely to participate in emotional caregiving (e.g., playing, teaching, and reading) than physical caretaking (e.g., feeding, diapering, taking to doctor). Noninteractive domestic work associated with child care (e.g., laundry, shopping, cooking) were the least shared tasks (see Table 12.2). Studies of U.S. fathers have also found such results (Lamb, 1987; Sandqvist, 1987; Vannoy-Hiller & Philliber, 1989). These items were later combined in a child care task scale (Cronbach's alpha = .82).

The third dimension of child care studied was time spent taking care of or being together with children. Time was the one area where fathers approached equity with mothers. Fathers were reported to spend an average of 10.50 hours with children on a nonworkday, which was 47% of all the time parents spent with children on nonworkdays. Looking at working couples only, fathers spent 3.15 hours with children on workdays, 39% of the time working parents spent on workdays. A time estimate for a week was created by multiplying the workday estimate by 5 and the nonworkday estimate by 2. In dual-earner couples, fathers spent an average of 36.81 hours per week with their children, which was 43% of all time working parents spent.

The present study yielded higher estimates of how equally parents share time spent with children than were found in an earlier study of Swedish fathers with small children (Lamb et al., 1988) or in one study of U.S. fathers by C. P. Cowan and P. A. Cowan (1987). In the Cowans' study, fathers were found to spend an average of 18% of the time the couple spent with children (26 hours a week, compared to mothers' total of 121). Another U.S. study, however, indicated that fathers might spend as much time with children as Swedish fathers do. Nock and Kingston's (1988) time

Table 12.2 Swedish Fathers' Participation in Specific Child Care Tasks ($N = 319$)

	Mean	*% equal*
"Who does the following things in your family?"		
Buys food for the child	1.92	25
Prepares food for the child	1.68	15
Feeds the child	2.03	25
Changes diapers	2.15	27
Bathes the child	2.44	38
Buys child clothes	1.35	6
Washes child's clothes	1.57	12
Arranges baby-sitting	2.19	33
Plays with child	2.76	58
Reads books to the child	2.59	50
Teaches the child to do something new	2.64	54
Comforts the child when sick or tired	2.32	36
Takes the child to doctor	1.64	12
Picks up child when it cries at night	2.45	40
Total scale	2.00	9

NOTE: Responses were coded as follows: 1 = mother mostly; 2 = mother more; 3 = both mother and father equally; 4 = father more; 5 = father mostly. "% equal" means the percentage of couples who reported that both parents did this task equally often. This figure also includes cases where the father actually did the task more often. This occurred in 1%-3% of the cases for 12 of 14 tasks. The exceptions were for getting up at night, which 16% of fathers did more often than mothers, and playing, which 7% of the fathers did more than mothers. The only significant difference between dual-earner couples and single-earner families was that fathers in dual-earner couples comforted children more, according to a one-tailed t-test.

budget data revealed that fathers spent 43% of the time the couple spent with children (27.12 hours a week for fathers vs. 36.42 for mothers).

The last aspect of child care sharing investigated was participation in parental leave programs. Some 27% of fathers in the study had taken paid parental leave for the child born in 1984. This figure was nearly the same as the national average for children born in that year (Röcklinger, 1987). Since then, however, the number of Swedish fathers taking parental leave has increased dramatically to 44% (Riksförsäkringsverket, 1990). This change seems to be the result of governmental efforts to increase fathers' participation. Campaigns were launched to convince fathers that taking leave was the right thing to do. To help fathers take leave after the period of full-time breastfeeding is over, the government increased the amount of well-paid leave time available from 9 months in 1984 to 12 months by 1989. Eligibility was also expanded by allowing fathers to take leave even if their partner was ineligible.

Swedish fathers' usage of parental leave benefits is much higher than in the few other (Nordic) countries where such benefits are available (Nordic Council of Ministers, 1988). Although Swedish fathers are clearly willing to stay home for child care when their children are very young, the length of time they stay home is short in comparison to mothers. For children born in 1989, fathers who stayed home did so for an average of 43 days, in contrast to mothers' average of 260 days. This means fathers take only about 14% of all parental leave days. Moreover, this percentage has remained almost constant for the past 10 years (Riksförsäkringsverket, 1990).

Swedish fathers take more advantage of parental benefits that do not involve staying at home for a long stretch of time. In the late 1980s, nearly all (85%) of fathers took the 10 daddy days available at childbirth. In addition, fathers took around one third of days used to care for sick children and to keep in contact with day care centers and schools (Riksförsäkringsverket, 1989).

Swedish parents' attitudes toward fathers' participation in child care were more egalitarian than the division of labor they actually practiced. The 1986 survey contained several questions designed to measure attitudes toward fathers' sharing child care. Two gauged their opinions about men's ability to perform child care, by asking for reactions to the statements: "A father can be as emotionally close to a child as a mother" and "A man can become a good at child care as a woman if he has the opportunity to learn." Parents were also asked if they agreed with the ideal of sharing child care: "If the woman works full-time, the man and woman ought to share equally in care of the child." The vast majority of Swedish parents strongly affirmed all three statements, but many still evidently have reservations about mothers and fathers equally sharing the child care role. Women were significantly more likely to believe in fathers' ability to perform child care than were men. Women were also more likely than men to think fathers should share equally in child care if both parents were employed full-time, with 85% of women agreeing absolutely to this, compared to 65% of men.

In short, findings from the 1986 survey of parents and from national statistics regarding fathers' usage of parental benefits suggest there is considerable public support for equality in child care and Swedish fathers participate a great deal in it. Yet their participation does not approach parity with mothers. Although much more inclined than Americans to give lip service to the idea of role sharing (DeStefano & Colasanto, 1990), many Swedish mothers and fathers evidently still have reservations about equally sharing child care responsibility.

Barriers to the Realization of Equality in Sweden

Progress toward gender equality has been made in Sweden, but considerable differences in the employment and child care responsibilities of fathers and mothers remain. What are the barriers to the elimination of the gender-based division of labor in Sweden? One type of potential barrier to gender equality is social-psychological in character, related to childhood and adult socialization and traditional gender role attitudes. The other relates to social structure, particularly the gendered nature of the labor market.

Social-Psychological Barriers

Until recently, gender differences in parenting have been attributed primarily to the social-psychological dispositions of individual men and women. With traditional parents as role models and gender differences in opportunity to develop appropriate skills, people may be socialized to become unwilling or unable to practice role sharing later in life (Herzog & Bachman, 1982; Hwang, 1985; Pleck, 1986; Russell & Radin, 1983).

Assuming that removal of social-psychological barriers to gender role change is necessary, Swedish policymakers have made deliberate efforts to resocialize men and women for the human being model. Children receive the same encouragement to develop career and child care skills in school regardless of gender. Adults are admonished by well-financed advertising campaigns to take on responsibilities once left to the other sex.

Results from the Gothenburg survey offer insight into whether policymakers are on the right track in emphasizing social-psychological barriers to gender role change. Three types of social-psychological variables were examined. The first measured people's exposure to traditional role models in childhood (i.e., whether they had an employed mother and a nurturing father). The second concerned previous experience with child care before becoming a parent, and the last was gender role attitudes (measured by an index composed of the 5-item attitudes toward breadwinning and child care described above).

Multiple regression analysis was used to see which variables had the strongest independent effects on role behavior. Evidence of the modest importance of all three types of variables was found. The division of labor in the family was affected almost evenly by exposure to traditional role models in childhood and gender role attitudes, and to a lesser extent by women's earlier experience with child care (see Tables 12.3 and 12.4).

Prospects for the decline of these social-psychological barriers seem good in Sweden. Increased numbers of Swedes will have egalitarian parental models as more women enter the labor force and men continue to increase their participation in child care. Educational efforts to change attitudes toward gender roles (particularly the latest campaigns launched by mostly male labor unions) and to level out gender differences in parenting ability are also continuing.

Although the Gothenburg survey found that social-psychological variables are related to role behavior, these explained less than 11% of the variance. We must therefore look elsewhere to further explain barriers to gender role change in Sweden.

Social Structural Barriers

Contemporary gender role theory focuses less on social-psychological determinants of the gender-based division of labor in the family than on the impact of social structure. Many authors now reject the notion that the family and outside social institutions form separate social spheres (the "private" and the "public") (Ferree, 1990). These authors view the economy in particular as structured so as to reproduce male power and authority as well as the gender-based division of labor in the family. Several aspects of the Swedish economy deserve attention as structural barriers to gender role change. Among these barriers are the availability of part-time work for women, the prevalence of sexual occupational segregation, and the gender gap in earnings.

Part-Time Work. Since the 1960s, businesses and especially public agencies have deliberately developed part-time jobs for women to recruit them into the labor force. Men's work hours were not restructured to allow them to participate more actively in child care. (Fathers as well as mothers are entitled to shorten their workweek to 30 hours while their children are of preschool age, but the corresponding loss of

Table 12.3 Hierarchical Regression Prediction Work Attitudes of Swedish Parents (Dual-earner couples only, $N = 242$)

	Standardized Beta Coefficients							
	Father's Work Preference		*Mother's Work Preference*		*Father's Work Importance*		*Mother's Work Importance*	
	Step 1: Social-Psych. Variables	*Step 2: Social Structural Variables*	*Step 1: Social-Psych. Variables*	*Step 2: Social Structural Variables*	*Step 1: Social-Psych. Variables*	*Step 2: Social Structural Variables*	*Step 1: Social-Psych. Variables*	*Step 2: Social Structural Variables*
Social-Psychological Variables								
For men:								
Whether mom was employed	–.05	–.04	.04	.05	.03	.01	.08	.10
Father's child care role	.04	.04	.07	.08	.07	.06	.02	.03
Previous child care experience	.07	.07	.08	.08	.01	–.03	–.02	–.01
Gender role attitudes index	.12*	.10	–.07	–.06	–.01	.01	–.03	–.01
For women:								
Whether mom was employed	–.12*	–.12*	.03	.03	–.09	–.05	.09	.08
Father's child care role	–.03	–.04	.12*	.11	–.04	–.03	.12*	.11*
Previous child care experience	.00	.01	–.25*	–.24*	.02	.02	–.20*	–.20*
Gender role attitudes index	.10	.09	.00	.01	.04	–.00	.01	–.00
Social Structural Variables								
Gender gap in hours (Man's hours – woman's)		.03		.00		–.18*		.10
If woman had nontraditional job		.04		.12*		.05		.07
If man worked in private sector		.03		.15*		.18*		.17*
If woman worked in private sector		.05		–.04		–.02	–.10	
If woman earned as much or more than partner		.14*		–.04		.06	–.08	
R^2	.05	.07	.09*	.12*	.01	.10*#	.06	.11*#

*significant at the .05 level; #significant increase in R^2.

Table 12.4 Hierarchical Regression Predicting Child Care Sharing by Swedish Parents (Dual-earner couples only, $N = 242$)

	Standardized Beta Coefficients					
	Responsibility for Child Care		*Child Care Tasks*		*Father's Relative Time Spent in Child Care*	
	Step 1: Social-Psych. Variables	*Step 2: Social Structural Variables*	*Step 1: Social-Psych. Variables*	*Step 2: Social Structural Variables*	*Step 1: Social-Psych. Variables*	*Step 2: Social Structural Variables*
Social-Psychological Variables						
For men:						
Whether mom was employed	–.08	–.03	–.10	–.06	–.08	–.06
Father's child care role	.14*	.12*	.07	.06	.13*	.11*
Previous child care experience	–.01	–.07	–.00	–.04	.03	–.01
Gender role attitudes index	.12*	.16*	.16*	.19*	.14*	.15*
For women:						
Whether mom was employed	–.10	–.04	–.09	–.05	.01	.04
Father's child care role	.09	.10	.01	.02	.10	.11
Previous child care experience	.08	.07	.14*	.14*	.07	.07
Gender role attitudes index	.08	.03	.12*	.09	.06	.04
Social Structural Variables						
Gender gap in hours (Man's hours – woman's)		–.30*		–.22*		–.23*
If woman had nontraditional job		–.07		–.04		–.05
If man worked in private sector		.17*		.16*		.04
If woman worked in private sector		.01		.03		.05
If woman earned as much or more than partner		.13*		.06		.07
R^2	.08*	.26*#	.09*	.19*#	.07*	.14*#

*significant at the .05 level; #significant increase in R^2.

pay and negative employer reaction makes it rare for fathers to do so.) The greater availability of part-time work for women encourages couples to retain traditional gender roles within their relationships, whereas the lack of availability of part-time work for those men who want it (24% of the sample in the Gothenburg study) prevents couples from breaking the old pattern. In the Gothenburg survey, the larger the difference between males' and females' work hours, the less sharing of child care on all three measures (see Table 12.4).

In the Swedish context, efforts to convince women to work more hours per week in order to be more equal to men are not likely to be successful. Even if more full-time jobs were available, the Gothenburg study suggests few women would voluntarily choose them. The 30-hour week most of them now work allows them to blend parenting and employment roles in a satisfactory way. What would seem more conducive to gender equality in the family would be a reduction in men's work hours via a 30-hour workweek for all. The 30-hour week has been a demand of feminists in the Social Democratic Party for two decades and was more recently taken up as a cause by two small political parties, the Environmental Party and the Left (formerly Communist) Party. This reform, however, is considered too utopian by employers and trade union leaders, who reject it as a threat to economic growth and workers' purchasing power (Pettersson, 1989; Scott, 1982).

Recent changes in the tax laws might actually increase the gender gap in weekly work hours. Previously, Swedish workers were discouraged from working extra hours by a heavily progressive tax policy that taxed extra earnings at a high rate. A 1989 tax reform lowered the marginal rate to encourage employees to work more hours. A significant increase in women's work hours seems unlikely, given their preference for combining work and family by working part-time. What seems more likely is that men, as the higher paid workers (see below), will be encouraged to work more hours (Hobson, 1990). This change would very likely reinforce traditional gender roles in the family.

Sex-Segregated Labor Market. A second structural barrier to changing gender roles in the family is the sex-segregated labor market. Previous studies have found that Swedish occupations are among the most sex-typed in the world (Ericsson & Jacobsson, 1985; Persson, 1990). Two thirds of employees in the public sector are women, compared to only one third in the private sector (Persson, 1990). Even within these sectors, women and men occupy different jobs. Only 7% of women and 6% of men work in jobs where the sexes are balanced within a 40%-60% range for each group (Statistiska Centralbyrån, 1990). Sex segregation in the labor market is also manifested in women's lack of access to top positions. For example, women hold only 3% of the senior executive positions in businesses and public agencies (Ericsson & Jacobsson, 1985).

If men's opportunities for success and achievement in the workplace are greater than women's, we can expect couples to decide that men should take more responsibility for family income and opt out of child care. When women's opportunities for self-fulfillment in the workplace are less than men's, they will tend to devote themselves more to family work and to express less interest in employment. When women are not widely dispersed at various levels in organizations, it becomes easier for organizations to remain based on traditional male values without seriously considering the goal of gender equality. Findings from the Gothenburg survey lend support to this hypothesis. Women holding jobs traditionally occupied by women expressed less interest in employment than women in nontraditional jobs. Men who worked in the male-dominated private sector (in comparison to men in the female-dominated public sector) felt work was more important, participated in child care less, and had partners who preferred to work part-time rather than full-time (see Tables 12.3 and 12.4).

Prospects for a sharp reduction in labor market segregation in the near future seem small. Government efforts to reduce segregation are directed mainly at individuals' career awareness. Increasing numbers of young people are choosing nontraditional subjects as majors in upper secondary school (Rhoadie, 1989; Swedish Institute, 1989a), but their future in nontraditional fields seems in jeopardy unless structural changes in the labor market occur. Traditional prejudices against women still operate to prevent them from pursuing a wide variety of occupational opportunities (Lindren, 1989). Economic incentives that might encourage women to try to overcome barriers to their entry into male-dominated work are also lacking, given the availability of jobs in female-dominated occupations and (as discussed below) the relatively low wage differences between traditionally male and female jobs. Lastly, traditionally male jobs require full-time (or overtime) work, which most Swedish women do not desire.

Earnings Gap. A third structural barrier to equality in Sweden relates to the earnings gap between Swedish women and men. Efforts on the part of labor unions to boost lower paid workers' salaries have led to Swedish women earning more relative to men and being less economically dependent on their spouse than women in other industrial societies (Hobson, 1990). Swedish women's average pay, depending on their job, varies from 70% to 90% of men's average pay (Persson, 1990). But the remaining 10%-30% gap in earnings is made greater by the tendency of women to work fewer hours than men do.

Gender theorists emphasize the importance of women's wages for the gender-based division of labor in the family. When women earn less, the structural opportunity for them to share the breadwinning role is limited (Ferree, 1990). This in turn means that women are therefore in a weaker position to press men to participate in domestic roles. In the Gothenburg survey, men were found to participate more in child care if their partner made as much or more money than they did; such men also expressed more interest in part-time work (see Tables 12.3 and 12.4).

Prospects for an equalization of women's and men's earning power seem slim. The earnings gap, which narrowed significantly from the 1970s through the mid 1980s, has again begun to widen (Gustafsson, 1991; Persson, 1990). This widening may reflect a change in approach to wage bargaining. After years of pushing a centralized "wage solidarity" policy to raise the earnings of low-paid workers, unions have now adopted a less centrally negotiated, more individualized wage-setting plan. Such a system has the potential to reduce women's earlier wage gains, as can be seen in Acker's (1991) study of women's declining wages in Swedish banks (1991).

Increase in Unpaid Family Work. The above obstacles to gender role change in Sweden directly concerned the economy. The last obstacle concerns the structure of the welfare state. Do social programs that enable women to be employed and encourage men to be involved in child care have unforeseen consequences? In 1975, the Swedish government set out to establish day care places for all children. Although an impressive number of high-quality places were created, to date the goal of complete coverage has not been realized. Since the late 1980s, places for the youngest children (under 2 years old in some places, typically 18 months in most) have been gradually replaced by places for older children (which are cheaper to provide). Day care for the youngest children still exists, but in scarce quantity. Because paid parental leave lasts only a year, families are forced to arrange their own child care assistance for an additional 6 months to 1 year. This policy often leads to mothers' remaining at home, and typically having another child in the interim, extending their stay out of the labor force and reinforcing the traditional division of labor. In other cases, mothers work part-time in the evenings or on weekends so that fathers can care for children.

Recent tax cuts and the election of a more conservative government promise to exacerbate the day care problem. In addition, access to social programs now provided to families to help them manage family work (e.g., parental leave) might be curtailed, given the current climate of fiscal austerity. Such changes may increase the amount of unpaid domestic work that has traditionally fallen on women's shoulders. If men begin to work more hours, they are less likely to be available for domestic labor.

In summary, both social-psychological and social structural factors impede the realization of gender equality in Sweden. Of the two, social structural barriers are more influential. In the Gothenburg survey, social structural variables measuring the gender gap in hours and earnings, as well as those measuring the types of jobs held by men and women, explained significantly more variance in work attitudes and child care sharing than social-psychological variables did (see Tables 12.3 and 12.4). These findings suggest that Swedish policymakers have not paid sufficient attention to the ways in which the structure of the labor market impedes progress toward the goal of men and women equally sharing breadwinning and child care roles.

Conclusion

For over 25 years, Sweden has officially promoted gender equality, encouraging men to become more nurturing toward children and women to become more involved in providing family income. The motives for this unique policy lie in serious economic concerns over a labor shortage and a low birthrate. To promote the policy, women were given greater opportunities to be employed, work-family programs such as paid parental leave and subsidized child care were enacted, and men received considerable encouragement to develop closer relations with children.

To a considerable extent, policymakers' efforts have been successful. Women, including those with small children, are almost as likely to be employed as men, and Swedish men participate in child care more than formerly and more than men in other societies. Swedes hold very egalitarian attitudes toward sharing breadwinning and nurturing. But here the revolution in gender roles has stalled. In only a minority of

Swedish families do fathers assume equal responsibility for care of children. Most Swedish mothers work part-time in a narrow range of jobs with modest pay. The gender gap in work hours and income promises to widen.

Further progress toward the goal of gender equality calls for more radical restructuring of social institutions outside the family than is currently envisioned. This restructuring requires an ideological commitment to eliminating the gendered character of the labor market. According to sociologist Joan Acker (1990), work organizations are based on the notion that workers should not have "other imperatives of existence that impinge upon the job" (p. 149), like child care or a partner who also has a job. Historically, the best workers were considered to be those (men) whose lives could center on permanent, full-time work, with personal needs and children being cared for by others. In this system, workers (typically male) who appear to demonstrate the greatest commitment to paid employment are rewarded with opportunities for a wide range of positions, authority, and material rewards. Other workers (typically female) are not so blessed.

Swedish policymakers at the national level have not fundamentally challenged the gendered nature of work organizations. There is no sign that they realize that the benefits to be gained by restructuring work in nongendered ways might outweigh the personal costs to male stakeholders. Some might argue that the creation of programs to help workers combine work and family (e.g., parental leave, days off for sick children, part-time work) does in fact suggest that policymakers have attempted to restructure the work place. The fact that women rather than men rely on these programs suggests that male workers typically do not take domestic responsibilities as seriously as women. The persistent and even widening gap in men's and women's wages and work hours also is evidence that such programs do not effectively eliminate gender disadvantage.

A promising area for future research is to explore how business practices and processes could be restructured to eliminate gender-related expectations and inequalities. A logical first step would be to conduct case studies of organizations to understand how everyday operations and corporate philosophy reflect and in turn influence men's and women's opportunities to be involved in breadwinning and child care.

References

Acker, J. (1990). Hierarchies, jobs, bodies: A theory of gendered organizations. *Gender and Society, 4,* 139-158.

Acker, J. (1991). Thinking about wages: The gendered wage gap in Swedish banks. *Gender and Society, 5,* 390-407.

Allen, J. P. (1988). European infant care leaves. In E. Zigler & M. Frank (Eds.), *The Parental leave crisis—Toward a national policy* (pp. 245-275). New Haven, CT: Yale University Press.

Arbetsgruppen om Mansrollen [Work group on the male role]. (1985). *Mannen i förändring* [The changing man]. Stockholm: Tiden/Arbetsmarknadsdepartementet [Department of Labor].

Arbetsmarknadsstyrelsen [National Labor Market Board]. (1977). *Equality in the labour market—Programme adopted by the Labour Market Board.* Solna, Sweden: Author.

Baude, A. (1979). Public policy and changing family patterns in Sweden: 1930-1977. In J. Lipman-Blumen & J. Bernard (Eds.), *Sex roles and social policy* (pp. 145-176). Beverly Hills, CA: Sage.

Cowan, C. P., & Cowan, P. A. (1987). Men's involvement in parenthood. In P. Berman & F. Pederson (Eds.), *Men's transitions to parenthood* (pp. 145-174). Hillsdale, NJ: Lawrence Erlbaum.

DeStefano, L., & Colasanto, D. (1990, February). Unlike 1975, today most Americans think men have it better. *Gallup Poll Monthly,* pp. 25-36.

Eduards, M. (1988). *Gender politics and public policies in Sweden.* Paper prepared for Conference on Gender Politics and Public Policy, New York.

Ericsson, Y., & Jacobsson, R. (1985). *Side by side—A report on equality between women and men in Sweden.* Stockholm: Gotab.

Falkenberg, E. (1990). *Far till 100%* [100% father]. Stockholm: Tjänstemännens Centralorganisation.

Ferree, M. M. (1990). Beyond separate spheres: Feminism and family research. *Journal of Marriage and the Family, 52,* 866-884.

Forsberg, M. (1984). *The evolution of social welfare policies in Sweden.* Stockholm: Swedish Institute.

Gustafsson, S. (1983). *Equal employment policies in Sweden.* Unpublished manuscript, Arbetslivcentrum [Center for Working Life], Stockholm.

Gustafsson, S. (1991). *An economic history of Swedish family politics.* Paper presented at the 5th annual conference of the European Society for Population Economics, Pisa, Italy.

Gustafsson, S., & Lantz, P. (1985). *Arbete och löner—Ekonomika teorier och fakta omkring skillnader mellan kvinnor och män* [Work and pay—Economic theories and facts concerning differences between women and men]. Stockholm: Almqvist & Wiksell.

Haas, L. (1982). Parental sharing of childcare tasks in Sweden. *Journal of Family Issues, 3,* 389-412.

Haas, L. (1986). Wives' orientation toward breadwinning: Sweden and the United States. *Journal of Family Issues, 7,* 358-381.

Haas, L. (1992). *Equal parenthood and social policy: A study of parental leave in Sweden.* Albany: State University of New York Press.

Herzog, A. R., & Bachman, J. G. (1982). *Sex role attitudes among high school seniors.* Ann Arbor: University of Michigan, Institute of Social Research.

Hiller, D., & Philliber, W. (1986). The division of labor in contemporary marriage. *Social Problems, 33,* 191-201.

Hobson, B. (1990). No exit, no voice: Women's economic dependency and the welfare state. *Acta Sociologica, 33,* 235-250.

Hochschild, A. (1989). *The second shift.* New York: Viking.

Hood, J. C. (1986). The provider role: Its meaning and measurement. *Journal of Marriage and the Family, 48,* 349-360.

Huber, J., & Spitze, G. (1983). *Sex stratification.* New York: Academic Press.

Hwang, C. P. (1985). Småbarnspappor [Fathers of small children]. In C. P. Hwang (Ed.), *Faderskap* [Fatherhood] (pp. 15-38). Stockholm: Natur & Kultur.

Kamerman, S. B., Kahn, A. J., & Kingston, P. W. (1983). *Maternity policies and working women.* New York: Columbia University Press.

Lamb, M. E. (1987). Introduction: The emergent American father. In M. E. Lamb (Ed.), *The father's role—Cross-cultural perspectives* (pp. 3-26). Hillsdale, NJ: Lawrence Erlbaum.

Lamb, M. E., Hwang, C. P., Broberg, A., Bookstein, F. L., Hult, G., & Frodi, M. (1988). The determinants of paternal involvement in primiparous Swedish families. *International Journal of Behavioral Development, 11,* 433-449.

Lamb, M. E., & Levine, J. A. (1983). The Swedish parental insurance policy: An experiment in social engineering. In M. E. Lamb & A. Sagi (Eds.), *Fatherhood and social policy* (pp. 39-51). Hillsdale, NJ: Lawrence Erlbaum.

LaRossa, R. (1988). Fatherhood and social change. *Family Relations, 37,* 451-457.

Lindren, G. (1989). *Kamrater, kollegor och kvinnor—En studie av könssegregeringprocessen* [Comrades, colleagues, and women—A study of the process of sex segregation]. *Sociologiska Institutionens Forskningsrapporter* [Department of Sociology Research Reports], University of Umeå.

Moberg, E. (1962). *Kvinnor och man* [Women and men]. Stockholm: Bonnier.

Natti, J. (1990). *A comparison of part-time work in the Nordic countries.* Paper presented at the annual meeting of the World Congress of Sociology, Madrid.

Nock, S. L., & Kingston, P. W. (1988). Time with children: The impact of couples' work-time commitments. *Social Forces, 67,* 59-85.

Nordic Council of Ministers. (1988). *Kvinnor och män i Norden—Fakta om jämställdheten* [Women and men in the Nordic countries—Facts about equality]. Stockholm: Author.

Persson, I. (1990). The third dimension—Equal status between Swedish women and men. In I. Persson (Ed.), *Generating equality in the welfare state—The Swedish experience* (pp. 223-244). Oslo: Norwegian University Press.

Pettersson, G. (1989, June). Working hours in Sweden (*Current Sweden, 368*). Stockholm: Swedish Institute.

Pleck, J. H. (1985). *Paternity leave* (Working paper #157). Wellesley College, Center for Research on Women.

Pleck, J. H. (1986). Employment and fatherhood: Issues and innovative policies. In M. E. Lamb (Ed.), *The father's role—Applied perspectives* (pp. 385-412). New York: John Wiley.

Qvarfort, A. M., McCrae, J., & Kolenda, P. (1988). Sweden's national policy of equality between men and women. In P. Kolenda (Ed.), *Cultural constructions of women* (pp. 161-193). Salem, WI: Sheffield.

Rhoadie, E. (1989). *Discrimination against women—A global survey.* Jefferson, NC: McFarland.

Riksförsäkringsverket [National Social Insurance Board]. (1989, October 16). Tillfällig föräldrapenning för vård av barn 1987 [Temporary parental leave for care of children in 1987] (*Statistisk Information, No. 26*).

Riksförsäkringsverket [National Social Insurance Board]. (1990). Uttag av föräldrapenning med anledning av barns födelse under barnets första levnadsår. [Use of parental leave during child's first year] (*Statistisk Information,* IS-I, 16).

Ruggie, M. (1984). *The state and working women—A comparative study of Britain and Sweden.* Princeton, NJ: Princeton University Press.

Russell, G., & Radin, N. (1983). Increased paternal participation: The fathers' perspective. In M. E. Lamb & A. Sagi (Eds.), *Fatherhood and social policy* (pp. 139-165). Hillsdale, NJ: Lawrence Erlbaum.

Röcklinger, A. S. (1987). Hur används föraldräförsäkringen? [How is parental insurance used?] In Socialdepartementet (Ed.), *Barnfamiljerna och arbetslivet* [Families with children and worklife] (pp. 85-99). Stockholm: Socialdepartementet/Gotab.

Sandlund, M. B. (1971). The status of women in Sweden—Report for the United Nations 1968. In E. Dahlström (Ed.), *The changing roles of men and women* (pp. 290-302). Boston: Beacon.

Sandqvist, K. (1987). *Fathers and family work in two cultures.* Stockholm: Almqvist & Wiksell International.

Scott, H. (1982). *Sweden's right to be human—Sex role equality: The goal and the reality.* London: Allison & Busby.

Sellström, E., & Swedin, G. (1987). Mot ett jämställdt föräldraskap?—En studie över nyblivna förstagångsföräldrars planering inför föräldraledigheten [Toward equal parenthood? A study of prospective first-time parents' planning for parental leave]. *Studier för Vårdutveckling* [Studies for progress in caregiving], *12.* Östersund, Sweden: Vårdhögskolan Östersund [Östersund's College for Caregiving].

Statistiska Centralbyrån [Central Bureau of Statistics]. (1990). *Pä tal om kvinnor och män* [Talking about women and men]. Stockholm: Author.

Swedish Institute. (1989a, September). Facts and figures about youth in Sweden. *Fact sheets on Sweden.* Stockholm: Author.

Swedish Institute. (1989b, March). Religion in Sweden. *Fact sheets on Sweden.* Stockholm: Author.

Vannoy-Hiller, D., & Philliber, W. W. (1989). *Equal partners—Successful women in marriage.* Newbury Park, CA: Sage.

Wistrand, B. (1981). *Swedish women on the move.* Stockholm: Swedish Institute.

13

Segmentation and Synergy

Two Models of Linking Work and Family

AMY ANDREWS
LOTTE BAILYN

"Work/family is not an issue here, because there are no women in this firm."

So speaks the received wisdom, in the words of a male management consultant responding to a questionnaire assessing issues of work and family. What this quote reflects is the gendered division between public and private that is characteristic of the industrial world. It reflects the belief that the public domain of work and the private domain of family are separate and distinct. Work is work, family is family, and the two spheres do not and should not intersect. And graphed onto this dichotomized framework is a second idea, the idea that the public sphere of work is "masculine" whereas the private sphere of family is "feminine." Men, of course, also have families, but they are identified with the public arena that is conceptually separate from the private domain where women have primary responsibility for family concerns.

Work on which this chapter is based was supported, in part, by a grant from the Ford Foundation (#890-3012) to the second author. We are grateful to Joyce Fletcher, Jane Hood, and Leslie Perlow for insightful comments on previous drafts of this chapter.

The effect of this cultural assumption of separate spheres is to privatize conflicts and concerns about family and child care that are in fact widely experienced and structurally determined. Relegating family problems to the private sphere limits our ability to imagine either alternative structures or alternative roles for men and women. Because the assumption of separate spheres is inherently gendered, it functions to reinforce and reproduce gendered roles for men and women.

In her 1977 review of the literature on work and family, Kanter began to debunk this "myth of separate worlds." She identified several arenas where people's work and family lives bump up against each other and intersect. Citing numerous studies, she showed how different types of work situations place different types of demands (temporal, emotional, physical, etc.) on workers and their families. She maintained that the myth of separate worlds persists at least in part because it serves the interests of emotionally greedy employers who need loyal and committed employees. Unable to eliminate the particularistic demands of the family, Kanter argued, employers marginalize their effects: "The compromise put into effect by the modern organization could be phrased as a dictate to members: 'While you are here, you will *act as though* you have no other loyalties, no other life'" (p. 15). Kanter also outlined an extensive research agenda that would uncover the links between these two institutional domains and reveal the constructedness of the separation model.

Although Kanter's work was enthusiastically adopted and widely cited by work-family researchers, the metaphor of separate spheres has continued to permeate the field. Indeed, the very term, "work-family," reflects the somewhat awkward compromise struck in attempting to merge and combine concepts that have traditionally been seen as separate. Researchers investigate strategies that individuals evolve to balance their responsibilities, accommodate family, or "juggle" predefined roles, but throughout all of this work is the assumption (or perhaps the recognition) that separate and distinct roles or responsibilities are inescapable.

More recent work, especially that of feminist scholars (e.g., Alcoff, 1988), has focused on the conceptual and empirical shortcomings of the idea of separate spheres and called for a move away from dichotomized formulations of the work-family issue. Acknowledging the tendency to equate "masculine" with public and "feminine" with private, these scholars have argued that the fundamental notion of separation must be replaced with a different view if gender is ever going to drop out of the analysis. Nancy Dowd (1989) is not alone when she writes:

> The struggle to think of work and family *together* requires overcoming the tendency to separate the two and conceive of them as opposites, in contradiction and conflict with each other. The family and the market are assumed to embody a fundamental and radical separation: "The market structures our productive lives and the family structures our affective lives." It is an unnatural separation, contrary to our felt connection of the two. (p. 100, quoting Olsen, 1983, p. 1498)

A particularly problematic aspect of this cultural separation of spheres is that organizational procedures are anchored in this assumption and are designed to fit a "typical" male employee who has no family responsibilities. So even as women enter the public world of paid work, the assumption remains that they, not the men, will deal with the link between work and family. Indeed, recent work amply demonstrates (Crosby, 1991; Hochschild, 1989) that women are more likely than men to deal with both of these realms simultaneously, by predilection or necessity or both. And yet, men too must negotiate the tensions arising from living in two domains. The constraints they encounter as they do this are different but no less severe than those facing women.

Men's response to this tension is the subject of this chapter.[1] Our thesis is that many men have a segmented mental model, a way of categorizing the world that keeps work and family spheres distinct. This mind-set, we suggest, stems from and reinforces the cultural separation of spheres into public and private. Such a mental model is important because it guides choices and responses, thereby limiting consideration of alternatives. Nonetheless, we see the beginning of a different approach in the way many women, and some men, link these two arenas of experience in a more synergistic way. We use data from MBA graduates, successful professionals 10 years after receiving their degree, to highlight differences between the synergistic and segmented models. And we pinpoint the strains accompanying the segmented model typical of men's beliefs about the relationship between their work and family lives.

Data From MBA Alumni

We start with two vignettes. Both men are white business school graduates who are well established in their career. Both are married to professional women and have children. Yet they respond in different ways. One has changed his aspirations and his definitions of success to better accommodate his private concerns. In the other man, we see no such accommodation, only the stresses, indeed the guilt, that result.

The first is a senior engineer in a large utility company. His wife works full-time as a contract administrator at a major university. Their two children, aged 8 and 10, are involved in YMCA after-school programs and attend day camps in the summertime. His day starts before his wife and children are awake. He leaves for work early so that he can pick up his children after day care in the evening. He works a 40-hour week, which he indicates is slightly unusual in his organization. He seems unconcerned about this "abnormality" and devotes a great deal of time to the youth soccer program and to church activities.

In contrast, the other man is an extremely work-oriented person. After a failed entrepreneurial venture, he now works as a venture capitalist in a city 200 miles from where his wife is employed as a banker. He has thrown himself into the new work wholeheartedly, working 60 to 80 hours per week and traveling 80% of the time. He rarely sees his wife and their two children. In spite of appearances, he values both his marriage and his children a great deal. He feels his relationship with his wife has facilitated his progress at work and values the fact that she can understand his interests and concerns. He considers her career as a banker a positive contribution to their relationship, although he does not see a similar boon from his own career. With respect to his children, he made arrangements to stay home for 3 weeks when his daughter was born and seems deeply disturbed by the fact that he now so rarely sees his children:

> In the past year, I've been lucky to get home on weekends and am often away for 6 weeks at a time without seeing my kids. A new child was born 6 months ago, and she doesn't even recognize me.

Nonetheless, he continues to work the same schedule, and his wife remains committed to her career. A live-in au pair cares for the two babies.

These two men have different relationships to their work. The former places value on interesting work with competent co-workers, but is not as interested in becoming financially independent as the latter. He values regular work hours, limited travel, and "a fair degree of responsibility," and is satisfied in these terms. But the second, despite his much more intensive involvement in his work, is still not free of the pressures emanating from his personal life. For him, however, it seems easier to manage his guilt than to alter his commitment to work. He has no plans to change jobs in the near future.

Both men experience a connection between work and family, even as they find themselves working in a world that appears to deny this link. Thus they face a common dilemma, although they react to it in different ways.

These two are part of a sample of MBA graduates we studied in 1989, 10 years after they had received their business degree.[2] One of the 41 men in the sample was not employed at the time of our survey. Most of the rest were still in corporate jobs (50%), though 13 (32%) had left the corporation for entrepreneurial ventures. A further four (10%) were in consulting and three had left the field of business altogether. All but five of these 41 men were married in 1989, and 24 were in dual-career marriages (15 with children, 9 without). These men worked an average of 55 hours/week (ranging from 30 to 80) with a mean salary in 1989 of $115,000 (median of $85,000). Thus, a picture emerges of the stereotypical successful career man.

Nonetheless, these men are not fully content with their life. Only two out of three are satisfied with their job, and less than half feel successful at work by organizational criteria. Although the men are more likely to feel successful by their own personal criteria, these standards also turn out to be overwhelmingly work oriented. Not surprisingly, the men's stress level is high, considerably higher, in fact, than it was 5 years after their graduation from business school.

We observed that men married to traditional wives did not differ much from single men in the extent to which they accommodate their working life to their family's needs; not many show any accommodation. Among men in dual-career families, in contrast, 80% of those with children and 67% of those without show some accommodation to their family. Those who do not accommodate, like the venture capitalist described above, indicate a higher degree of stress from both their work and their personal life. They also report feeling a great deal of interference between work and family more frequently than do their more accommodating peers.

In general, the men in dual-career families, when compared to those in a more traditional family situation, seem to be more satisfied with the balance between work and family and are more likely to feel that these areas of their life do not interfere very much. And yet, although they are more accommodating than their traditional peers, this accommodation is considerably more likely to have an effect on their career.

This is an interesting group: a group of men trying to accommodate work to family needs and finding that because of this, their career has been affected. Compared to men whose accommodation has not affected their career, who locate stress primarily in work, these men identify stress from both public and personal life, as well as from cultural expectations about their roles. They also report more interference between work and family and are less satisfied with the balance in their life. In general, these men are more likely to feel that their family relationships constrain their work and that their career as well as their partner's career creates problems for their marital relationship. It seems that the synergy they seek is hard to fashion, given current organizational and cultural expectations.

All in all, those men who try to adjust their career to their family needs, like the senior engineer mentioned above, live in a complicated, unexpected, uncharted world. The difference is highlighted when we compare men in dual-career families with the women in the sample. Here there are dramatic differences in the way the two groups describe the intersection of their personal relationships with their work and the work of their partner. The women tend to see a positive interrelation among their own work, their partner's work, and their marital relationship; everything helps (Crosby, 1991). Not so for the men. They either see no effect of one sphere on the other or are likely to feel that their career causes problems for their personal relationships.

This comparison suggests that women find it easier to conceive of a synergy between their personal and work lives. They have found ways to bridge the public and private domains so as to live with less stress. In contrast, the men, although appearing to live according to cultural expectations, find the discordance between these expectations and the actuality of their life more difficult to manage. The same gendered structure of social roles that makes it difficult for women to find equal opportunity in the workplace also places great constraints on men's options for linking work and family. The gendered character of organizational expectations, which persists even in firms committed to gender equity, also does not help.

The difficulties men face in challenging these basic assumptions are illustrated by comments from our respondents. For example, one manager in a large, successful, and progressive company had made a number of innovative arrangements with some of his best female employees when they needed more flexibility to care for their children. But when asked if he would entertain such a request by a father he said, "It would feel a little funny." Another man, who works for a medium-sized health care organization where he is able to work a standard 40-hour week without much difficulty is married to a woman who has a demanding job. When they had a child, he thought about the possibility of scaling back to a modified schedule. He acknowledged that women in professional positions in his organization had been able to negotiate reduced work schedules in order to care for children, and he could easily describe the characteristics of the job that would allow an employee to work with such an arrangement. Critically, however, when asked what would happen to a *male* employee who met all these criteria, he felt it would be more difficult for him to negotiate a reduced schedule and then to be viewed positively afterward. As he struggled to make sense of this apparent inconsistency, he offered the following explanation:

> It would be viewed rather negatively. Why do I say that? I guess because it would be such a novelty around here and people are often aghast at novelties. . . . It would be a "break the ice" kind of thing. As I say that, I want to think a little bit more about that. Most of the senior managers . . . in order to become a senior manager, you have to have been a relatively driven person career-wise or otherwise you probably wouldn't be there. And driven people like to be working with other driven people, people who want to create a better organization, make more money, do greater things, whatever. . . . For a manager to come forward and say, "Yeah, I've been driving right along with you guys for a while but I don't want to drive this fast any more, I want to spend some time with my family"—that would be like saying "I don't want to be a part of this club anymore." Although it may be arranged on an individual basis, I think the individual would lose a lot of effectiveness in the organization, the ability to influence the other senior managers.

What was imaginable for a female professional, though subject to critical limitations, was not thinkable for a male professional. Same type of job, same type of employee: different gender. Another man we talked to, who had a female peer working a reduced schedule, was also unable to imagine a man working the same type of schedule. Though a modified schedule was appealing to him, he said he would change careers rather than challenge the norms of the workplace in which he worked.

The power of these gendered expectations is affirmed by the fact that women have as much difficulty imagining their male counterparts in modified schedules as the men do. As one female manager said:

> If you want to get ahead, males are not going to be able to do that. I don't know, maybe lower down, depending on the job, you can. It depends on who

> you're dealing with. If you're in senior management, middle management, I don't think you're going to find as much of that.

And another woman, describing a man who stays home with his children, put it this way:

> He's really the nurturer. . . . It's very clear . . . but I think he's a unique person. He is not—he is a unique man. Just in general. He doesn't feel like the typical man out there. Different personality totally.

In both reactions, the message is that men who work such schedules are different, not necessarily respected, and certainly not rewarded in the organization.

But what happens when men and women are freed from the constraints imposed by organizations on their career? What happens when they strike out on their own and start their own enterprise? Do we still find evidence of these distinctions? For if we do, then we can see that these are not merely external constraints, but are deeply internalized social norms that profoundly affect the options people feel they have in life. The small group of entrepreneurs in our sample allows us to investigate this issue. They show how difficult it is for men to bridge the culturally defined separation between the public and private spheres.

The male entrepreneurs in our sample are generally in dual-career relationships, very stressed both personally and professionally and suffering from a great deal of work-family conflict. Female entrepreneurs are also in dual-career relationships, but very accommodating of family needs and generally satisfied with the balance. Their enterprises are different, reflecting different ways of conceptualizing the link between work life and private concerns. Women seem to structure these opportunities around their personal life and needs; two thirds of them say that their organization fits their personality. In contrast, only 2 of 13 men say the same, with three fifths saying that they have had to modify their behavior either some or a lot to fit into their *own* organization. The difference is illustrated in the following comparative story.

Karen and Bill received MBAs from the same school in 1979. The paths they pursued during the first several years after graduation were almost identical. Both of them began in a prestigious, high-profile corporate position, moving on to a venture capital start-up a few years later. In both cases, the venture capital concern failed to take root. Karen then launched a consulting company of her own, combining her experience and expertise in biotech and computers, and Bill opened the doors of his own investment company. Along the way, each of them married and began a family.

The point at which these two professionals broke from established organizational settings and set out to design their own opportunities marks the beginning of significantly different lives for Karen and Bill. Karen's decision to strike out on her own came as a result of a reevaluation of her aspirations and priorities: "Five years ago, I wanted to be a power player and run something. Now, I don't care about the fast track. I just want an interesting way to make money and stay flexible with my time." Karen chose the sector in which she was going to offer her services based on her two substantive interests, computers and biotechnology. She considers her work well respected and thinks that she could generate more income if she so desired. However, she is not willing to invest all of her time in work.

Karen sees her work as a complement to the rest of her interests. She has traveled extensively for pleasure in the past 5 years, and at the time of the survey, was taking 6 months off to stay with her new baby. Karen feels that her relationship with her husband, a software developer/consultant, has facilitated her progress in her career. She thinks that each of their respective careers has allowed them the money and time to pursue their personal interests together. Karen names her husband as her primary source of emotional support and says that she has no problems with stress whatsoever.

Bill's journey is quite different. Bill named three reasons for becoming an entrepreneur: "(1) Dissatisfaction with corporate life and management; (2) Identification of significant business opportunity; (3) Need to get wealthy." Driven by the desire to build a successful business from scratch, Bill works long hours and travels extensively.

Other claims on Bill's emotional or temporal energy create stress because they limit his ability to invest all in the new venture. He characterizes his relationship with his wife as a "constraint" on his progress at work; he also includes "presence of a 2-year-old son" in the list of constraints. He says his wife, a business student, "has deferred to [his] career goals and resents it."

Bill identifies work as a primary source of stress and says that he copes with stress "poorly." Stress affects both his performance at work and his personal life. Asked who provides support when problems arise, he wrote "no real support." He spends zero hours per month in non-work-related activities outside his home.

Although Karen and Bill began their careers on parallel tracks, the 10-year follow-up found them living very different lives. They have both chosen to strike out on their own, to design and create their own professional opportunities. What is different is the degree to which they capitalized on their freedom from organizational constraints to design their work to fit with their personal and family lives. Whereas Karen has taken advantage of this freedom to create an innovative arrangement, Bill's set of options seem limited by the cultural expectations that he has internalized. Thus, internalized gender norms combine with the gendered cultural assumption that work and family are separate to create different options as well as different strategies for men and women.

For both women and men, entrepreneurship is a way out of the dilemmas created by large bureaucratic organizations. What is different is the extent to which their new organizations reflect a different image of the link between work and family. Bill has carried the model of segmentation between work and family into his entrepreneurial life. He perceives his family responsibilities to be a constant drain on his ability to work and vice versa. Karen, on the other hand, has used this route as a way to integrate her life. The former is a model that reflects the mind-set of segmentation; the latter reflects synergy.

In an attempt to corroborate this distinction by data from the full sample, we looked at all the respondents in dual-career relationships who had answered questions on how they saw the connection between their career and their relationship.[3] Of the 38 respondents for whom these data were available, almost half (47%) viewed their work and family lives through segmented lenses (see Table 13.1). They generally saw their work and personal lives as separate and distinct arenas. To the extent that they sensed any link at all between these spheres, the link was negative. Thirty-seven percent, however, characterized this link as positive and synergistic. They felt that their work experiences had a positive influence on their relationships at home and thought that their personal life contributed positively to their performance at work. Finally, 16% of the respondents were ambivalent about the links between these two areas of their life.

We found a strong association between sex and perceptual framework: 65% of the men applied a segmented model to these questions about work and family; in contrast, 67% of the women used a synergistic framework. Only one male entrepreneur was synergistic in his outlook, and only one female entrepreneur had a segmented framework.

Table 13.1 Number of Respondents Indicating Segmented, Synergistic, and Mixed Perceptual Frameworks by Sex

	Perceptual Framework			
	Segmented	*Synergistic*	*Mixed*	*Total*
Men	15	4	4	23
Women	3	10	2	15
Total	18	14	6	38

This comparison suggests that women find it easier to evolve a synergy between their personal and work lives by finding ways to bridge public and private domains. For the majority of men, in contrast, the links between the two spheres are viewed segmentally, either as entirely distinct or as involving trade-offs, both emotionally and temporally. Men seem to find it significantly more difficult than women do to bridge the culturally defined separation between work and family.

Discussion

How should we think about the two strategies identified in our sample, the segmentation model typical of the male respondents and the synergistic model more typical of the women?[4] Clearly the latter has some advantages, as our data show: less stress, more satisfaction. However, the synergistic model is incompatible with the assumed demands of the workplace and thus ensures that the top posts in our organizations and in society will be held by those willing and able to segment their life.

The commonly held view is that employees who are willing to commit all of their resources, emotional and temporal, to the organization's goals are most prized and most effective. From this perspective, designing policies that enable employees to integrate their family life with their work life is costly. Such policies may be a necessary concession, occasioned by the shifting demographic realities of the new work force, but they are concessions nonetheless. Although the idea that such policies might actually enhance the performance of employees is difficult to comprehend, a number of our respondents told us that they are better, more effective employees *because* they have other commitments and other loyalties.

Still, the culturally presumed separation of these spheres is pervasive. This separation of public and private emerged during the industrial revolution as paid work became isolated temporally and geographically from family life (Cott, 1977). At the same time, work and family roles became even more closely correlated with sex; men were in the public arena earning the wages, women remained privately domestic taking care of the home and its occupants. This distinction led to the cultural assumption that men have a right to be "ideal" workers by putting work above everything else in life, whereas women have a right to be with their children, hence unable to be "ideal" workers (Williams, 1989). Women have some "choice" in such a gendered structure. By remaining childless, possibly single, they might also aspire to "ideal" worker status (without the home support that is available to men in a "traditional" family structure). But men have very little choice, as we have seen. What is needed, therefore, is for all people, whatever their sex, to be able to model the links between their work and family in a multiplicity of ways, without becoming marginalized and devalued in society.

Such flexibility, however, would require a radical change in the structure of the workplace (Dowd, 1989), in the demands of organizations on people's commitment and time, and in the assumptions underlying occupational reward structures. Men's segmentation strategies are deeply embedded in received assumptions about work, individualism, privacy, and gender (Dowd, 1989). They reflect a workplace that assumes that women will meld employment with care, but makes it difficult for men to do the same. And that construction of the world of work profoundly determines the course of men's lives as well as women's.

Moreover, as indicated by our data, the change in women's roles away from purely domestic involvement increases the stress the segmentation strategy creates for men. Although this strategy permits men to retain their access to positions of influence and power, as men face greater demands to augment their family roles, it also heightens the constraints under which their life unfolds.

Concluding Note

In spite of the apparent consensus among work-family researchers regarding the need to transcend the "myth of separate worlds" and to reconceptualize the links between work and family, constructing a suitable alternative to the separate worlds metaphor has been problematic. We have argued that the alternative metaphor has remained elusive at least in part because the image of segmentation is consistent with gendered institutional arrangements and gendered social norms about appropriate behavior.

Prevailing notions of careers and work are based on segmentation. They embody a zero-sum assumption similar to that underlying the strategies of our male respondents. Some of the women in our sample, on the other hand, have found a way to bridge the public and private domains, thereby living more integrated and satisfactory lives. They alert one to a model of work and family that embraces the notion of time at home as potentially *valuable* to the organizations in which they work. Their model is based on synergy, not on trade-offs.

Our story has highlighted two strategies of linking work to family. And though we see some advantage to the synergistic mode, that model loses some of its advantage by not being freely available to both men and women. Nor do we mean to imply that these are the only two available models. Rather, they represent two examples from what ought to be a multiplicity of possibilities available to people in our society, each of which could be chosen depending on interest, circumstance, life stage, or perhaps luck, but not sex.

Notes

1. For recent views of men's experiences, see Bell, 1982; David & Brannon, 1976; Pleck, 1985; Segal, 1990; Weiss, 1990.

2. This group was selected from a study of five classes that had been followed for their first 5 post-MBA years by Phyllis Wallace (1989). There were 64 men and 29 women in the Wallace sample for the MBA class of 1979. Of these, 22 women and 41 men responded to a follow-up survey in 1989. We also did a number of networked interviews with members of this sample, i.e., interviews with the respondents, their spouses, their colleagues, and their bosses. All the quotes in the chapter are taken from these interviews.

3. Two questions were used: "How has your relationship affected your progress or performance at work (i.e., does it constrain, have no effect, facilitate, etc.)?" and "How has your career affected your relationship?" Responses to these questions were then combined into a new variable indicating the extent to which the respondents perceived the connection between their work and family lives as segmented, synergistic, or mixed. People who revealed by their replies a negative interaction between work and family or no connection whatsoever were assumed to be displaying a segmented model. Those who described the positive ways in which their work and family lives reinforced each other were assumed to have a synergistic perceptual framework, and those who indicated both positive and negative interactions between the two spheres were coded as ambivalent or mixed.

4. It is important to remember that the correlation between the way people view the intersection between work and family with sex is not perfect. Seven respondents (3 women and 4 men) in our sample did *not* fall into their "appropriate" sex-stereotypical category. Thus, we do not view the distinction as based on any essential difference between the sexes. Rather, we see it as a reflection of the gendered structure of the workplace (Acker, 1990; Dowd, 1989; Williams, 1989).

References

Acker, J. (1990). Hierarchies, jobs, bodies: A theory of gendered organizations. *Gender and Society, 4,* 139-158.

Alcoff, L. (1988). Cultural feminism versus post-structuralism: The identity crisis in feminist theory. *Signs: Journal of Women in Culture and Society, 13,* 405-436.

Bell, D. H. (1982). *Being a man: The paradox of masculinity.* Lexington, MA: Lewis.

Cott, N. (1977). *The bonds of womanhood: Woman's sphere in New England, 1780-1835.* New Haven, CT: Yale University Press.

Crosby, F. J. (1991). *Juggling: The unexpected advantages of balancing career and home for women and their families.* New York: Free Press.

David, D. S., & Brannon, R. (Eds.). (1976). *The forty-nine percent majority: The male sex role.* Reading, MA: Addison-Wesley.

Dowd, N. E. (1989). Work and family: The gender paradox and the limitations of discrimination analysis in restructuring the work place. *Harvard Civil Rights/Civil Liberties Law Review, 24,* 79-172.

Hochschild, A. R. (1989). *The second shift: Working parents and the revolution at home.* New York: Viking.

Kanter, R. M. (1977). *Work and family in the United States: A critical review and agenda for research and policy.* New York: Russell Sage.

Olsen, F. E. (1983). The family and the market: A study of ideology and legal reform. *Harvard Law Review, 96,* 1497-1578.

Pleck, J. H. (1985). *Working wives/Working husbands.* Beverly Hills, CA: Sage.

Segal, L. (1990). *Slow motion: Changing masculinities, changing men.* New Brunswick, NJ: Rutgers University Press.

Wallace, P. A. (1989). *MBAs on the fast track: Career mobility of young managers.* New York: Ballinger.

Weiss, R. S. (1990). *Staying the course: The emotional and social lives of men who do well at work.* New York: Free Press.

Williams, J. C. (1989). Deconstructing gender. *Michigan Law Review, 87,* 797-845.

Author Index

Subject Index

About the Contributors

Amy Andrews is a graduate assistant at the Poynter Center for Research on Ethics and American Institutions at Indiana University. She holds a master's degree in industrial and labor relations and is completing work on a master's degree in secondary education. She has worked with Lotte Bailyn on several research projects exploring work-family and gender issues in organizations and is the author of *Flexible Working Schedules in High Commitment Organizations: A Challenge to the Emotional Norms?*

Lotte Bailyn is T. Wilson Professor of Management at the Sloan School of Management, MIT. She has a Ph.D. in social psychology from Harvard University and has been at the Sloan School since 1969. Her recent research has centered on the careers of men and women and on the organizational practices that facilitate or constrain them. She is the author of *Living With Technology: Issues at Mid-Career* (1980), co-author of *Working With Careers* (1984), and has just finished *Breaking the Mold: Women, Men, and Time in the New Corporate World* (1993).

Theodore F. Cohen is Associate Professor and Chair in the sociology-anthropology department at Ohio Wesleyan University, where he teaches a variety of courses, including The Family, Gender in American Society, and Masculinity and Men's Roles. He received his Ph.D. in sociology from Boston University in 1986. He has published articles on men's friendships, the impact of marriage and fatherhood on men, and men's attachments to work and family. He is currently working on an interview study comparing the work and family attachments and conflicts experienced by women and men in three different occupations.

Scott Coltrane is Associate Professor of Sociology at the University of California, Riverside. His research on families, gender inequality, and the changing role of fathers has appeared in *American Journal of Sociology, Social Problems, Journal of Marriage and the Family, Journal of Family Issues, Gender & Society,* and *Men's Studies Review.* He is co-author with Randall Collins of *Sociology of Marriage and the Family: Gender, Love, and Property* (3rd edition, 1991) and is presently studying media images of fathers and investigating the evolution and impact of joint custody legislation.

Alfred DeMaris is Associate Professor in the Department of Sociology at Bowling Green State University, Bowling Green, Ohio. He received his Ph.D. in sociology (with emphases in family social psychology and quantitative methods) from the University of Florida in Gainesville in 1982 and an M.S. in statistics in 1987 from Virginia Polytechnic Institute. His interests are about evenly divided between statistical applications and the study of the family. He is the author of *Logit Modeling: Practical Applications* (1992) as well as additional papers on logistic regression in *Psychological Bulletin, Social Forces, Proceedings of the American Statistical Association,* and *Journal of Marriage and the Family.* He has authored or co-authored a number of other articles on three primary topics: premarital cohabitation and its relationship to subsequent marital quality and stability, violence in intimate relationships, and single fathers. His current interest is the application of exchange theory to the study of marital violence and marital instability, and statistical methods for dealing with dyadic data.

Katherine Dennehy is a Ph.D. candidate in the Department of Sociology, University of Minnesota, and research assistant for the Youth Development Study. Her research interests are in the areas of gender, work and family, and historical sociology. She is working with Professor Barbara Laslett on an analysis of household structure and family strategies in 19th-century Los Angeles. Currently she is conducting research on the impact of child care policy on women's work and family roles in contemporary Germany.

Polly A. Fassinger is Associate Professor of Sociology at Concordia College in Moorhead, Minnesota. In 1987, she completed her Ph.D. at Michigan State University and received the Dissertation Paper Award from the American Sociological Association, Section on Sex and Gender. The chaper included in this volume was awarded the 1991 Outstanding Contribution to Feminist Scholarship Award from the National Council on Family Relations, Section on Feminism and Family Studies. Her current research involves a survey project on gender and classroom interaction.

Geoffrey L. Greif is Associate Professor of Social Work at the School of Social Work at the University of Maryland at Baltimore. He has published several books and articles on single parents and also leads support groups for divorced parents. He is author of *The Daddy Track and the Single Father* (1990) and co-author of *Mothers Without Custody* (1988) and *When Parents Kidnap* (1993).

Linda Haas is Associate Professor of Sociology and Women's Studies at Indiana University-Indianapolis. She has published articles on the obstacles to gender equality in the family and the labor market in the United States and Sweden in *Family Relations, Journal of Marriage and the Family, Sex Roles, Journal of Family Issues,* and in several anthologies. She recently published *Equal Parenthood and Social Policy: A Study of Parental Leave in Sweden* (1992). Her latest research concerns the impact of organizational culture on fatherhood.

Jane C. Hood is Associate Professor of Sociology at the University of New Mexico. Her research focuses on the intersection of work, family, and gender. Publications include *Becoming a Two-Job Family* (1983) and "The Provider Role: Its Meaning and Measurement" (in *Journal of Marriage and the Family,* 1986). She has also done research on janitors, images of male and female gender tokens, and substance abuse among nurses. Currently she is doing life history interviews for a book about growing up in U.S. leftist families during the McCarthy era (tentatively titled *Growing Up Red*).

Masako Ishii-Kuntz is Associate Professor of Sociology at the University of California, Riverside. She received her Ph.D. from Washington State University. She has published several articles on family, gender, aging, and social support networks from cross-cultural and cross-ethnic perspectives. Her earlier publications focused on how the AIDS epidemic influenced sexuality among college students and their families. Her work has appeared in *Journal of Marriage and the Family, Journal of Family Issues, Sociological Perspectives, Sociology and Social Research, The Gerontologist, International Journal of Aging and Human Development, Research on Aging,* and *Journal of Applied Social Psychology.* She recently completed a book manuscript exploring how modern Japanese immigrants and their families adapt to the United States by forming a unique ethnic identity. At present, she is conducting research comparing Chinese, Japanese, Korean, and Filipino American families.

Daphne John is Assistant Professor of Sociology at Oberlin College, where she teaches gender stratification and research methods. Her research interests include work and family linkages, with emphases on ethnic differences in family roles, patterns of child care use, and comparisons between cohabiting and married couples' family roles. She received her Ph.D. from SUNY-Buffalo in 1992. Her dissertation is titled "Patterns of Childcare Use and Consumption Among Married and Single Employed Mothers."

Jeylan T. Mortimer is Professor of Sociology and Director of the Life Course Center at the University of Minnesota. Her research examines the interrelations of work, family, and psychological change, using several longitudinal data sources. Her earlier study of a panel of Michigan graduates assessed the interrelationships between work experiences and attitudes among men in early adulthood. Subsequent research compared the impacts of work on men and women of different ages. She is currently directing a panel study focused on the impacts of work experience on adolescent mental health, psychosocial adjustment, and achievement. Her publications include *Work, Family, and Personality: Transition to Adulthood* (with Jon Lorence and Donald Kumka, 1986), *Work Experience and Psychological Development Through the Life Span* (co-edited with Kathryn Borman, 1988), "Adulthood" (in the *Encyclopedia of Sociology,* 1992), and "The Social Psychology of Work and Organizations" (with Jon Lorence) in the forthcoming *Sociological Perspectives on Social Psychology* (edited by Karen Cook, Gary Alan Fine, and James House).

Joseph H. Pleck is Research Associate at the Wellesley College Center for Research on Women and was formerly the Henry R. Luce Professor of Families, Change, and Society at Wheaton College. He is the author of *Working Wives, Working Husbands* (1985) and co-author of *The Impact of Work Schedules on the Family* (1983). He also co-edited *Families and Jobs* (1983) with Helena Z. Lopata. His other research interests include adolescent male sexual and contraceptive behavior, and men's roles.

Beth Anne Shelton is Associate Professor of Sociology at the State University of New York at Buffalo. She does research on the sociology of gender and work and family. Her primary research focus is the trade-off between women's and men's household and labor market roles. Recent publications include *Women, Men and Time: Gender Differences in Paid Work, Housework and Leisure* (1992) and numerous articles on work and family issues.

Haya Stier is Lecturer in Sociology at the University of Haifa, Israel. Her current research focuses on the Israeli marriage market, with specific attention to stability and change of ethnic intermarriage. Other research in progress examines mothers' employment patterns and the work and welfare consequences of living in concentrated poverty neighborhoods. She is a consulting editor for the *American Journal of Sociology.*

Marta Tienda is Professor of Sociology at the University of Chicago and co-author of *The Hispanic Population of the United States* (1987). Currently she is studying ethnic variation in the school-to-work transition (with V. Joseph Hotz), the dynamics of minority underemployment (with Franklin Wilson and Larry Wu), and contextual determinants of minority educational achievement (with Ross M. Stolzenberg). She is editor of the *American Journal of Sociology.*

Elsa O. Valdez is Professor of Sociology at California State University, San Bernardino. She received her Ph.D. degree in sociology from the University of California, Riverside, in 1991. Most recently her work has focused on dual-earner Chicano couples, with an emphasis on paid work and family roles. She co-authored "Work, Family, and the Chicana: Power, Perception, and Equity" in *Employed Mothers in the Family Context* (1993). Among her future research goals is a study of Latino families living in East Los Angeles.

Norma Williams received her Ph.D. from The University of Texas at Austin in 1984 and is now Associate Professor of Sociology at the

University of North Texas. She is the author of *The Mexican American Family: Tradition and Change* (1990) and recently published (with Andrée F. Sjoberg) a lengthy chapter on ethnicity and gender in *A Critique of Contemporary American Sociology* (1993). She is working on a long-range project studying the Mexican-American elderly in Dallas, Texas.

Beth Willinger is Director of Newcomb College Center for Research on Woman and Assistant Professor of Women's Studies and Sociology, Tulane University. In addition to her interest in changing definitions of masculinity and the male role, she is engaged in research on the higher education of women and a longitudinal study of the self-concepts of college women and men.